THE GREAT SOUTH CAROLINA KU KLUX KLAN TRIALS, 1871–1872

STUDIES IN THE
LEGAL HISTORY OF THE SOUTH
Edited by Paul Finkelman and Kermit L. Hall

This series explores the ways in which law has affected the development of the southern United States and in turn the ways the history of the South has affected the development of American law. Volumes in the series focus on a specific aspect of the law, such as slave law or civil rights legislation, or on a broader topic of historical significance to the development of the legal system in the region, such as issues of constitutional history and of law and society, comparative analyses with other legal systems, and biographical studies of influential southern jurists and lawyers.

THE GREAT SOUTH CAROLINA

KU KLUX KLAN TRIALS, 1871–1872

Lou Falkner Williams

The University of Georgia Press
Athens and London

University of Georgia Press paperback edition, 2004
© 1996 by the University of Georgia Press
Athens, Georgia 30602
All rights reserved
Designed by Betty Palmer McDonald
Set in 11/13 Bodini by Books International, Inc.
Printed digitally

Printed in the United States of America

The Library of Congress has cataloged the hardcover
edition of this book as follows:
Library of Congress Cataloging-in-Publication Data
Williams, Lou Falkner.
The great South Carolina Ku Klux Klan trials,
1871–1872 / Lou Falkner Williams.
        p.   cm.
Includes bibliographical references and index.
ISBN 0-8203-1795-0 (alk. paper)
1. Trials—South Carolina. 2. Reconstruction—South Carolina.
3. Civil Rights—South Carolina—History.   I. Title.
KF220.W537   1996
975.7'00496073—dc20   95-4615
ISBN 0-8203-2659-3 (pbk. : alk. paper)

British Library Cataloging-in-Publication Data available

FOR MY THREE SONS

Randall Lee Williams

Scott Kendrick Williams

AND

Jeffrey Alan Williams

WITH LOVE

Contents

Acknowledgments

Perhaps the nicest thing about completing a project as large as this one is the opportunity to express my gratitude to those who have helped me along the way. I can never repay the debts I owe, both professional and personal, but I will remember. To the best of my ability I will pass the favors along to students, colleagues, family, and friends.

First I want to thank Kermit Hall, to whom I owe my greatest professional debt. Hall suggested that I take a look at Judge Hugh Bond when my plans for a seminar paper on another topic fell through. The constitutional issues of Reconstruction grabbed me, and the paper eventually grew into a book. Hall shepherded the project through the dissertation stage, constantly exhorting me to probe more deeply and think more broadly. His encyclopedic knowledge and editorial good sense kept me moving in the right direction whenever I was prone to lose my way. His friendship has encouraged me through many a dark day and continues to sustain me. He is a credit to his profession, an inspiration to his students and friends.

Three other professors deserve special thanks. Bertram Wyatt-Brown, Milbauer Professor of History at the University of Florida, provided the Milbauer Fellowship that financed my graduate education for four years. He has set a standard of scholarship to which those of us who are privileged to have been his students in Southern history will long aspire. I am especially indebted to Wyatt-Brown for his careful scrutiny of chapter 2. Johanna Shields and Carolyn White of the University of Alabama in Huntsville turned me on to Southern history and constitutional history respectively. These extraordinary women have for many years provided intellectual stimulation, tough criticism, sweet friendship, and the role models that have inspired me.

Other friends and critics have provided valuable assistance along the way, praising me when I did things well and insisting that I rethink when I had erred. Donald Nieman and Paul Finkelman each read two drafts of the manuscript for the University of Georgia Press. Their exacting criticism forced me to strengthen and clarify my argument and doubtless saved me much embarrassment. Nieman's penetrating evaluation and suggestions for revision were particularly valuable; his friendship and encouragement, moreover, have helped me to find my way in the profession. Les Benedict's insightful criticism of an early version of chapter 4 helped me to improve my analysis. Sue Zschoche, Peter Knupfer, and Marion Gray, colleagues at Kansas State University, generously critiqued my treatment of the Klan. I am particularly grateful to Zschoche for her assistance with my analysis of gender issues. My department chairman, Donald Mrozek, deserves much credit for creating a professional atmosphere that has fostered my work. I sincerely appreciate his continuing guidance and interest in this project— as well as his friendship. Wherever I have stubbornly refused to heed the wise counsel of my colleagues in the profession, I am of course solely responsible.

I am grateful for the institutional support that made this book a reality. The University of Florida provided a generous dissertation fellowship that financed travel to North Carolina and Ohio. A liberal travel grant from Kansas State University enabled me to spend several weeks in Washington and South Carolina in the summer of 1992. Portions of chapters 3, 4, and 5 were drawn from articles previously published in *Civil War History*, the *Journal of Southern Legal History*, and the *Maryland Historian*. I am grateful to the editors of these journals for permission to reprint.

Without the help of librarians and archivists this project would have been impossible. I wish to thank the people at the South Carolina Historical Society in Charleston, the Maryland Historical Society, the Southern Historical Collection at the University of North Carolina, Chapel Hill, the Perkins Library at Duke University, the Alderman Library at the University of Virginia, and the Alabama State Department of Archives and History. I owe a special thank-you to Mary Ronan of the National Archives, Mary Ann Hawkins and Charlie Reeves of the National Archives Atlanta Branch, and Laura Costello of the South Caroliniana Library at the University of South Carolina. The South Carolina Department of Archives and History became my home for many weeks. To the professional staff and student assistants there I am most grateful. They provided not only their expertise but also their friendship to a visiting scholar. My special thanks to Robin Copp and, above all, Steve Tuttle, who went into the inaccessible "green files" again and again in hopes of finding *something* to help with the black militia.

The people at the University of Georgia Press have been professional, helpful, and kind. Malcolm Call earned my everlasting gratitude by showing up at the American Historical Association meeting with glowing readers' reports just when I thought the entire project had fallen into a black hole never to be retrieved. Special thanks to managing editor Kelly Caudle for her patience when my auto accident delayed production. Copyeditor Trudie Calvert has an incredible eye for detail; this book is much improved because of her expertise.

I am blessed with special friends and family who have encouraged me in my academic endeavors. Several deserve special recognition. Michael Justus, my closest friend and colleague at the University of Florida, kept me sane and provided a cookie break whenever I needed it. Sylvia McCullars, Susan Sheppard, Ann and Ronald Blanton, and Cille and Andy Ouzts provided the "family" ties I lacked in Gainesville. My cousins, Martha and Hayes Harris, took me in for many weeks when my research took me to the Washington, D.C., area. Dorothy and Ed Clark believed in me, encouraged me, and provided room and board in Huntsville. Louise and Louis Williams have lovingly maintained our family ties despite the many changes in our lives. Sherrill and Bob Boyd and Virginia Nystrom have become "family" in Kansas. One of the best things about teaching at Kansas State has been the opportunity to renew family ties with my borther and sister-in-law, Frank and Carol Falkner. Trips to the Colorado mountains make it easier to enjoy living in Kansas. All these wonderful people have given me the love that makes life worthwhile and academic work endurable.

I deeply regret that neither my mother, Eloise Hoffman Falkner Tollett, nor my aunt Gladys Falkner lived to see this book completed. Although my mom never understood my compulsion to study history, she encouraged me and gave sacrificially to see me through the tight spots in graduate school. Aunt Gladys, an independent woman and a scholar in her own right, understood and did everything she could to foster my work. They would have been proud, and I trust that, somehow, they know the book is finally in print.

My three sons, Randy, Scott, and Jeff Williams, have tolerated an absentee mom and learned over the years to take pride in my work. They didn't type, edit, critique, or proofread, but they made me laugh and helped me keep my perspective about the things that are most important in life. I am deeply grateful. They are wonderful young men, and it is to them I dedicate this book.

THE GREAT SOUTH CAROLINA KU KLUX KLAN TRIALS, 1871–1872

1
Introduction

When white South Carolinians laid down their arms in 1865, most quit the fight only because the Confederacy had been thoroughly whipped by the Union army. Never did they concede that their peculiar institution and the Southern way of life had been anything but right and good. These white Southerners grimly determined that freedom would not substantially alter the condition of the former slaves. Southern intransigence in the face of Republican efforts to provide and enforce constitutional rights for the former slaves precipitated a spiraling effect of action and reaction as the Republican national government provided increasingly stronger measures to protect the freedmen. South Carolina responded to the end of slavery with Black Codes calculated to restrict the liberties of the black population. The Republican Congress, in turn, determined that the white South would bow to the inevitability of change. The Reconstruction Amendments, the Enforcement Act of 1870, the Ku Klux Klan Act of 1871, the suspension of habeas corpus in nine upcountry South Carolina counties, the arrest of hundreds of Ku Klux Klansmen without the usual procedures of due process, and subsequent prosecutions in the Ku Klux Klan trials of 1871–72 were all designed to effect a social and political revolution in South Carolina. But white South Carolina resisted federal encroachment on every front. In the upcountry whites opposed the establishment of Yankee values in the time-honored Southern way—with violence.[1] Whites from all parts of the state employed laissez-faire constitutional principles to protest the work of the Republican state government. In their relations with the national government, white South Carolinians used traditional notions of dual federalism to weaken the effect of the Reconstruction Amendments. The unrepentant, unreconstructed former Confederates stood on their constitutional principles and eventually won the peace they desired.

The great South Carolina Ku Klux Klan trials of 1871 and 1872 present a unique opportunity to observe the dynamics of federal efforts to enforce the Fourteenth and Fifteenth Amendments in the face of white South Carolinians' unwavering determination that traditional Southern social values and constitutional principles would not yield.[2] Resistance to Reconstruction was nowhere stronger than in upcountry South Carolina, where night riders terrorized black citizens almost nightly over a period of several months in 1870 and 1871, forcing the freedmen to sleep in the woods and swamps for fear of their lives.[3] Powerless to protect the citizens of his state, carpetbag governor Robert K. Scott turned to President Ulysses S. Grant for assistance. Grant suspended the writ of habeas corpus in a nine-county area. Grant's action—unprecedented in the United States in peacetime—facilitated mass arrests of Klan terrorists and enabled the federal government to bring many of them to justice.

The South Carolina Klan trials were the national government's most determined effort, aside from the Thirteenth Amendment itself, to use constitutional amendments and federal statutes to change the political and social structure of the South. In the trials the nationalistic goals of the prosecution stood in sharp contrast to the traditional ideas of state sovereignty and dual federalism. The dynamics of the legal process in South Carolina demonstrated the deep divisions within the nation over the meaning and scope of the Reconstruction Amendments and proved the difficulty of implementing ambiguous national policy in conflict with the unflinching localism of white South Carolina. Although the Ku Klux Klan trials secured numerous convictions, they failed to secure legal changes drastic enough to change the minds and hearts of white South Carolinians steeped in the tradition of white supremacy, dual federalism, and laissez-faire constitutional principles. The juxtaposition of national interests with local determination in the South Carolina Ku Klux Klan trials explains in microcosm why the best efforts of the Republican government failed to secure constitutional doctrines and a national rule of law strong enough to secure the civil and political rights of the four million freedmen.[4]

The Civil War brought poverty and shame to white South Carolinians, but defeat never convinced them to change their racial attitudes and constitutional principles. "The Master he says we is all free," one South Carolina freedman reported, "but it don't mean we is white."[5] The enormous physical, emotional, and economic hardships caused by war in South Carolina hardened racial attitudes among the whites and diminished whatever paternalism had endeared the slaves to their masters and protected them from other whites.[6] Whites felt betrayed when "their" people deserted the plantations to find freedom in the trail of the Union army. It was beyond their understanding that the blacks did not plan to stay in their place and behave like slaves. If the slaves were as happy and the masters as benevolent as their proslavery rhetoric had convinced them, surely the blacks had no need to be free. To make matters worse, defection was more prevalent among the favored domestic slaves than among the field hands. Defeat and the end of slavery came as a double shock to white South Carolinians; many simply could not believe that the United States government stood ready to enforce emancipation. Accordingly, many of the stunned masters delayed reporting their new status to the blacks, hoping a miracle would occur and life would go on as before the war. When the slaves inevitably learned that their bondage had ended, whites resolved to perpetuate a system as nearly like slavery as possible.[7]

Having long understood free blacks to be dangerous to their society, whites considered a strict system of racial control to be absolutely mandatory to the new order. Conjuring up the specter of a bloody race war, South Carolinians rushed to institute the infamous Black Code of 1865,[8] which severely limited the freedom of the recently emancipated slaves. No black could aspire to any occupation other than farmer or servant without obtaining a license and paying a special tax, designed to be confiscatory. The old patrol laws were reinstituted; blacks were required to make contracts, work from sunup to sundown, and obtain permission before leaving the premises or entertaining visitors. No black could join the militia or keep a weapon. Vagrants—unemployed freedmen—were to be severely punished.[9]

White South Carolinians enacted the Black Code to reestablish order and perhaps even to protect the former slaves, but the laws demonstrated above all the white Southerners' fundamental assumption that blacks were inherently, immutably inferior to whites. Some white South Carolinians allegedly believed the freedpeople needed protection because they were a race of children who were incapable of reaching a civilized state. Without the guidance and direction of white men, they would be incapable of functioning in society. More important, however, was the white population's profound fear of the freedmen; white South Carolinians had maintained a state of paranoia over the possibility of slave insurrection for so long that they were convinced free blacks would rise in retaliation against their former masters. Locked into their traditional assumptions concerning blacks, South Carolinians feverishly predicted a war between the races. Absolute control of the labor supply was mandatory. "If the Government expects to establish voluntary labor as the future of these people," an Aiken man wrote Provisional Governor Benjamin F. Perry, "then indeed will much of the most productive and richest portions of the Southern States become a howling wilderness and a war of extermination with all of its horrors ensue." A system of compulsory or organized labor was the only answer to the problem, he continued, the sole means by which the blacks could ever understand that freedom meant work. "Moderate corporeal punishment" would keep the workers in line.[10]

However much they despised the idea of black freedom, whites recognized, nonetheless, their absolute dependence on black labor. Although some whites left the state and others made elaborate plans to attract white immigrant labor, most conceded quickly their need for the former bondsmen. "The white citizens must show much more energy and willingness to work in the fields than they have yet manifested," a Freedmen's Bureau agent explained succinctly, "before they can be in any respect independent of negro labor."[11]

The former slaves were equally dependent upon the whites, but they seized the opportunity to test the meaning of liberty before they were willing to settle down and contract their labor. Freedom initially meant simply the right to pick up and go. Most blacks in South Carolina left their masters—the symbol of their bondage. There was a tremendous amount of movement among the former slaves in South Carolina as family members sought one another, and slaves who had fled to the Union army from their masters or from the Union army with their masters returned to their old neighborhoods. But when all the moving around was over, most of the freedpeople settled near their former homes. Some even returned to work for their former masters.[12]

Blacks expected more from freedom than the ruling class was willing to grant. They were pleased at first to have the opportunity to legitimize their marriages, adopt or perhaps reveal surnames, worship in their own churches, and make contracts. Inevitably, however, these freedoms were not enough. The freed black people of South Carolina had a strong sense of the labor theory of value. Having sweated long and hard on their masters' land, they were convinced that the land should belong to them. For years after emancipation blacks agonized over signing their annual labor contracts lest obligation to a contract prevent them from accepting the anticipated government grant of forty acres and a mule. Education was another important goal of black Carolinians. They eagerly sent their children to school, and adults labored hard to learn to read and write.[13]

As much as anything else, the freedmen of South Carolina desired access to the political process. During the heady early days of freedom, black delegates gathered in Zion Church in Charleston to discuss their goals and make them known to the white people of their state. "Lifted up by the providence of God," they declared,

> We ask for no special privileges or peculiar favors, we ask only for even-handed Justice, or for the removal of such positive obstructions and disabilities as past, and the recent legislators have seen fit to throw in our way and heap upon us. . . . We simply desire that we shall be recognized as men; that we have no obstructions placed in our way; that the same laws which govern white men shall direct colored men; that we have the right of trial by a jury of our peers . . . that we be dealt with as others in equity and justice.[14]

Black males in South Carolina demanded to be treated as men—not hired men, or colored men, or even freedmen—but men. Nothing less would satisfy their craving for justice and equality.

It was precisely in their capacity as men that blacks seemed most threatening. Most white South Carolinians were incapable of thinking of granting blacks equal rights as citizens. Blacks were innately inferior in the white South Carolina mind and must at all costs be prevented from rising to a higher level. Sharing rights with freedmen was unthinkable. While blacks wanted equality, whites inevitably jumped to the conclusion that granting the rights of manhood and citizenship to the freedmen would mean either black supremacy or a bloody war of extermination between the races. There was no middle ground. A. C. Garlington of Newberry, for example, predicted a bloody race war if the Radicals insisted on absolute equality. J. M. Anderson complained that the political equality of the Negro was "the *ne plus ultra* of all evils . . . alone and of itself utterly intolerable and certainly ruinous. It will certainly bring every other evil in its train," he predicted. "Give the negro political equality and he will legislate social equality." Another South Carolinian carried the hysteria surrounding the idea of social equality to its illogical extreme, fearing the United States Congress would someday require "that your daughter and mine shall either marry negroes or die unmarried." White men were convinced that they needed to protect their women from "insult and abuse" by black men. Constant vigilance was necessary to maintain the customary order of society.[15]

Freedmen's Bureau representatives in South Carolina were in a unique position to observe the stormy racial relations between the former slaves and masters during this transition period. The Yankee officers reported evenhandedly the struggle between the races, whether it was petty thievery by the blacks or attempts by the landowners to cheat the laborers out of their just portion of the crop. Like local whites, bureau officers became impatient with the freedmen. Unlike white South Carolinians, however, the Northern officers more generally believed the blacks could mature into their responsibilities as citizens. Bureau representatives recognized the intransigence of the whites, however, and noted that in some ways the freedmen were better off as slaves "for then it was certainly to the interest of their owners to at least preserve their property from abuse, but now being no one's possession, any one may injure them at pleasure." The former rebels were unrepentant and unreconstructed, according to Freedmen's Bureau representatives; if there were any hope of success, they would gladly take up arms again. "Miniature Hamilcars, bringing out their Hannibals," the South Carolinians still believed "that secession was right, that the negro is fit for nothing but a slave, and that Northern men will find it out so." More thoughtful bureau officials recognized that the whites needed Reconstruction to fail so they could continue to believe that slavery was just:

> It is not to be expected that the former slave owners will now go to work and teach their former slaves how to get along as free men, because they fear that if the freed people have sufficient opportunity given them, they may show to the world that they are worthy of their freedom; no they will do the opposite; they will try and prevent such improvements in order to show to the world that liberty is a curse to these people and that they need masters.[16]

Their willingness to promote the cause of freedom earned bureau agents the hatred and ostracism of the majority of whites in South Carolina. It was a "wearisome and almost thankless work," William Stone, a future South Carolina attorney general and U.S. attorney, wrote in 1869. Nevertheless, he understood the long-term significance of his job: "Were it not that this is so interesting a period of our history, I should almost be inclined to let all this work go by the board for the sake of being among civilized beings again. As it is, I am deeply interested in this great social and political problem we are working out and look to the future full of hope and confidence."[17]

Because approximately 60 percent of the state's population was black, the whites obviously feared the changes in their way of life that an enfranchised black majority could bring. Southern obstinacy about the freedmen dictated a more radical Reconstruction policy on the part of the national government. The Reconstruction Act of 1867 called for new state constitutions that would provide for manhood suffrage, their approval by a majority of registered voters, and ratification of the Fourteenth Amendment as conditions for readmission to the Union. Recognizing the inevitability of black suffrage, a few white leaders in South Carolina called for cooperation, hoping to control the votes of the former slaves. Confederate cavalry hero Wade Hampton, for example, thought initially that "all who can do so should vote, and every good man who can go to the Convention, even if sent by negroes and with negroes should go. We can control and direct the negroes if we act discreetly."[18] Controlling the black vote proved an elusive goal, however. Hampton changed his mind before the convention. "I think it far preferable the State should remain . . . under military rule, than that it should give its sanction to measures which we believe to be illegal, unconstitutional and ruinous," he argued.[19]

Many South Carolinians refused to take part in a political process on an equal basis with their former slaves. A convention of whites served notice that the "property and intelligence" of South Carolina "would never acquiesce in Negro equality or supremacy." Preferring military rule to a constitution that called for universal suffrage, many whites boycotted the polls, hoping to prevent the necessary majority from voting in favor of a constitutional convention.[20]

If some whites deliberately avoided the polls, many others had no choice. All who had sworn before the war to uphold the U.S. Constitution and then participated in the Confederacy were disfranchised. The Reconstruction Acts eliminated not only the men who had previously held important federal offices but also those who had participated at the state and local levels. So thorough was the disfranchisement policy, which excluded "the whole body of the capital, the experience, the intelligence and the character of the State," William Henry Trescot argued, "it is the destruction of society."[21] With the vast majority of white South Carolinians either unwilling or unable to go to the polls, the freedmen and their allies voted in favor of a constitutional convention. Thus the new constitution of South Carolina was drafted without the aid of the former leaders of the state.[22] Eligible whites went back to the polls in June 1868, but their efforts to defeat the proposed constitution and the Republican party slate were unsuccessful. The Democrats managed to elect only 6 of 31 senators and 15 of 124 representatives. They carried ten counties. The freedmen, with the help of Northern whites who had moved to South Carolina and local white Republicans, elected a Northern-born Republican governor, Robert K. Scott, a senate with a solid Republican majority, and a lower house with a large black majority.

Neither the whites who had deliberately deprived themselves of a voice in creating the state government nor those who had been disfranchised by federal action felt obligated to support the constitution and government of the state. Constitutions and the laws under them, if they are to enjoy legitimacy, must be sanctioned by the people. White South Carolinians overwhelmingly considered their constitution and state government a fraud. Former provisional governor Benjamin F. Perry expressed the attitude of most of the white people of his state:

> Is it not infamous that such an assemblage of negroes and yankees should be forming a constitution for the once proud, honored, and glorious old state of South Carolina. Can there be anything more abhorrent to the feelings of an honorable man than to see these renegades & adventurers, black & white, from all the northern states coming here associating with our former slaves and the vilest of the white race in order to form organic laws for the gentlemen of South Carolina. . . . There is not a single member of this infamous convention who would even have dared, before the war, to enter the house of a gentleman except on a message or matter of business. And this body styling themselves the representatives of the people have undertaken to reconstruct the Palmetto State.[23]

The situation was too grievous for many white South Carolinians to bear. The Republican government in Columbia "which calls itself the state" contradicted everything they perceived to be constitutional liberty and republican government. "We live under a government put over us by usurpation, fraud, military power, and violence. *It is not our government,*" Democratic leader James Campbell wrote from Charleston. In a letter to Governor Scott, William Henry Trescot noted similarly that the white people of Anderson District "have not believed that the present state government was legitimate."[24]

Thus to most white South Carolinians the Republican state government was unauthorized from the beginning. Never would they recognize the legitimacy of their "Black Republican" state government. For many the freedmen's insistence on behaving and being treated as equals was provocation enough to warrant Klan atrocities. Klan support was strongest in the upcountry, but the Klan found many allies among men of property and intelligence throughout the nation. Conservative whites who would have personally disdained the violence and refused to participate in the Ku Klux Klan overlooked the atrocities and contributed to defense efforts because they shared the racism and constitutional principles of the Ku Klux Klan of South Carolina.

Laissez-faire constitutional principles embodied the notion that the purpose of government was to promote the general welfare, not to serve the interests of one class or interest group at the expense of another.[25] To achieve this purpose, government should rest squarely on the shoulders of the educated and propertied classes, for they alone possess the intelligence, vision, and virtue to understand the general good and establish government policy accordingly. "It is a maxim founded in truth that virtue and intelligence alone can sustain a republican form of government," former governor Perry put it.[26] Deprived of a voice in their state government, the property owners insisted that they had been denied their constitutional right to a republican form of government.[27] "Let me impress upon you a truth which I do not think you or your friends realize," William Henry Trescot wrote Governor Scott:

> The foundation of your difficulty, of our difficulty, is that the local government of the state has passed out of the hands which ought to hold it. . . . The guardians of the law do not represent the character, the intelligence, or the property of the country. That great body of substantial men whose moral support all the world over, makes the strength and power of the law, are aliens and criminals in their own homes. Is it any wonder that in such a condition of things, the bad and the violent defy the laws?[28]

If their constitutional tenets persuaded white South Carolinians that their state government was unlawful, their overwhelming racism exacerbated the problem. The majority of white South Carolinians considered blacks ignorant and venal; clearly they could not possess the intelligence and virtue necessary to recognize and promote the common good. Yet the unthinkable had occurred: "A black colony succeeding the reign of chivalry and truth. A Negro legislature framing laws for men born under the Palmetto." Most of the former ruling class would have agreed with Alfred Huger, who declared that he would "rather die in chains than be participant criminal in this unholy work."[29]

At the head of this "unholy work" was Governor Robert K. Scott, a Republican from Ohio by way of the United States Army and the Freedmen's Bureau. As the head of the Freedmen's Bureau in South Carolina Scott had earned the reputation of being fair to blacks and whites alike. Scott had made money in land speculation before the Civil War. While working for the bureau, he had given his own funds generously to private relief in the state. Republicans drafted Scott as their choice for governor. A sense of duty convinced him to run despite his initial hesitation. As governor, Scott was in a precarious position. Most whites despised him for his close social relations with black Republicans, yet he depended on the black vote for his office. When he brought friends from outside South Carolina to fill state offices, both sides complained. Accusing Scott of entering politics simply to line his own pockets, historians have traditionally held him responsible for the state's Reconstruction financial disasters—bond fraud and railroad problems. Richard N. Current has reevaluated Scott, however, and argued that the state was already in serious financial trouble before he took office. Current blamed the state Democrats as much as the Republicans for the bond problems, suggesting that the whites deliberately sabotaged the state's credit. For Current, "Scott was at least as much a hero as anyone else . . . in South Carolina politics."[30]

Daniel Henry Chamberlain, a Massachusetts abolitionist, was another prominent Northerner in the South Carolina government. Serious and scholarly, Chamberlain had attended both Harvard and Yale and was probably the best educated of all the state's Northern-born politicians. Fearful that the war would end before he had his chance to serve, Chamberlain had quit law school in 1864 to join the army. As an officer of black troops, he spent the remainder of the Civil War at a desk job. Chamberlain traveled to South Carolina after the war to settle the affairs of a friend who had died. There he tried his hand at cotton planting in the low country, hoping to make his fortune. He soon discovered, however, that his talents were better suited to politics. Chamberlain played a prominent role at the

South Carolina constitutional convention, where his eloquent speeches often won the day. When elected state attorney general in 1868, Chamberlain had yet to argue his first case in court.[31]

The Republican legislature of South Carolina was considered a "convention of baboons and pickpockets" by many white South Carolinians, who complained that they were subjected to the absolute control of their former slaves; the black legislators, in turn, they considered to be under the control of the hated "carpetbaggers." White racism combined with the traditional notion that the virtuous, intelligent, property-owning class should govern for the good of all blinded whites to the positive work that was accomplished by their state legislature.[32]

Despite the myths perpetuated by white South Carolinians and reiterated by early historians, most of the legislators of the "Black Republican" government took their work seriously.[33] Blacks held a majority in the lower house in South Carolina between 1868 and 1877, although they never controlled the state senate. Although they lacked experience in government, most of the black lawmakers did not venture to the statehouse directly from the cotton fields. Antebellum free blacks, freedmen who had served in the Union army, and Northern blacks made up a large proportion of the state legislature. Most had at least a common school education; some had excellent college and professional training; only a few were illiterate. The black lawmakers did not create a monolithic block, nor did the white Republicans control the actions of the black majority. Important class differences among the Republicans divided the party on many issues. Legislators from the prosperous antebellum free mulatto class tended to hold values that differed widely from those of the former slaves; their conservatism on economic issues often aligned them against other blacks. On civil rights issues, however, black and brown lawmakers stood together.[34]

White members of the Republican party in South Carolina suffered ostracism and contempt from the majority of their race. Local white Republicans, or "scalawags" as their Democratic opposition labeled them, had generally displayed a stronger attachment to the Union before the war than the average white South Carolinian. Many of the Northerners who served in the state government were idealists, strongly committed to the elevation of the freedmen. These "carpetbaggers" were not the "bootless opportunists" of Southern myth but were usually young army officers who had remained in the state at the war's end.[35] The refusal of the South Carolina white leadership to participate in politics alongside the freedmen doubtless promoted Northerners to positions of authority and power they would not have enjoyed otherwise.

To provide needed services for their constituency, the Republican lawmakers of South Carolina raised taxes to unprecedented heights. Tax revenue was absolutely necessary if the state was to fund public education, hospitals, insane asylums, internal improvements, and other needed facilities. But the Republican tax policy was a vast change from the prewar era, when a head tax on slaves had provided most of the state's income. Real estate had been consistently undervalued for tax purposes, particularly in the upcountry, where the small farmer's tax bill was negligible. After the war, when land values fell and money was scarce, property was assessed at a much higher rate. High property taxes, the primary source of state revenue in Reconstruction South Carolina, enraged the whites who already considered the state government illegal. White South Carolinians observed, moreover, that revenue was not the only purpose of the Republican tax program. The Radicals legislated high taxes in a deliberate effort to redistribute land to the freedmen. The Republicans expected the high taxes on unused land to force property on the market so the state could purchase it for resale or private individuals could buy it. "The owner cannot afford to keep thousands of acres idle and unproductive," Governor Scott announced; "stern necessity . . . will compel him to cut up his ancestral possessions into small farms, and sell them to those who can and will make them productive; and thus the masses of the people will become property holders."[36]

The Republican tax program did indeed release vast quantities of land forfeited to the state for nonpayment of taxes. But it also increased the antagonism of the majority of the white citizens of the state—the property owners—toward the government. Times were hard in Reconstruction South Carolina, and taxpayers resented the new financial burden. An unexpected result of the tax program was that it fell particularly hard on small farmers, both black and white. Freedmen who had been able to acquire land often lost it to the government that was supposed to protect their interests. Resentment of the high taxes they had never had to pay before bound the white yeomen to the planters and undermined the authority of the Republican government as surely as did the racism that bound the whites together. Because most taxpayers were white and Republicans were generally black, taxpayers complained loudly of taxation without representation. The undeniable excesses of the Republican government in Columbia further aggravated the problem.[37]

Republican efforts to establish a genuine democracy, redistribute land, and provide services and facilities for black citizens were to conservative white South Carolinians nothing more than class legislation, a serious violation of their constitutional rights. Laissez-faire constitutionalism dictated that public policy be neutral. Government should never promote the interests of one group at the expense of another.[38] Yet conservative whites believed the Republicans planned "to convert the whole state government into a vast sponge to suck up money from the whites & squeeze it out to the blacks & their unprincipled leaders."[39] The intelligence and wealth of South Carolina were "crushed into the dust by ignorance, pauperism & rascality." Reduced to "sackcloth and ashes," the qualified, "native-born" leaders of South Carolina were suffered to "stand at the door" of the statehouse and "pay the expense of those who caroused within."[40] Accustomed to a laissez-faire system that had fostered their own class interests as slave owners, whites objected fundamentally to obviously redistributive legislation that favored a different class. Thus racism combined with a traditional understanding of constitutional legitimacy to foredoom the democratic governments Republicans sought to establish.

It was taxation without representation, pure and simple, or so the majority of white South Carolinians believed. Those "whose property had been taxed only by those who paid the taxes, beheld the whole thing suddenly subverted and themselves placed at the mercy of ignorance and of corruption," James Chesnut complained.[41] Frustrated whites held a taxpayers' convention in Columbia in 1871 to protest state policy. There the delegates routinely referred to the redistributive measures of the government as "confiscation." W. D. Porter of Charleston, president of the convention, for example, considered the state's increased tax policy and "reckless expenditures" calculated to bring about a "wide-spread confiscation of property. And the worst feature of the matter," he continued, "is the curious and anomalous fact, without parallel in the history of any representative government, that they who lay the taxes do not pay them, and that they who are to pay them have no voice in the laying of them. Can greater wrong or greater tyranny in republican government be well conceived," he asked.[42]

Their refusal to concede constitutional legitimacy to the state government obviously colored the reactions of white South Carolinians to the tax measures passed by their lawmakers. If legitimate government rested on the consent of the governed, if republican government depended upon the participation of the virtuous and intelligent members of the polity, if

the purpose of government was to foster the welfare of the entire community, if government was responsible for protecting property rights, then
white South Carolinians were living under an "absolute despotism." The
state government violated the principles of liberty as they understood
them. Whites frequently complained that they were the oppressed, "subjected" to the "absolute rule of dishonest strangers and the domination
of their own slaves."[43] Reconstruction had enslaved the Anglo-Saxon
and "decreed the Negro his superior," Alfred Huger insisted.[44] David
Schenck expressed the views of many South Carolinians when he prayed
"that God may now 'execute justice and judgement for the oppressed'
and this year deliver us from the political tyranny of carpet-bag thieves
and negro ignorance and that Constitutional liberty may once more be
restored."[45]

The Republican program in South Carolina was absolutely unacceptable to most white South Carolinians. They perceived it as humiliating
and totally foreign to their social reality, a government imposed by self-
righteous conquerors and carried forward by outsiders, traitors, and inferiors, or "carpetbaggers, scalawags, and niggers" as they preferred to
call them. It had little or no support among the recognized white leaders
of the state. When the "property and intelligence" of the state became
aroused from political lethargy to take charge again, the Republican party
in South Carolina had neither the power nor the tradition to maintain itself. Political frustration, racial antagonism, economic hardship, and a
deep conviction that the Republican state government was illegitimate
convinced whites that change was essential.

Whites proclaimed 1870 the "Year of the Happy Deliverance"—the
year in which they would reclaim the governorship and the state legislature. The Democratic press urged a conciliatory policy toward the blacks
and a united white vote as a necessary strategy in a state where blacks
constituted about 60 percent of the eligible voters. Because the freedmen
had rejected the Democratic party in 1868, Democrats united with dis-
affected Republicans to form the Union Reform party. Their candidate for
governor was Judge Richard B. Carpenter, a Republican; for lieutenant
governor the party chose Matthew C. Butler, a native of Edgefield County.
Blacks ran for office on the Reform ticket but only at the local level.[46]

The Reform party actively courted the black vote. Candidates stumped
the state, playing to racially mixed audiences. Posing as the true friends
of the freedmen, the whites insisted that Republicans used the blacks for

their own self-interest. They urged blacks to desert the Union Leagues and vote their own consciences. Reformers recognized the legal rights of the freedmen, including the franchise, but their general attitude made clear that they were able to do so only by holding their noses. Reformers concentrated on high taxes and corruption in the Republican ranks.[47] Republican candidates reminded the blacks that the Republican party had consistently befriended them. They intimated, moreover, that the Reformers would attempt to reenslave the freedmen. A vote for the Republican party thus signified a desire to remain free. Denying the corruption charges, the Republicans reminded the freedmen of benefits accomplished by the party, including public education and a homestead act.[48]

Fearing that persuasion alone would not carry the election, both sides resorted to more forceful means of strengthening their chances at the poll. Economic coercion was a favorite method among the whites, who threatened to discharge any workers who failed to vote the Reform ticket. Governor Scott and the Republicans used the black militia and Union Leagues to maintain black solidarity, and the freedmen were actively hostile to blacks who planned to desert the Republican ranks. But the work of the Union Leagues and the social ostracism of black Democrats by black Republicans pales in comparison with the threats of violence and outright brutality employed by the Democrats in several upcountry counties where the ratio between blacks and whites was very close. Republicans appealed to Governor Scott for arms and ammunition before the election, reporting that whites were killing blacks in Laurens County and a large fight was expected in Newberry. Whites in Spartanburg County mounted a campaign of violence before the election, whipping Republicans, turning them off their lands, and in some instances even shooting those who refused to deny their Radical principles. Republicans testified after the election that many Spartanburg blacks refrained from voting from fear of losing their livelihood and even their lives.[49]

Neither side was willing to risk a free and fair election. Armed whites surrounded the polls in some precincts of Spartanburg County and turned black voters away, insisting that "this is a white man's government." Whites from the Augusta, Georgia, area flocked into Edgefield County to swell the Reform party's numbers. Not to be outdone, the blacks imported voters from North Carolina. Voters did not have to be registered so the possibilities were endless. Some men allegedly voted more than once; some underage blacks voted; and rumor had it that some sick freedmen sent their wives to cast their votes for them. The worst excesses probably occurred after the precincts closed. Election laws allowed the ballots to be held by the election officials—all Republicans—for several days before they were turned in, a practice that invited fraud. One election manager in Laurens County, the notorious Joe Crews, who was a candidate for the legislature, first returned a large vote for himself which reversed the 1868 Democratic majority in his precinct and then destroyed the ballots. Despite the fraud and intimidation, however, both sides recognized that the Republicans had scored a tremendous victory at the polls. The totals for Republicans and Democrats very nearly matched the corresponding votes for blacks and whites.[50]

The Reform party failed basically because conservatives were willing to offer the black electorate nothing more than "ballyhoo and barbecue." Whites found it humiliating to recognize the freedman as a political equal and scarcely disguised the campaign effort to restore white supremacy and their traditional notions of constitutional liberty. Despite their lack of political experience, blacks clearly understood that it was the Republican party that represented their interests. They recognized, as a prominent black politician explained to a newspaper correspondent, that those who considered slavery a God-ordained institution had not changed so quickly.[51] Having failed in their attempts to restore constitutional liberty as they understood it, white South Carolinians, in their frustration, mounted a campaign of violence designed to restore the familiar social standards and constitutional liberty—Southern style.

The Ku Klux Klan was the white solution to a black population that refused to defer to the "property and intelligence" of the state. In November 1870, the Klan initiated a reign of terror throughout upcountry South Carolina which continued unabated until September 1871. Hooded night riders swept through the countryside, their horses draped, relentlessly persecuting the Republican population. Again and again they whipped black and white Republicans for no offense greater than voting the party ticket. Republicans who escaped with only a whipping were fortunate. The South Carolina Klan in its fury committed some of the most heinous crimes in the history of the United States.[52]

The Klan was not new to South Carolina in 1870. It had existed in the state since 1868, when a Klansman from Pulaski, Tennessee, had organized a Klan in York County. Ku Klux Klan violence and intimidation played an important part in the presidential election of 1868 in South Carolina, when the Klan focused on breaking up the Union Leagues and preventing blacks from voting. Night riders killed several Republican leaders, whipped others, and threatened many more with eviction if they dared to vote. The brutal campaign was successful in keeping blacks from the polls in the up-country. In several counties that had reported a Republican majority in the April state election, Horatio Seymour led Grant by a substantial majority. Clearly the Klan could make a difference in counties where the racial mix was close. Blacks needed protection in order to vote.[53]

A period of relative calm in Klan activities followed the election of 1868, but for the white population violence remained a viable solution for racial antagonism. Although Democrats insisted that "profound peace" existed in the state, Republicans continued to write their governor requesting protection. A correspondent from Newberry County reported that some "malicious devils" had set fire to the black school he had built on his property. Another wrote from Spartanburg that there was not a "sufficient number of loyal and law abiding citizens in this county to execute and enforce the laws." Disguised night riders had destroyed his barn, his carriage house and carriage, and all his household effects. Although his son and daughter had identified some of the assailants, local officials refused to punish them. The leading Democrats, he said, "rejoice at my misfortunes."[54] A magistrate reported from York County that an organization of disguised men was burning the houses of good citizens—Republicans—and threatening their lives. From Edgefield a man who made it his practice to hire Republicans wrote that he was being run off his property because the local whites "would not suffer a raticule [radical] in the neighborhood." A deputy constable from Abbeville admitted the need for more law enforcement officers in the county and suggested to the governor that arming a strong force of black militia was the most efficient means of enforcing the laws and protecting the black population.

Governor Scott found himself in an untenable position. As governor of the state he was duty bound to protect the people; as a Republican he was dependent on the black vote. Yet he recognized that the majority of the white citizens of his state did not recognize the validity of his administration. To mount an armed force of former slaves against the "property and intelligence" of South Carolina was certain to cause serious problems. His mail warned him that the "formation of Negro regiments . . . would most unquestionably lead to a war of races." Hoping to put a halt to the violence and assure a Republican victory at the polls in 1870, Scott began to organize and equip a black militia. This militia, according to Herbert Shapiro, was largely responsible for the Republican victory in the South Carolina upcountry in 1870.[55] The policy of intimidation that had carried the upcountry for the Democrats in 1868 failed in the presence of armed black troops. The Reform party had humiliated white citizens by "pandering" to the black vote and then failed to produce a white majority in the upcountry.

Never again, upcountry whites vowed, would they be so humiliated. South Carolina Democrats understood precisely how to solve the Negro problem, and racial cooperation in the political arena was not the answer. The Ku Klux Klan mounted a campaign of terror following the election of 1870 designed to halt the growth of the Republican party, put the freedmen in their proper place, restore the familiar social customs of the South, and reinstitute constitutional liberty—Southern style.

2

Klan Crime and
the South Carolina Whites

Ku Klux Klan violence during Reconstruction assumed its worst form in the state of South Carolina, where masked riders rode almost nightly over a period of several months immediately following the election of 1870. Although the low country with its large black majority remained relatively free of violence, Klan brutality reached its most fearsome proportions in nine counties of the upcountry, where the black-white ratio was more equal: Chester, Fairfield, Laurens, Newberry, and Union in the lower piedmont, Lancaster, Spartanburg, and York in the upper piedmont, and Chesterfield in the sand hills.

Although Ku Klux Klan outrages were common in both the upper and lower piedmont, the population and economy of the areas were very different. Blacks outnumbered whites in every county of the lower piedmont, whereas the upper piedmont, taken as a whole, had a majority of white people. The proportion of blacks to whites was very close in Lancaster and York counties (49 and 51.9 percent, respectively), which could make a little intimidation go a long way toward a Democratic victory at the polls. But a clear majority of whites did not diminish the Klan's wrath. Spartanburg County, with only 32.6 percent blacks and a safe Democratic majority throughout the Reconstruction period, was one of the most violent Klan counties. Spartanburg whites were obviously opposed to blacks participating in politics regardless of whether they succeeded or failed.[1]

The racial differences between the upper and lower piedmont reflected the economies of the two areas. Throughout the upcountry, plantations were smaller and the people less wealthy than in the low country. Cotton production and a plantation economy dominated the lower piedmont.

Plantations were rarer and planters less likely to dominate the economy in
the upper piedmont, where white yeomen prevailed. Yeoman farmers in the
upper piedmont had practiced "safety-first" agriculture before the Civil
War, concentrating on their own subsistence crops first and then producing
a small amount of cotton for the market. When railroads penetrated the upcountry in the 1850s, the upper piedmont became more market oriented
and "safety-first" was sacrificed for increased cotton production. Towns
grew, and local merchants prospered, a transition that continued throughout Reconstruction. The upper piedmont continued to produce a large volume of subsistence crops despite the increased importance of cotton, but
the small farmers suffered from falling cotton prices and high taxes. Thus
during Reconstruction, many independent yeomen lost their land and became renters or sharecroppers.[2]

Emancipation complicated the shift that was already taking place in
the upcountry economy. Freedmen made clear that they were no longer
willing to work the gang system in the cotton fields. The change from gang
labor to share wages or tenant farming was more difficult in the lower
piedmont than the upper because planters there were more accustomed to
working large numbers of slaves. Farmers were desperate for labor, however, and were forced by black recalcitrance and continued financial
losses to accept the new arrangements. Freedmen all over South Carolina
preferred rental agreements to sharecropping. Under South Carolina's lien
law, renters qualified as owners of the crop and were thus able to give
liens for supplies independent of the landowner, a system that increased
the freedmen's autonomy. Sharecroppers worked under closer supervision
of the owner, who paid and supplied them. The growing independence of
the workers alarmed the landowners, who complained that the freedmen
preferred politics to farming. They run off to political meetings, A. B.
Springs, a wealthy York County planter wrote, "leaving fodder and cotton
to take care of itself." Freedmen's Bureau reports noted the same preference for politics. The freedmen leave for days without "any reason or
right," one representative reported, "causing the planters much inconvenience and loss, and not improving their own chances for a respectable
crop."[3]

Upcountry blacks were much in earnest about politics. Having worked
on smaller plantations and farms where they had more contact with whites
than low country slaves, the freedmen of upcountry South Carolina were
correspondingly more politically astute. Thus they quickly grasped the
meaning of the franchise. They flocked to Union League meetings where

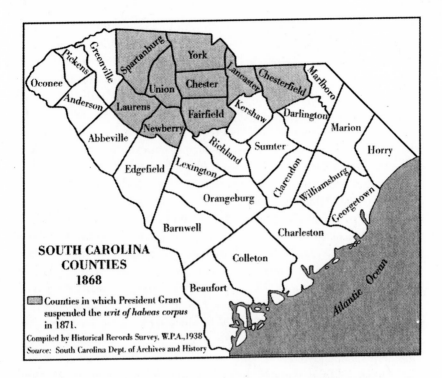

SOUTH CAROLINA
COUNTIES
1868

Counties in which President Grant
suspended the *writ of habeas corpus*
in 1871.
Compiled by Historical Records Survey, W.P.A.,1938
Source: South Carolina Dept. of Archives and History

Republican party organizers educated them in their rights as free men
and their duties to the Republican party. The Union Leagues were initially secret, oath-bound clubs—not from any desire to do harm to the
white citizens but in deference to the real fear held by the former slaves
that political organization was dangerous. The secrecy reassured anxious
blacks and eased their introduction to politics. The political education
provided by the Leagues emboldened the freedmen and promoted local
leadership among them. Because of the Leagues, blacks were staunchly
Republican, tightly organized, and zealous in their devotion to the party
that had delivered them from bondage. They were vocal, moreover, in
their opposition to the political and economic goals of the Democrats.
Members of the Union Leagues took seriously their responsibility to discourage—physically if necessary—any blacks who threatened to desert
the party ranks and go over to the opposition. Southern whites, predictably, perceived the Union Leagues as dark and sinister organizations that
needed to be eradicated. The freedmen's preference for political meetings
over field work compounded the problem, and mutual distrust grew.[4]

If most of the white citizens of South Carolina refused to welcome the freedmen as their political equals—and virtually all whites in the state agreed that political domination by their inferiors must and would end—upcountry whites took special exception to the political organization of the former slaves. Perhaps the overwhelming black majority in the low country counseled a more patient attitude there. Pringle Smith, for example, wrote from Charleston that "bayonet rule can't last always and, that over, the superior race will assert itself." That hope, however, was "only for a far off future." In the meantime one simply had to make the best of a bad situation. Upcountry whites impatiently determined to make more immediate changes. Irritated that a group of Union League members had been rowdy at a Reform party rally, W. R. Robertson of Winnsboro proposed a solution to the problem of "stupid leading darkies . . . determined to provoke a conflict with the white race." Meet the problem "promptly and *terribly*," he insisted. "Kill up a few hundred of them" and thus "put a stop to their incendiarism in short order." The *Yorkville Enquirer*, ordinarily a voice of restraint for a Democratic newspaper, considered the Union Leagues "a perpetual source of irritation" that would inevitably "give rise to counter organizations and thus endanger the public peace."[5] Public peace, on white terms, depended on the political subjection of the blacks; upcountry whites objected fundamentally to any organized, effective political effort among blacks. Black assertiveness and solidarity were inimical to white supremacy.

The political organization and assertiveness training provided by the Union Leagues precipitated a spiraling reaction of white counterorganization. Gearing up to protect themselves from the perceived threat, whites stockpiled large numbers of Winchester rifles and prepared for a "war of the races."[6] White reaction necessitated further political action among the Republicans. Neither individual Republican party members nor the party itself could stand against armed, organized former Confederates. Recognizing the antipathy of the majority of the white citizens to the possibility of an armed black electorate, Governor Scott nonetheless determined to organize a state militia strong enough to protect both his constituency and his own chances for reelection in 1870.

The South Carolina Militia Law of 1869 authorized the governor to employ as many persons as he thought necessary to suppress insurrection or resistance to the laws and forbade under penalty of fine or imprisonment any unauthorized military organizations. Technically the militia was not intended to be a strictly black organization, but the racial attitude of the vast majority of South Carolina whites foredoomed any possibility of a racially mixed organization. Republican politicians and personal friends of the governor traveled throughout the state organizing companies of black volunteers, many with black officers at the local level. A few white companies were organized, but they failed to gain the necessary acceptance and authorization of the governor as commander in chief. Black militia leaders complained that Scott even considered accepting white companies. Because most whites considered the Republican party program completely unauthorized, the governor realized that he could trust only the black militia companies to uphold the laws. It was almost impossible to find whites loyal to the state government. Questioned whether he would obey the governor as commander in chief in the event of an armed collision resulting from an attempt to enforce the laws, the captain of a white company responded, "In case of difficulty, I will go with my race."[7]

If the governor's initial purpose in creating a state militia was to protect his constituents from white violence and intimidation, the militia quickly assumed an overtly political nature. Indeed, the protection of the black electorate and the success of the Republican party were so dependent on each other that it is impossible to separate them. Scott's constables and militia organizers constantly advised the governor in 1870 of the political situation and his chances for reelection. "I will carry the election here with the militia," one wrote from Laurens. "I am giving out ammunition all the time. Tell Scott he is all right here now." The black militia was most effectively armed and equipped in the upcountry, where the black-white ratios were close and the Ku Klux Klan had resorted to violence and intimidation to keep the freedmen from the polls in 1868. Armed black militiamen accompanied Republican politicians to party rallies to protect them from Reform party interference. The militia made clear, also, that the freedmen should not even consider deserting the Republican party ranks.[8]

Whites in the South Carolina upcountry viewed the presence of an armed black militia as an intolerable affront, an insult "too grievous to bear." Indignation swelled as they watched the freedmen drill and march in the streets of the towns. The *Yorkville Enquirer* recommended the immediate organization of white companies to "appease this outraged sense of right." Tradition long grounded in the institution of slavery insisted that guns were for white men only.[9] Every armed black seemed a potential threat to the entire white community. To the white mind, whole companies of armed, trained black soldiers, left unchecked, signaled inevitable disaster. The martial airs assumed by the blacks further offended the honor of every South Carolinian who took pride in the region's military tradition.[10]

Black soldiers had been a serious matter of contention for white South Carolinians ever since the war's end. "Nothing seemed more contrived to humiliate white manhood, insult white womanhood, and demoralize the ex-slave," historian Leon Litwack wrote, "than the 'vindictive and revengeful' act of Federal authorities in stationing black troops in their midst." South Carolinians wrote provisional governor Benjamin F. Perry in 1865 expressing their alarm over the "unmixed evil" of black occupation troops who incited the freedmen "almost to a state of revolt." The editor of the *Charleston Mercury* warned that if blacks were allowed to bear arms, they would become "swaggering buck niggers" and would attack white women. When the federal government planned to organize a black militia in 1865, even the United States military commanders in South Carolina agreed with the governor that it would be "disastrous in the extreme, and would undoubtedly inaugurate a war of races."[11] Plans for the black militia were canceled. This white attitude remained unchanged in 1870. When Governor Scott actually organized a black state militia, white South Carolinians grimly determined to disarm the freedmen. Black participation in the state militia was both fearsome and offensive to the white mind.

Taking courage from their guns and their comrades in arms, some of the black troops engaged in behavior that seemed to whites deliberately calculated to provoke people accustomed to a slavelike demeanor from every black. The freedmen clearly enjoyed drilling and firing their guns. The black troops gloried in their uniforms, parading through the streets in red, yellow, and white, complete with epaulettes, some even sporting ribbons and feathers. Every company had a drum, a possession legally denied to blacks in slavery. The drumrolls alarmed whites, often disturbing their sleep. Whites complained that the militia insisted on marching "company front" in town, taking up the entire street and refusing to step aside for whites. Insulting language was not unusual from these black militiamen, John A. Leland complained to Governor Scott, "and in these insults neither age nor sex was spared and the most diabolical threats were constantly made and heard." The militia accompanied Republican candidates to political meetings and sometimes created a loud disturbance when Reform candidates tried to speak. In Chester, for example, a large crowd of blacks "singing John Brown and hooting" made it impossible for the candidates to go on with a meeting.[12] Some drunken black militia actually murdered one white man, a one-legged former Confederate bootlegger, who sold the blacks enough whiskey to get them drunk but not enough to satisfy their craving for liquor. This unfortunate event doubtless increased the hysteria of the white population.[13] The record indicates, nonetheless, that acts of violence by the black militia were extremely rare.

While the rank and file of the militia, including the company commanders, were black, many of the officers were white—most of them political allies of the governor. Having these officers on the state payroll assured the governor a statewide network of white friends. Most native white South Carolinians objected to the men Scott chose. The most infamous of the lot was Lieutenant Colonel Joe Crews of Laurens County, a former slave trader turned "scalawag" or "nigger trader turned nigger lover" as one critic labeled him, notorious for making "incendiary" speeches to the blacks. According to reports of white spectators, Crews insisted that the blacks were the rightful owners of the land and promised them that they should get it through the Republican party's tax policies. Judge Carpenter, the Reform party candidate for governor in 1870, testified to the congressional investigating committee that Crews encouraged the freedmen that if they wanted property "they should go and take it, and if the white people made a fuss about it they should burn down their houses." Regardless of whether Crews actually made such inflammatory speeches, the sight of him parading on horseback while his militia companies drilled was more than enough to make the whites despise him.[14]

The state of South Carolina spent enormous sums of money to recruit, arm, and equip the militia that was so despised by the white population. Many of the higher-level officers were Governor Scott's friends from Ohio. They traveled throughout the state at the expense of the taxpayers, organizing the blacks for the election of 1870. The number of men actually enrolled in the militia was between ninety and one hundred thousand, most of them unlettered freedmen determined to protect their newfound rights. Company captains were generally blacks who were leaders in the community. The common soldiers, like the officers, were on the state payroll, which was interpreted by the majority of the white population as "but another excuse and pretext intended and used to enrich and secure in power the great wire-pullers of the Republican party by taxes wrung from an oppressed and helpless people."[15]

The white population objected in equal measure to the method by which the black militia was armed and equipped. Governor Scott sent his adjutant and inspector general F. J. Moses, to Washington to appeal to the federal government for weapons. Moses procured some ten thousand Springfield muskets and all accouterments at no charge to the state. He then made contracts with the Remington and Roberts Breech Loading Rifle Companies to change the guns to breechloaders at a cost of approximately $9 each. Of this amount Moses was to receive a kickback (he called it a commission) of $1 per gun. This amount was discounted by the state paymaster, but Moses nevertheless lined his pockets with an easy $7,000. Governor Scott insisted that the secondhand army weapons were virtually useless until changed, but Democratic testimony, doubtless meant to discredit the Republicans, later maintained that the guns were actually more useful before they were modified. The state purchased another thousand Winchesters, complete with bayonets and ammunition. The "commissions" on these items were even more generous, an estimated total of some $1,675 split between Moses and another Republican state official.[16]

With a total of only eleven thousand weapons—distributed primarily in the upcountry, where violence had been most threatening before the election of 1868—among the ninety thousand or so militia members, it seems evident that the majority of the blacks were never armed.[17] Still, eleven thousand armed former slaves must have seemed enormously threatening to a white population long established in the belief that one black with a squirrel gun represented a serious danger of insurrection. Assessing the level of fear among the whites is difficult. Although many whites insisted that the black militia spread terror among the entire white population, saner voices recognized, as a white militia officer expressed it, that "a lot of ignorant colored men with clumsy muskets in their hands" could never "catch a squad of experienced soldiers on blooded horses." Judge Richard Carpenter, Reform candidate for governor in 1870, testified before the congressional investigating committee that "the people felt they had no security at all; that they might be attacked at any minute." Still, the judge recognized that the militia was never intended "to have any war with the white people." In Carpenter's estimation, the militia was organized strictly to guarantee a Republican victory at the polls. The *Yorkville Enquirer* reported during the election of 1870 that the purpose of the black militia was not to "terrify the white population so much as the colored. The main purpose is to prevent colored men from leaving the Republican ranks and voting with the Reform Party." In a letter to the *Charleston Daily Courier*, Julius J. Fleming similarly remarked that the militia was understood to be "intended to marshal the black and to convert peaceful laborers into armed auxiliaries for party purposes."[18]

If some whites recognized that the black militia posed no real dangers, the Ku Klux Klan nonetheless deliberately played on traditional fears to mass the white population in opposition to the blacks. Charles W. Foster of York County testified in the Klan trials, for example, that he knew of no alarm within the white community at the time the Klan began outraging the neighborhood. He was personally not at all afraid of the militia. Still, he stated, there was so much talk about the "negroes being up in arms" that he was eventually persuaded that he should join the Klan for mutual protection from the freedmen: "I was not afraid at the present time; but if everybody was afraid, I might be injured, too." By appealing to white fears, the Klan gained support and convinced the white community generally that the danger was acute. James Long of York insisted during the Ku Klux Klan trials that "folks were pretty much scared" in his neighborhood; "they did not know but what the niggers might come with their arms and kill them."[19]

In its efforts to consolidate white public opinion against the black militia, the Ku Klux Klan successfully appealed to white paranoia concerning armed blacks which had been nurtured in South Carolina for over a century. White South Carolinians were convinced that the master race alone should have the privilege of bearing arms. Any armed black was a potential assassin. Slavery had united the white community in its eternal vigilance against the possibility of insurrection. Virtually every white man of military age—whether a slave owner or not—was required to belong to the patrol, the instrument whites used to maintain racial control.[20] The patrols served as "courts on horseback" with authority to "try, judge, sentence, and punish offenders on the spot." The patrols had control not only over the slaves but also over free blacks and any whites suspected of conspiring with blacks. The patrols rode the highways at night breaking up meetings of blacks, arresting those who were found away from their homes, and searching for guns. The patrol had the responsibility for stopping insurrection before it began.[21]

The Ku Klux Klan was to a large degree a continuation of the old patrol system. The presence of armed black troops conjured up the specter of insurrection which had haunted South Carolinians for so long. When rumor got out that black militia members had threatened to "kill from the cradle to the grave," reason gave way to traditional racial fears. "Placing arms in the hands of the colored men," the *Yorkville Enquirer* later reported, "gave a feeling of insecurity to the whites, and caused a feverish feeling of alarm to pervade every community. Whether this feeling was well grounded, or otherwise, made no difference to the fact that such a feeling actually existed, and so long as that feeling existed there was imminent danger of a collision upon the slightest provocation." Arming black citizens convinced whites that they, too, must arm themselves for self-protection.[22] Like the antebellum patrol, the Ku Klux Klan rode the highways at night as courts on horseback to control the blacks. That the black militia posed little or no genuine danger was lost on the majority of the white community.

As important as the fear that bound whites together in support of the Klan was their inability to accept the black militia simply because it violated tradition and offended the honor of the whites. The military tradition was strong in South Carolina, but it was for whites only. The sight of armed, uniformed blacks drilling in the town squares infuriated white South Carolinians. It suggested that blacks were citizens—equal to whites—and capable of taking up arms to defend themselves and their families. An outraged sense of honor demanded that the black militia be disarmed.

Thus through its appeals to traditional Southern fears and to the honor of white men, the Ku Klux Klan was successful in uniting most of the white population. Klan membership was drawn from every class of white society and in the upcountry included the greater part of the adult male population. The organization's leaders came from the planter and professional class, many of them former Confederate officers. Ordinary Klansmen tended to be poor whites who were often as ignorant and illiterate as the blacks they attacked. Whites who preferred to remain aloof were pressed into service through threats and night attacks so that the Klan would represent a unified white community consensus. With white support of Ku Klux Klan outrages established, the night riders were free to terrorize their victims at will. Until the federal government intervened, Klan outrages went unreported and unpunished.[23]

With white support assured, the Ku Klux Klan instituted in upcountry South Carolina following the election of 1870 a sustained wave of terror that lasted for months. Sweeping through the countryside late at night, masked riders burst into the homes of Republicans, dragged hundreds of them from their beds, and whipped them severely. Driven from their homes, large numbers of freedmen spent the night hours in the woods and swamps. If whippings were the most frequent manifestation of Klan violence, they were hardly the most atrocious. Robbery, rape, arson, and even murder were common. It is impossible to determine exactly how many people lost their lives to the South Carolina Klan. The Klan reports documented thirty-eight murders between the election of 1870 and the suspension of habeas corpus in April 1871 in four of the nine upcountry counties where President Grant suspended the writ of habeas corpus. For the entire upcountry this body count is undoubtedly low.[24]

Klan violence in South Carolina aimed to preserve traditional white community values. Although most of the South Carolina Klan's nocturnal activities demonstrated the fear of armed black men and determination to check the freedmen's political progress which have dominated historiographical assessments of the Klan, Klan goals extended beyond politics to preserve the community status quo.[25] On the typical Klan visit, recounted time and time again in the two thousand pages of testimony in the South Carolina Klan reports, night riders forced their way into the freedman's home, demanded to talk to the man of the house, questioned him about his political activities, ordered him to renounce the Radical party, dragged him outside, then delivered a severe whipping. Almost every Klan visit included a search for weapons. Some blacks were spared a whipping on the first visit if they agreed to publish a notice that they had repudiated the Republican party. The blacks who told this story were almost always Republicans. Many were also involved in the Union Leagues or the black militia. Black leaders were a special target for Klan wrath. In these model Klan visits, contempt for the black man, fear of an armed black militia, and desire to suppress the Republican state government were so inextricably intertwined that it is impossible to separate them. Because the Republican party had extended political rights to the freedmen, the effort to "put down Radicalism" was less a movement against the Republican party per se than an all-out effort to reinstitute traditional white values. Put more simply, the Klan attacked Radicals, as one man testified, because "you damned niggers are ruining the country."[26]

White Republicans, like blacks, were resented by the Ku Klux Klan. Both Northern-born and native Republicans renounced their party membership at the insistence of the Carolina night riders. Many white Republicans received whippings. If Klan visits to whites served a political purpose—to

suppress the Radical party—they also demonstrated a demand for white
solidarity and an overarching desire to halt the black man's progress.
John Neason, for example, owned a country store at which he allowed
blacks to hold political meetings. The Klan forced Neason to close his
business and leave town. While they were on the premises, Klansmen
burned the wooden building Neason had built for a black school. Klansmen raided John Plowden, a native Southern Republican, beat him, and
left him tied up in the swamp. To the local whites, Plowden was a "traitor" to his race.[27]

The Klan's attack on William Champion, another Southern Radical
and an election official, was perhaps its most graphic statement that
white support for black rights would not be tolerated. Klansmen shot
into Champion's home about a hundred times, blindfolded and abducted
him, then took him to a clearing where they were holding several blacks.
After whipping Champion until he was faint, Klan members shamed him
further by forcing him to kiss the posterior and "private parts" of a black
woman and the posterior of her husband, demanding that he have sexual
intercourse with the woman (which he declared he was unable to do), then
asking him how he "liked that for nigger equality." After removing the
blindfold, the night riders forced Champion to whip the black man.[28] All
three of these attacks blended political purpose with racial hatred in support of a traditional Southern norm—white supremacy.

As dispensers of justice and repositors of Southern values, Ku Klux
Klansmen rode in support of other societal norms unrelated to politics.
Often this violence was directed against blacks. Klansmen beat Pressly
Thompson, for example, because he wanted to be buried in a white persons' graveyard. They whipped another black man, born free, because he
taught a black Sunday school. Klansmen whipped blacks who made good
wages in railroad construction and forced them to return to farms, where
their income was significantly lower.[29]

The moral structure of the white community was another focus of the
Klan's attention. The night riders warned a Democrat to stop abusing his
wife. Apparently he did not because several nights later the Klan whipped
him. Similarly, night riders warned Richard Roberts that he should close
his bar and stop selling whiskey on the Sabbath. Roberts's place of business was too close to the church to suit Southern propriety.[30]

These varied offenses all violated Southern community standards. To
see the black man rise economically and socially was unthinkable to

whites indoctrinated to believe blacks were inherently inferior. To accept a political party that promoted political equality for the freedmen was inconceivable. To allow lapsed moral standards was impossible at a time when society seemed to be falling apart. Hugh Lennox Bond, the federal circuit court judge who presided over the South Carolina Ku Klux Klan trials, keenly observed that white South Carolinians "preferred to live in amongst this outrageous Klan rather than under the government of law."[31]

For most white Southerners, however, the traditional mores carried a force greater than the laws the Yankees sought to impose. Two separate and distinct legal systems struggled for supremacy in Reconstruction South Carolina. Established Southern white perceptions of justice and how it should be accomplished strained against the Yankee values the Republican administration attempted to force on South Carolina. It was white supremacy versus black equality, vigilante justice and the code of honor versus the rule of law. By and large, white Southerners were convinced that the Ku Klux Klan's nocturnal raids were a necessary, if unfortunate, means of enforcing order and defending the South's traditional values.[32]

The value system that distinguished antebellum Southern society, as both Bertram Wyatt-Brown and Edward Ayers have demonstrated, was its code of honor. Honor was an ascriptive quality possessed by the individual as a feeling of self-worth, which depended upon the opinion of others. A man was what public opinion held him to be. Fear of being shamed, more than conscience or guilt, dictated Southerners' behavior. Honor stressed family and kin, the sanctity of white women, and the necessity of defending one's good name. Slavery and race fostered the hierarchical society and bestowed honor on all white men. Taking pride that they were neither slaves nor blacks, the poorest whites "legitimized the principles of honor."[33] At its core, the Southern code of honor embodied white male values and demanded conformity from women and blacks, who were excluded from this fraternal system.

If the Ku Klux Klan rode to support traditional local values, the value system the Klan's violence enforced was Southern honor—the sacred, ethical rules of the white male order. The code of honor justified the various crimes the night riders committed. Honor dictated that freedmen be kept in a servile position. It was important to the ethic of honor that blacks demonstrate heartfelt respect and deference for the dominant class—indeed, for all white men. A mere pretense on the part of the black denied the white man—who depended on others for his good feelings about himself—his honor.[34] Honor demanded the suppression of the Republican party and reinstitution of legitimate constitutional government as whites understood it. Acceptance of Republican party policy would legitimate the blacks' claims to equality and contradict traditional notions of white supremacy. Finally, honor prescribed gender behavior for men and women.

Although the Ku Klux Klan reports are replete with evidence, historians have directed little attention to the Klan's violence against women.[35] Both black and white women suffered at the hands of the night riders, although blacks were victimized far more often. These attacks, like the crimes Klansmen perpetrated on men, supported the usual white masculine values: the integrity of the white family and determination to keep blacks in their accustomed place.

The Southern code of honor dictated expected gender behavior for white Southerners. White males demanded chastity from their unmarried daughters, submission and unerring faithfulness from their wives. White Southern men considered women to be both physically frail and childlike, a condition that allegedly rendered them easy to manipulate and morally weak. Women, in this view, required strong male protectors. Because a "tarnished woman" brought public shame to her menfolk, the Southern system suppressed the white woman's sexuality and encouraged the familiar sexual double standard. Lustfulness was an accepted fact of life for the male; a healthy sex life presumably prepared the young man for marriage. Even for the married white Southern male, discretion was more important than fidelity. The object of white male passion—outside the marriage union—was very often the black woman. Indeed, the presence of so many blacks allowed white men to maintain a sexual double standard.[36]

Whites agreed, nevertheless, that racial amalgamation was unthinkable; black blood would taint the bloodlines of the master race. Despite strong legal and moral pronouncements against miscegenation, however, the number of mulattoes increased steadily throughout the antebellum period. White men blamed their weakness for black women on the blacks' aggressive sexuality and animalistic nature. Because blacks were naturally lascivious, white men could hardly be blamed for succumbing to the charms of black women. At the same time, whites believed the aggressive promiscuity of the Negro race dictated unwavering attention to the purity of white women. Black blood in a white womb was the ultimate racial taboo in the antebellum South. White men were certain that blacks lusted after their women. These racial fears, as Winthrop Jordan has suggested, may have been a matter of transference or projection of their own sexual attitudes. It is more likely that these fears for the safety of white women masked the white male fear of humiliation by the black. There was no greater offense to the white man's honor than the ruination of his women.[37] No one has yet proved that black men were particularly interested in white women, yet the notion has persisted well into the twentieth century that white Southern women needed special protection from the "black beast rapist."

There is no evidence in the Klan reports for South Carolina that any black man raped or even attempted to rape any white woman, but it is clear nevertheless that this traditional Southern fear was at least partially responsible for Klan outrages. The whites feared that black equality and political empowerment would encourage interracial mixing. During a particularly savage attack, Klan members accused Elias Hill, a hopelessly crippled black preacher and minor Republican party official, of encouraging black men to ravish white women. Across the border in North Carolina, attorney David Schenck wrote that one purpose of the Klan was "to protect female virtue from negro violence or his embraces." These examples demonstrate the irrational white male fear of sexual humiliation by black men which drove the Ku Klux Klan. As late as 1916, John Lucas, a former South Carolina Klansman, justified the Reconstruction Klan's "defense" of white womanhood and determination to halt social and political progress of black citizens:

> It is as necessary now here as it was then to uphold White Supremacy and to protect the White Women of the South from insult and outrage. . . . His [the black's] criminal propensities and disposition to criminally assault our white women appear to increase in proportion to the educational opportunities furnished him. . . . When the illeterate [*sic*] negro acquires education, he aspires to obtain social equality, and knowing how utterly impossible that is, South, he broods on that thought and reads on the subject until becoming obsessed he by stealth and cupidity waylays and victimizes an unprotected white woman. Then he finds himself dangling at the end of a short rope, without judge or jury. Such summary punishment is as necessary here now as the Ku Klux Klan was then.[38]

Klan members served warning that no racial mixing between black men and white women—however willing the women might be—would be tolerated. Six to eight night riders shot a black man on the steps of the house where he allegedly lived in adultery with two white spinsters. The Klan reports do not mention the fate of the two white women. If they escaped the wrath of the Klan they were fortunate. Their alleged sexual aberration had shamed the entire white community.[39]

Another white woman received hideous treatment from the night riders for her association with black men. When the Klan arrived at her home she was discovered hiding two black men under the floor of the house. The two men managed to escape, but Klan members ordered the woman out of her house, forced her to lie down on the road, then poured hot tar into her "private parts" and ordered her to leave town within three days. The Klan reports give no indication of the woman's moral character or her relationship with the blacks. The Klan's punishment for her behavior was obviously planned ahead so one can only assume that her conduct had been outrageously offensive to the white male psyche. The Klan reports refer to one raid on a prostitute, but it is impossible to determine if this was the same incident. Whatever the woman's offense, this atrocity was a graphic statement that emancipation had not changed traditional Southern sexual mores. Any interracial sex between white women and black men was forbidden by the white male value system.[40]

Just as the Ku Klux Klan's attitude toward white women reaffirmed the South's moral structure, so too did Klan outrages restate the white male's traditional power over black women. Night riders threatened and cursed black women, knocked them down and kicked them around, pistol-whipped them, beat their heads against the walls of their homes, whipped them by the hundreds, and sometimes raped them. Testimony revealed that attacks on black women were likely to be as severe as the crimes perpetrated against black men—thirty to forty hard licks with a hickory were not at all unusual. Jane Surratt, for example, testified that Klansmen complained that she did not work hard enough. For her poor working habits the night riders gave her forty lashes with sticks as wide as her thumb. Wounded from her ankles all the way up her backside, the woman was unable to hold her baby on her lap. She had to stand beside the bed to nurse the child.[41] Samuel Bonner testified that Klansmen whipped his mother and sister as hard as they did him. The reason the white men gave for whipping the old woman: "D———n her, she is a nigger; just whip it on her."[42] That the Ku Klux Klan demonstrated no respect for black women is not surprising. Slavery had muted gender differences among blacks.

Black women worked alongside men in the fields and had been subjected to the same punishment as the men.

Like the whippings, the sexual assaults Ku Klux Klan members committed on black women were a restatement of the white male's traditional authority. Sexual exploitation of black women was institutionalized under slavery. Whether sexual liberties were granted as a part of the master-slave relationship or taken by brute force, black women were completely vulnerable to white men. Rape of a Negro woman was not a crime at law. The behavior of the Klan members demonstrated their assumption that black women were still available to them sexually. Bursting into her home late at night, Klansmen spit on Harriet Simril and threw dirt into her face until she was blinded. The night riders ate the food the woman had stored in her cupboard. Then three of them dragged the woman into the road and raped her in succession while the others carried on a lewd conversation. The Klansmen left the woman lying senseless in the road. Later, when the family had taken to sleeping in the woods, the Klan burned their house to the ground. During another Klan raid, freedman Amzi Rainey watched helplessly from a loft while several Klansmen beat his wife and threatened to kill her if she refused to reveal her husband's whereabouts. When Rainey's small daughter begged, "please don't kill my pappy," a Klan member threatened to blow the child's brains out, then shot her in the forehead. wounding her slightly. In the next room, an unspecified number of night riders allegedly raped another daughter in full view of the other children.[43]

These atrocities were not simply gratification of the night riders' lust for black women, however, nor were they primarily expressions of male power over the female. No one could deny that the Klan's sexual attacks on Harriet Simril, Amzi Rainey's daughter, and other assorted black women violated their persons and expressed the male desire for dominance, yet the rape of the women appeared almost incidental to the Klan's original intent. Klan members did not ride to Simril's home hoping to find a black woman to rape. Rather, they came looking for her husband, a Radical Republican. They claimed they would not bother the husband if he would promise to vote the Democratic ballot. Thus the rape of Harriet Simril was more than a matter of sadistic lust, more than a crime against women. It was layered with social and political meaning directed primarily against the assertion of black male political power rather than against women per se. Similarly, Klan members did not break into the home of Amzi Rainey to ravish his daughter. Their business was with the man of the house.[44] With few exceptions, the same rule holds true for most of the black women who were whipped. The night riders were searching for their husbands. While the black men hid in the woods, as one female victim of the Klan's wrath testified, Klansmen "took the spite out on the women."[45] In short, the Ku Klux Klan did not go out looking for black women to exploit. The outrages upon black women were part and parcel of the white males' efforts to render black men powerless.

The ancient notion that women are the property of men was still prevalent in the male-dominated, paternalistic society of nineteenth-century South Carolina. Paternalism decreed that a man protect and defend his family. Abuse of a man's possession—his wife—was, by extension, an attack on the man. In addition to this male perception of women as property, the Southern code of honor taught white males that their personal moral worth resided as much in their women as in themselves. Thus an attack on wife, mother, or sister, according to Wyatt-Brown, was an attack on the man. A man, in other words, was subject to rape through his women. By whipping and raping the wives and daughters of black men, Ku Klux Klan members were making a ritualized statement of the black male's powerlessness. The man who whipped or raped a black female, as Susan Griffin put it, simultaneously aggrandized his own manhood and reduced that of another. Violence against black women, like other Klan crime, served to reaffirm the community value of white male authority.[46]

Indeed, white male authority was the driving force behind the entire value system of Reconstruction South Carolina. The unchallenged political power of the white man, the sanctity of the white family, the unfeigned submission of white women and all blacks, the continuity of things as they had always been—these were the important things in life. Antebellum tradition was too firmly entrenched to give way simply because outsiders wanted to establish Yankee values and a rule of law. White South Carolinians resisted the federal government, the Republican state government, the black state militia, and the inevitability of change in the traditional Southern way—with violence.[47]

The Ku Klux Klan's ritualistic vigilante justice cleansed the community of impurities and upheld the proper standards of conduct. If many South Carolinians believed the Klan's methods too extreme, with violence inexorably breeding more violence, they nevertheless agreed that the organization's purpose was a necessary reaffirmation of local values in the face of imminent danger. "Of course whites adopted some plan of counter-organization," Professor John Leland wrote in 1879. "They would have been less than men, if they had left their family hearths, and their wives and children, exposed to all manner of violence and insult, without some scheme."[48] The masked night riders of South Carolina's Ku Klux Klan believed that they rode to protect themselves, their womenfolk, local customs, and the right to constitutional government as they understood it from encroaching outside authority. The unprecedented wave of violence they sustained was for the sake of honor and tradition.

Because the majority of white South Carolinians supported the goals of the Ku Klux Klan, the state's criminal justice system was inadequate to stop the violence. Blacks who dared to report the crimes perpetrated against them often found that the local trial justices turned a deaf ear to their complaints. Some of these magistrates, appointed by the governor, were white Democrats who were personally involved in Klan activities. Others acquiesced silently to the goals of the Klan, refusing to use their authority to investigate outrages or issue warrants. These officials had earned a bad reputation with Freedman's Bureau officers, one of whom reported that they were "afraid to enforce the laws or will not risk their positions in society by attempting to arrest criminals who have only injured colored men." Generally speaking, as another Freedman's Bureau officer put it, when a freedman was the "aggressor" in a quarrel with a white man, public opinion acquitted the white of any guilt "without the tedious formality of a judicial examination." Republican trial justices, whether black or white, were threatened, intimidated, and sometimes even murdered when they attempted to uphold the rights of freedmen. John Hubbard, chief constable for the state, reported to Governor Scott in February 1871 that trial justices had been brutally murdered in Union, Spartanburg, and Laurens counties. Many other Republican county officials were forced to resign. When Ku Klux Klan terrorism was at its peak, local magistrates "did not dare to take up the cases and proceed with them." [49]

When blacks did get their day in court, they still found it extremely difficult to obtain justice. State law had denied blacks the right to testify against whites before the war, and the Fourteenth Amendment's equal protection clause had not changed Southern minds. When whites were tried for crimes against freedmen, they were often acquitted despite the evidence against them. In some cases, the attorneys were "sure to impress upon the jury that the evidence just taken is *nigger* and they must not believe it before white evidence." The presence of blacks on the jury did little to alleviate the problem. According to David T. Corbin, federal attorney for South Carolina, racially mixed juries usually split along political lines, again despite the evidence, resulting in hung juries and mistrials.[50]

When blacks were accused of crimes, the picture was likely to be very different. Retribution against black criminals was apt to be swift and terrible, whether it was informal and extralegal or within the state's judicial system. H. E. Hayne of Marion County reported to Governor Scott in late 1868 that several blacks were being held unduly for petty crimes. One freedman, for example, had already been locked up for seven months awaiting trial for stealing a bushel and a half of peas. Another black, accused of hog stealing, had been denied the right to have his witnesses heard when he was tried in the district court. A third was falsely accused of stealing bacon from his employer, then indicted for stealing a plow (which he had purchased) found in his possession. In each of these cases, Hayne insisted, the freedman was indicted primarily "because he would not sell his principles to his employer." Stealing was apparently a serious problem among the freedmen, as it is likely to be among poor people anywhere, but the evidence suggests that whites accused some blacks falsely of stealing goods they had come by honestly so as to have them incarcerated. Hayne, a white Republican, made this connection, as did Edward Lipscomb, a yeoman farmer from Spartanburg County, who put the matter bluntly: "We think in the year 1870 we will be able to chang [sic] the law making power for the negroes are leaving the upper districts a grate [sic] many has run away for stealing and a heap goes to the penotensuary [sic] & all that is convicted for stealing is done voting."[51]

A white population that was willing to imprison freedmen unjustly to prevent them from voting was obviously not going to exert itself to bring the night riders of the Ku Klux Klan to justice. Indeed, many whites insisted that the Klan did not even exist. One freedman who attempted to prosecute his assailants was tried for perjury and false arrest and landed in the penitentiary.[52] No serious investigation of Klan atrocities in South Carolina was attempted until the United States Army sent Major Lewis Merrill to York County. Initially skeptical concerning the level of both Klan brutality and community consensus among the whites, Merrill soon learned that the violence surpassed anything the Republican national government had imagined. The major documented eleven murders and more than six hundred whippings in York County, yet the civil authorities in the county were unwilling to address the problem. When the county grand jury met in September 1871, Merrill reported, "the whole effort appeared to be to devise some means of avoiding the knowledge" he tried to furnish. According to Merrill, at least one-third of the members of both the grand and petit juries were members of the Ku Klux Klan, some of them high-level officers; at least two grand jury members had been accessory to Klan murders. The few members of the grand jury who were actually interested in doing their duty were "browbeaten and overruled by the rest." Not surprisingly, the court session ended with no relief for the victims of the Ku Klux Klan. Indeed, Merrill labeled the grand jury proceedings "so broad a farce that it was very distasteful to be forced in contact with it."[53]

Because local civil officials all over the upcountry, as Major Merrill put it, were "either in complicity with the Ku-Klux conspiracy, or intimidated by it," a major federal effort would be required to stop the Klan and restore the civil and political rights of its victims. Governor Scott appealed to President Grant for help. Despite his fears of being labeled a military dictator, Grant moved quickly to restore order. Acting under authority of the Ku Klux Klan Act of April 1871, the president declared a nine-county area of piedmont South Carolina to be in a state of rebellion, then two weeks later, on 17 October 1871, he suspended the writ of habeas corpus in those nine counties, enabling the federal government to make mass arrests without the usual niceties of procedure. All over the upcountry local whites screamed that they were being torn from their homes unjustly in a time of "profound peace."[54]

3

Federal Intervention and Southern Resistance

The inability of the Republican state government under Robert K. Scott to suppress the Klan's terrorism, provide justice for the freedmen and white Republicans, and restore law and order moved the upcountry inexorably toward federal intervention. The governor found himself in an untenable position. A mutually reinforcing combination of racism and laissez-faire constitutional principles had convinced most South Carolina whites that the state government was illegitimate. Thus the majority of the white population either openly supported the goals of the Ku Klux Klan or silently acquiesced to its reign of terror. Scott recognized, moreover, the futility of declaring martial law or calling out state troops when the militia was one of the primary points of contention and the opposition consisted of mounted, trained former Confederates committed to disarming the black troops. The use of black troops was certain to incite further violence against blacks and white Republicans. Instead Scott attempted to reason with the white state leaders. The whites promised peace in return for disarmament. Scott proceeded to disarm and disband the black troops, only to find that he had exchanged the freedmen's means of protection for empty assurances.[1]

Scott's position was as precarious among the members of his own party as among the whites. Threatening impeachment, the Republican members of the state legislature passed a joint resolution in January 1871, demanding to know why the governor had not called out a militia force sufficient to dispel the violence in the upcountry. Fearful of returning to the upcountry, where they might be killed, many of the state lawmakers were virtual prisoners in the state capital. Scott made public pronouncements which discounted the need for armed forces in a time of "profound peace." "Such a remedy," the governor stated, "would be as bad as the disease, and would be a public declaration that there was no Civil Government in South Carolina, and that we are living in a condition of social anarchy." Quietly, however, Scott sought federal assistance for his strife-ridden state.[2]

Klan violence in South Carolina and throughout the South had spurred congressional Republicans to provide statutory authority to protect the freedmen and enforce the Fourteenth and Fifteenth Amendments. These extraordinary Enforcement Acts expanded the power of the federal government in relation to the states and provided a legal basis for the federal intervention Governor Scott sought. The first Enforcement Act of 31 May 1870 stated that citizens otherwise qualified to vote were entitled to do so without regard to race, color, or previous condition of servitude. Although the law was directed primarily toward discriminatory state interference with black suffrage, it recognized that a state's failure to protect black voters was often the problem. Thus the law prohibited private interference with the right to vote. Section 6, which targeted the Ku Klux Klan, made it a felony to conspire or ride the public highways to deprive any citizen of "any right or privilege granted or secured to him by the Constitution or laws of the United States" or to punish him for having previously exercised his rights. Section 7, one of the act's most controversial provisions, extended federal power to ordinary crimes committed by the Klansmen in the process of violating other sections of the law. A Klansman who committed murder on a Ku Klux Klan raid, for example, could be prosecuted in federal court. Technically, the federal offense was the civil rights violation, not the murder. But the state penalty for the crime determined the punishment for the civil rights violation. Thus the federal courts could possibly prescribe the death penalty—the state punishment for murder— for a civil rights violation. The law reenacted the Civil Rights Act of 1866 under the authority of the Fourteenth Amendment and guaranteed black citizens "full and equal benefits of all laws and proceedings for the security of person and property."[3]

The first Enforcement Act of 1870 had little effect on the situation in South Carolina. Klansmen were totally unimpressed with the federal law. Violence escalated. Responding to the pleas of Governor Scott, President Grant in March 1871 sent additional federal troops under the command of Major Lewis Merrill to Spartanburg, Union, and York counties. The troops calmed the problems in the towns where they were stationed, but violence in the countryside continued unabated. Indeed, several Klan murders in York County were committed after the arrival of the troops.[4]

Continued reports of outrages throughout the South, and particularly in upcountry South Carolina, produced a growing public demand for a stronger enforcement act. President Grant provided Congress with the evidence he hoped would persuade the Republican lawmakers to act. Congress appointed a special joint committee to investigate the problems in the South. The committee, which initially limited its investigation to North Carolina, confirmed the worst reports on conditions in the South. Despite their increased understanding of the Klan, however, the national lawmakers adjourned without providing the president any new power to deal with the problem. Believing that the role of the president was primarily to execute the will of the people as expressed through their congressmen and doubtful that the present law afforded him sufficient authority to halt the Klan, President Grant called the new national legislature into special session in March 1871. Congress balked initially, then acted on the "urgent" written request of the president to provide legislation to "effectually secure life, liberty, and property and the enforcement of law in all parts of the United States." On 20 April 1871 Congress passed a tough new law designed to enforce the provisions of the Fourteenth Amendment.[5]

The third Enforcement Act[6]—quickly labeled the Ku Klux Klan Act— like the first Enforcement Act, attempted to provide a remedy for private lawlessness. The statute outlawed conspiracies to deny civil rights and increased the power of the president to use military force to suppress domestic violence that deprived citizens of their "rights, privileges, or immunities, or protection named in the Constitution." It authorized the president to suspend the writ of habeas corpus temporarily when such violence existed. The president could send federal troops with or without the state's request. The Klan Act required every petit and grand juror in Enforcement Act cases to take an oath that he had never taken any part in Klan activities whether voluntarily or involuntarily.[7] Democrats and conservative Republicans complained that the law exceeded federal constitutional authority over individuals and worried about the extended power of the president. Indeed, the Democrats in Congress were more concerned about federal encroachment than about the atrocities committed by the Ku Klux Klan. Radical Republicans, however, perceived the Klan to be a paramilitary organization that could not be dealt with through normal law enforcement procedures. Thus they determined to use the full extent of their power to combat it.[8]

Following the passage of the Ku Klux Klan Act, the Forty-second Congress expanded the role of the Joint Select Committee to Inquire into the Condition of Affairs in the Late Insurrectionary States to investigate the rumors of Klan activity throughout the South, although Congress's purpose in forming the committee is not entirely clear. The Justice Department and the secretary of war were already taking steps to enforce the new law before the committee began its work. Congress probably intended the committee to confirm the necessity of the Klan Act and the controversial task of enforcing it. The committee produced thirteen volumes of evidence covering every aspect of Southern life. The reports remain one of the most fertile sources of information on the Reconstruction South. The subcommittee of three that investigated conditions in South Carolina interrogated people of every station in life from Confederate heroes and Democratic leaders to the humblest former slave. Although Southern white leaders discredited the atrocity stories and professed no knowledge of the Klan's nocturnal activities, eyewitness accounts—both black and white, Klansmen and victims—confirmed again and again the enormity of the problem and the complete failure of the state government to restore order. The Ku Klux Klan reports stand today as solemn testimony to the brutality of many white Southerners and the total breakdown of law and order in Reconstruction South Carolina.[9]

Attorney General Amos T. Akerman decided that the United States Justice Department would also conduct an investigation of affairs in South Carolina. A recent appointee, Akerman was the first attorney general to administer a department of his own. The Justice Department had been formally created in July 1870, at least partially to stop the flow of government money to expensive special counsel. The attorney general and his assistants were to perform all legal services necessary to enable the other departments of government to discharge their duties. The attorney general directed the activities of the district attorneys and all other legal officers, supervised their accounts and expenses, made rules and regulations for the management of the new department, and reported annually to Congress, in addition to writing legal opinions and arguing cases before the Supreme Court.[10] The workload would have been great under any circumstances, but the large number of Enforcement Act cases swelled the Department of Justice's burden to unmanageable proportions.

The only former Confederate to reach cabinet rank during Reconstruction, Attorney General Akerman was totally committed to the goals of the Republican party in enforcing the Fourteenth and Fifteenth Amendments. Born and educated in the North, Akerman had migrated to Georgia after finishing Dartmouth College. There he taught school while he studied law with former attorney general John M. Berrien. Akerman remained loyal to his adopted state during the war, even volunteering for the Confederate forces. After the war, however, Akerman considered it a point of honor to lay down his loyalty to the Old South along with his arms. He recognized, as he put it, that "a surrender in good faith really signifies a surrender of the substance as well as of the forms of the Confederate cause." Unlike most former Confederates, who "consulted the past rather than the future" and let "resentment rather than reason" determine their politics, Akerman joined the Republican party because he considered its ideas "both expedient and right." The position of United States district attorney for Georgia was Akerman's first reward for his change of heart. Congress granted a special dispensation because the lawyer was unable to take the test oath required of federal officers. Akerman's vigor in prosecuting violations of the Civil Rights Act of 1866, added to his efforts to build a strong Republican party in the South, earned him the position in the national cabinet when Grant wanted a Southern candidate.[11]

Akerman traveled to South Carolina to investigate personally the reports of atrocities in the upcountry. He first stopped in the state capital to consult with Governor Scott, South Carolina attorney general Daniel H. Chamberlain, United States district attorney David T. Corbin, and Major Lewis Merrill, commander of U.S. troops in York County. Fully concurring with Akerman's plans to implement enforcement procedures in South Carolina, Governor Scott was able to advise the attorney general about which counties should be included in the proposed suspension of habeas corpus. From Columbia, Akerman traveled to Yorkville, where he spent more than two weeks with Corbin and Merrill reviewing the evidence Merrill had gathered and examining witnesses. Merrill's evidence demonstrated that "the worst reports which had been heretofore made of the power and of the infernal purpose and conduct of the order fell far short of the facts." Akerman left South Carolina convinced that "from the beginning of the world until now," no community "nominally civilized, has been so fully under the domination of systematic and organized depravity." The Ku Klux "combinations amount to war," Akerman concluded, "and cannot be effectively crushed on any other theory." Accordingly, Akerman recommended to President Grant that he use the full extent of his powers under the recent act of Congress to suppress the Ku Klux Klan in South Carolina.[12]

Evidence painstakingly accumulated by Major Lewis Merrill convinced Akerman of the necessity of federal intervention; indeed, Merrill was the person primarily responsible for uncovering the information that would enable the federal government to bring the Klansman to justice. Merrill had begun his investigation of the Klan upon his arrival in York County in March 1871. Incredulous at first, Merrill gradually began to recognize that Klan brutalities surpassed anything the government authorities had perceived. Accumulating evidence was no easy matter in York County, where most of the white population was committed to the Klan's goals. Merrill used spies hired by the Justice Department and spent a "moderate sum" of money, which he obtained from the governor, to "supply all the missing links in my chains of evidence." Perhaps more important, he sheltered victims of the Ku Klux Klan in the army camp, where they were protected from the consequences of relating information to the federal officer. Merrill accumulated reliable evidence of some eleven murders and more than six hundred whippings and other brutal outrages in York County alone. He furnished this information to the York County grand jury in September 1871. Rather than acting on the evidence, however, the grand jury spent its time "avoiding the knowledge" of what Merrill termed a "carnival of crime not paralleled in the history of any civilized community."[13]

Attorney General Akerman was thoroughly impressed with Major Merrill and the job he had done. Akerman considered the major "bold, prudent with a good legal head, very discriminating between truth and falsehood, very indignant at wrong, and yet master of his indignation." In short, Merrill was "just the man for the work." The information Merrill furnished Akerman convinced the attorney general that "the local law is utterly unable to cope with the criminals." He called for measures that would put fear in the hearts of white Southerners. The Republican government was in the South by right, he had previously insisted, "and not by tolerance of the population." Thus in Akerman's opinion, "nothing is more idle than to attempt to conciliate by kindness that portion of the Southern people who are still malcontent. They take all kindness on the part of the Government as evidence of timidity and hence are emboldened to lawlessness by it." If it was impossible for the federal government to win the affection of the South, the government could, nonetheless, command respect by exercising the full extent of its powers under the law. When Akerman left South Carolina, he met with the president to recommend vigorous enforcement of the laws.[14]

President Grant determined to do everything in his power to stop the lawlessness in South Carolina despite his sensitivity to the charge that he was a military despot. Following the recommendation of Akerman and Senator John Scott, chairman of the joint congressional investigating committee, Grant issued a proclamation on 12 October 1871 which commanded "all persons composing the unlawful combinations and conspiracies" to turn their weapons and disguises over to a United States marshal and disperse to their homes within five days. Such a proclamation was required by law before the writ of habeas corpus could be suspended. As expected, Klansmen in South Carolina ignored the presidential order. Thus the president issued a second proclamation on 17 November that declared a nine-county area of upcountry South Carolina to be in a state of rebellion. Grant suspended habeas corpus in those counties, an act that was unprecedented in the United States during peacetime—if the Reconstruction era in South Carolina can properly be called a time of peace.[15] The suspension of habeas corpus was tactically important because it enabled federal officials to make mass arrests quickly. Large numbers of Klansmen were arrested and jailed without the usual procedures of due process. Klan members languished in confinement, unable to secure their release and desperate to learn the charges against them while United States officials concentrated their efforts on securing more prisoners. Newspaper accounts insisted erroneously that South Carolina suffered under martial law. Eventually, however, the suspects were properly charged and tried by civilian authorities.[16]

The suspension of habeas corpus and subsequent arrests spread fear and panic throughout upcountry South Carolina. Government efforts centered initially in York and Spartanburg counties. Federal marshals, assisted by the Seventh Cavalry, spread out from Yorkville into the county, depending on the element of surprise to catch the Klansmen before they had a chance to flee. The officers had done their homework. Mary Davis Brown of Bersheba Community reported in her diary that several men from her neighborhood had been arrested at a "shucking" that had been planned for the young people. Several others decided to forgo their social life when they heard about Grant's proclamation and thus eluded the federal officers. Government authorities made large numbers of arrests quickly, most of them in the daytime and with very little resistance. Finding suspects became more and more difficult as the Klansmen took to the mountains. Many of the more affluent Ku Klux members had fled the country as soon as Grant issued his initial proclamation. Others left when word got out that federal officers had commenced rounding up the criminals. Thus Major Merrill reported that many of the most wanted criminals were known to be as far away as Canada, Texas, and Pennsylvania. James W. Avery, who was head of a Klan unit and the person allegedly most responsible for planning and executing the murder of Jim Williams, a black militia captain, for example, had fled to London, Ontario, where he was staying with the Manigault family, also formerly of York County.[17]

Many Klansmen who did not flee decided to surrender; several entire Klans turned themselves in to the federal officials. The resources of the officers in charge were strained in attempting to take confessions from these "pukers," as they were called. Some of those who puked were poor, ignorant country boys who had been coerced or threatened into joining the Klan by leading citizens. Others doubtless had gone along with the crowd because of their race prejudice and desire to participate in socially legitimized bullying and brutalization. Whatever their motives for joining the Klan, they now perceived that the flight of their leaders had left them to bear the brunt of federal enforcement measures. Thus they willingly availed themselves of the opportunity to tell all they knew. From these Klan members Major Merrill learned of six murders in York County which his previous investigations had failed to uncover. Most of those who surrendered voluntarily were allowed to return home after they had made their statements, but some of them had committed outrages of such extreme criminality that they were incarcerated along with those the government arrested. A few of those who made voluntary confessions asked to be arrested to avoid the Klan's retribution for their action. Some were granted clemency for turning state's witness.[18]

It is difficult to overestimate the effect of the arrests on the upcountry, particularly York County, where the government was most active. Virtually every family was affected. After venturing to town to see what she could learn of the government's intentions, Mary Brown reported that the streets were deserted. Merchants were boxing up unsold goods to send back to the distributors. Business was ruined. The suspension of habeas corpus had a similar effect in the countryside. Families were separated. Women and children were left to cope with farm chores without the assistance of their menfolk. Mary Brown's diary testifies to the fear and excitement that overcame the upcountry as federal troops commenced the arrests. "Oure children and grandchildren is all under oure roof tonight," she wrote, "but it has the apperance that it may all never meet again." Her sons fled, leaving a "broken harted Farther & Mother." Her daughters, too, were heartbroken as fiancés left for "parts unknown." Other family members and friends "put on their hats this evening and steped off," with no knowledge of when they might be able to return. A praying woman, Brown committed each of these loved ones to the care of the Lord. "Enabel me," she pleaded, "to say thy will be done." Brown was not the only person driven to prayer. She related a scene she "had never seen ore heard before." She witnessed her uncle Bille as he knelt "in prayer before Almighty God pleading with him fore his care & protection in these times of sorrow and trouble. I pray God that he will make him faithful in his good work," she continued, "so that manny more will follow his exampell so that it can be said of Bershaba they are a praying people."[19]

If the streets of York were emptied, the local jail was full. Klansmen of all social classes and situations sat in jail and waited to learn the charges against them. The influential planter Iredell Jones complained to his wife in October that he was enduring his "persecution" as "the fruit of military rule to be innocent of any crime whatever, & yet be called upon to suffer a heavy penalty without even being allowed a hearing." Jones "felt keenly the responsibilities of home" and sent instructions for work to be done. He assured his wife that most of the men were innocent. They had been arrested on suspicion only, according to his story, "with the hope of getting testimony after arrest." He labeled the suspension of habeas corpus an unconstitutional exercise of executive authority. Convictions would be made because of political necessity, he predicted, with false evidence and packed juries provided for the purpose. A month after his incarceration Jones was still waiting for the government to advise him what the charges were.[20] The authorities were too overwhelmed with taking confessions and making additional arrests to take time to attend to the prisoners' anxieties.

The jailed Klansmen suffered little. The government allowed them exercise and visitors after the first few days. They marched regularly through the streets of town under guard. Local women outdid themselves to provide for the prisoners' appetites, bringing baskets of delicacies daily.

Some of the captives seemed to enjoy the attention they received as martyrs. While the men in jail protested their innocence and Democratic newspapers throughout the nation decried government policy, the *Yorkville Enquirer*, a Democratic paper, remained a voice of calm restraint. Printing the full text of both the Enforcement Act of 31 May 1870 and the Ku Klux Klan Act of 20 April 1871, the paper made clear that the government had no intention of arresting anyone innocent of crime. The *Enquirer* listed the names of the night riders who had been incarcerated and generally kept the community informed, "deeming conjectures and sensational paragraphs . . . as quite superfluous, and in tendency injurious."[21]

The federal government achieved remarkable success in arresting only legitimate suspects. Major Merrill reported the difficulty of the task. He was unable to find reliable local white men to help locate suspects; to use blacks, according to his judgment, would invite resistance. Federal officers were generally unfamiliar with the appearance of those they sought. Despite these difficulties, Merrill reported that of the 169 military arrests in York County before January 1872, only nine men were taken into custody by mistake. In each case the person arrested had the same name as the one desired. All were released as soon as the mistaken identity was revealed, usually within a few hours. Approximately two hundred men were incarcerated in the York County jail for serious crimes. At least five hundred more had surrendered voluntarily, given confessions, and been released. Twenty had turned state's evidence; six were arrested at their own request because they were afraid to testify unless it appeared that they were forcibly required to talk. Although York County was the primary focus of the initial prosecutions, the arrests extended into several other counties, most notably Spartanburg, Union, Chester, Newberry, and Laurens. Approximately six hundred men had been taken into custody by December 1871. Most of the arrests had been accomplished by the end of the year, but they continued off and on until 1873. Despite the large numbers of arrests, however, the federal effort never touched the majority of the offenders.[22] The mass of prisoners caught in the federal net nonetheless turned out to be far too great for the courts to handle.

Anticipating the flood of business Reconstruction would bring to the federal courts, Congress had expanded the federal judiciary in 1869. The Judiciary Act of 1862 had substantially altered the regional balance on the Supreme Court and in the circuits in favor of the North. To strengthen the federal judicial presence in the South without creating new Southern circuits, which would add Southerners to the Supreme Court, the Judiciary Act of 1869 provided for nine independent circuit court judges, one for each of the existing circuits.[23] The circuit judges were required to be residents of the circuits to which they were appointed. Within their respective circuits they held the same power as the U.S. Supreme Court judge assigned to the circuit. The law also aimed to reduce the circuit court responsibility for members of the Supreme Court. Supreme Court justices still had to ride circuit, but the circuit judges generally held court jointly with the district judge. Republican lawmakers hoped that this two-headed court with one judge from outside the immediate area would enhance the national interest by decreasing the favoritism toward parochial interests which was often displayed in the district courts.[24]

The Ku Klux Klan trials in South Carolina were to be tried jointly by High Lennox Bond of Maryland, circuit judge of the Fourth Federal Circuit, and George Seabrook Bryan, district judge for South Carolina. President Grant appointed Bond to the federal bench because of his demonstrated courage, commitment, and determination to enforce civil rights for the recently emancipated freedmen. Judge Bond had already demonstrated, however, a Unionism tempered by constitutional scruples that leaned toward states'-rights federalism. A member of an old and respected Baltimore family, Bond had grown up in New York. Returning to Baltimore after he graduated from New York University, Bond read law and was admitted to the bar in 1851. He was a founding member of the Republican party in Maryland. From 1860 to 1868 he served as a judge of Baltimore's criminal court. As a wartime border-state judge, Bond balanced his personal devotion to the United States with a keen regard for the constitutional liberties of his fellow Marylanders, who were deeply divided between the Union and the Confederacy.

In 1861 citizens of Baltimore had mobbed the Sixth Massachusetts Regiment as it passed through the city. Several people died, soldiers as well as civilians, and many more were wounded. In his charge to the grand jury Bond insisted that those who took part in the riot were guilty of murder. His support for the Union was clear. Bond's determination to punish all the guilty, moreover, foretold his reaction to the Ku Klux Klan. Later in the war, however, Bond courageously instructed a grand jury to indict United States military commissioners appointed to try civilians on the grounds that Maryland was not under martial law. Here, too, Bond presaged his future actions. He upheld states' rights and seriously ques-

tioned the federal government's constitutional authority to exceed its traditional powers, even in wartime.[25]

Bond's performance on the city bench also indicated his concern for
black rights. After the emancipation of Maryland's slaves, Bond used his
official position to fight the vestiges of slavery. A discriminatory appren-
ticeship system in Maryland required that black "orphans" be bound to
some white person, usually the former master. In effect, these youths were
reenslaved. As many as ten thousand blacks may have been apprenticed,
even though many had parents willing to provide for them. Hugh Bond issued writs of habeas corpus to release many of the apprentices and even
provided free legal advice to Freedmen's Bureau officials who worked to
eradicate this anachronistic system.[26]

Bond's approach to race relations in Reconstruction Maryland was a
Christian paternalism. Whether "by the grace of God or accidental circumstances," Bond considered himself superior to the blacks. But his
sense of superiority persuaded him to follow the scriptural injunction "to
help his neighbor up not put him down." Bond considered the "safe rule"
the one the "Almighty prescribes to himself: 'God is no respecter of
persons.'" Thus Bond supported equality before the law and worked to
provide free public schools and voting rights for Maryland's black citizens.
Concern for the legal rights of African Americans did not convince Judge
Bond that it was his duty to associate with them socially, however. "To
make a man equal before the law," he reassured a relative, "does not nec-
essarily make it obligatory on me to eat, sleep, or drink with him." Bond
had no desire to "intermingle with low irish, dutch, rebels, or Negroes."[27]

Bond ran for governor in 1867 on a Republican platform that appealed
for black voting rights. Although Bond made clear to the blacks that
they must be willing to work to enjoy the fruits of their liberty, he was
considered "too severely radical" by most of the state's Republicans. The
campaign ended with the Republican party seriously divided and the
Democratic machine in power.[28]

The commitment to black rights that rendered Hugh Bond unacceptable to Maryland voters made him an attractive candidate to President
Grant, who chose him for the federal judiciary in 1871. Senate confirma-
tion did not follow automatically, however. Radical Republicans supported Bond's nomination, but his racial attitudes made him an unpopular
candidate among Democrats and conservative Republicans, particularly
those from the border states. Nominated in April, Bond was not confirmed

by the Senate until 18 July and then only by a vote of twenty-eight to twenty-one. Soon after his appointment to the Fourth Circuit Court, Bond presided over the Ku Klux Klan trials, first in North Carolina and then in South Carolina.[29]

Judge Bond was determined to end the Klan's reign of terror. He did not perceive his role in the South Carolina Klan trials as that of an impartial jurist but rather as a pivotal member of a federal team determined to pursue successful prosecution. The Klan had "engaged in a war with the U.S. Courts," he wrote his wife. Bond vowed to punish Klan offenders "even if it costs me my life." But the circuit judge's support of Republican party objectives as he assumed the task of interpreting the substantive constitutional meaning of the enforcement legislation was tempered by his judicial independence and long-standing constitutional scruples.[30] Bond's ability to construe constitutional law was also influenced by District Judge Bryan, who would preside jointly with Bond at the Klan trials.

George Seabrook Bryan was a Democrat and former slave owner who could be trusted to represent local interests in the two-headed circuit court. Bryan received his appointment to the federal judiciary by virtue of his prewar political sentiments when he had been an outspoken anti-secessionist. When the first legislature convened in South Carolina following the Civil War, the state lawmakers recommended Bryan for the post of federal judge. President Andrew Johnson followed their advice. The Senate confirmed, and Bryan took his seat on the bench in 1866. Thus it was Judge Bryan who reopened the civil courts of the United States in South Carolina for the first time since the war. There he set about to restore constitutional order—Southern style. Bryan stood up to the military commander in Charleston, General Daniel Sickles, insisting on open courts and the right of trial by jury rather than martial law, a position that demonstrated his judicial courage. When the judge's pronouncements failed to sway the general's opinion, Bryan appealed to President Johnson as commander in chief. It was District Judge Bryan also who first ruled that Southern lawyers did not have to take the test oath to appear in federal or state courts, a principle that was followed throughout the South. His opinion was later affirmed by the Supreme Court in *Ex parte Garland*.[31]

Bryan's conduct during the first Enforcement Act cases in South Carolina demonstrated the need for Judge Bond's strong judicial direction in the Klan trials. Bryan had presided alone over the United States District

Court (with full powers of a circuit court) in Greenville during August and September 1871. Upon the insistence of the acting district attorney, Bryan had required the grand and petit jurors to take the required oath under the Ku Klux Klan Act of 1871. The grand jury found true bills against several persons indicted for conspiracy against a citizen for voting and intimidating a citizen because of voting. But the prosecution had absolutely no luck at trial in Judge Bryan's court. The juries would not convict. Federal efforts ended in mistrials and acquittals.[32] Clearly Judge Bryan failed to give the firm direction necessary to bring a successful prosecution.

Judge Bond recognized that Bryan would be a problem to the enforcement effort. "I am in a peck of trouble with old Bryan," he wrote. "The democrats have got hold of him—visit him in crowds & persuade him to be a stick between our legs at every step." The Democrats were indeed making every effort to influence Judge Bryan's interpretation of the law. Wade Hampton, Confederate military hero, future Redeemer governor of South Carolina, and certainly one of the most influential men in the state, urged upon Judge Bryan the "vital necessity of his taking his seat upon the bench with Bond." According to Judge Bond, "they have stuffed him full of the idea that the Democrats will make him Gov[ernor] if he differ with me." Bond was equal to the challenge, however: "I went to him [Bryan] the other day & frightened him half to death," Bond told his wife. "I stormed at him and told him . . . he had better not keep the court sitting doing nothing but posing about the smallest matter in the world day after day."[33]

South Carolina Democrats were as interested in providing a good defense for the "unfortunate people" who had suffered such enormous "trials and wrongs" from the Enforcement Acts as they were in influencing the bench. Wade Hampton spearheaded a subscription campaign to secure the soundest conservative legal talent available to defend the Ku Klux Klan and—more important—question the constitutionality of the Enforcement Acts. Hampton thought that eminent counsel from outside the state would "have more weight than our own advocates and could speak more freely."[34]

People from all over the state supported the defense effort, demonstrating that the night riders of the Ku Klux Klan and white South Carolinians who had abstained from the violence shared a deeply held racism that was layered—among those sophisticated enough to think about constitutional ideas—with laissez-faire principles. Racism convinced the majority of

white South Carolinians that blacks were inherently inferior and utterly
unworthy of respect. Laissez-faire principles satisfied them that the state
government was an illegitimate tyranny of class rule by those least qualified to govern: "carpetbaggers, scalawags," and, worst of all, Negroes.
Because the conservative effort to unseat the Republican state government
had failed, the Klan had seemed a necessary evil. J. M. Wallace expressed
the feelings of white people throughout South Carolina:

> While I am strongly opposed to all lawlessness, & the assumption by
> private individuals of meting out public justice—yet such is the
> tyranny & usurpations of our powers in authority that I cannot in my
> heart condemn those who assume the privilege of righting themselves.
> It is but self-defense properly—the last desperate remedy of the
> feeble & downtrodden. The poor worm turns to sting the foot that is
> crushing it, & if darkness & the mask can afford it any security—who
> can blame it for striking in the night.[35]

Just as racism and constitutional values bound white South Carolinians
together in support of the Klan, so too did the conviction that the federal
Enforcement Acts were unconstitutional. The Ku Klux Klan trials would
afford an excellent opportunity to air their opposition to the laws in court.
Democrats raised a reported $10,000 to hire Senator Reverdy Johnson of
Maryland and Henry Stanbery of Ohio.[36]

An outspoken critic of Republican Reconstruction measures, Democratic senator Reverdy Johnson was a natural choice for defense counsel.
Johnson, like Judge Bond, was a Unionist from Baltimore. He had wel-
comed the end of slavery, yet his sympathies were aligned with Southern
white sentiment. As a minority party member of the Joint Committee of
Fifteen on Reconstruction, Johnson had recommended immediate restoration of the Union with a general amnesty for all Confederates. Negro
suffrage, in his opinion, should have been postponed until the blacks
were sufficiently educated to understand the duties of citizenship. Johnson believed that the Enforcement Acts exceeded the constitutional authority of the Congress and seriously interfered with the reserved powers
of the states. President Grant, he thought, had recklessly suspended
habeas corpus in a state where no rebellion existed. He therefore wel-
comed the opportunity to defend the Carolina night riders, understanding
that the fate of individual Klan members would be less important to the
outcome of the trials than the constitutional questions that would arise.[37]

Johnson was as much at home in the courtroom as he was in the Senate chambers. His counsel was sought on many fine points of constitutional law; for example, he had argued the Southern side of the *Dred Scott* case before the Supreme Court. His biographer reported that Johnson commanded the highest legal fees of any lawyer of his day. If he believed in a cause, however, he might donate his services. Judge Bond reported that Johnson came to South Carolina well equipped to take on the federal prosecutors: "He has made every preparation to fight every inch. Has made himself (or has been posted by others) acquainted with the local statutes & practice and knows more about both than Judge Bryan who has been on the bench this six years." Bond not only admired the defense attorney's legal skills, he enjoyed his company. They had rooms close by each other, took their meals together, and Bond read the newspapers to Johnson, who was almost blind. "I would like to have the old gentleman with me all the time," Bond told his wife, "but on the other side." Although Johnson denied the constitutionality of the Enforcement Acts, he was shocked, after his arrival in South Carolina, to learn the depth of the Klan's depravity. Ironically, it was Johnson's son, the United States marshal in South Carolina, who filled his father in on the details of the Klan outrages.[38]

Henry Stanbery of Ohio was the second defense attorney hired by South Carolina Democrats to handle the Klan's defense. An outspoken critic of Reconstruction, he opposed all federal encroachment on traditional state power. "Restoration" rather than Reconstruction was Stanbery's policy. A Whig turned Democrat, Stanbery served as the first Ohio state attorney general when the office was created in 1846 and was, like Johnson, a former attorney general of the United States. He had served in Andrew Johnson's cabinet, then resigned to serve as defense attorney in the president's impeachment trial.[39] Several South Carolina attorneys, who reportedly donated their services for the cause, worked with Stanbery and Johnson on the defense. The local attorneys attended to the day-to-day defense of individual Klansmen while the eminent counsel concentrated their efforts on the important constitutional issues. The defense focused on securing a division of opinion between Judge Bond and Judge Bryan that would force the Supreme Court to consider the constitutionality of the Enforcement Acts.

Responsibility for planning and implementing prosecution strategy fell to David T. Corbin, United States attorney for South Carolina from 1867 to 1876. Corbin was a prominent South Carolina Republican with the "reputation of being one of the most conservative and fair of the Republican Party." Corbin had graduated from Dartmouth College and established a law practice in Vermont before the Civil War. He served in the Union army, then came to South Carolina to serve in the Freedman's Bureau. As a Freedman's Bureau agent, Corbin observed firsthand the stormy relations between white South Carolinians and the former slaves. An ambitious politician, Corbin also served in the state senate from 1868 to 1872, as solicitor for the constitutional convention of 1868, and as commissioner to revise the South Carolina statutes in 1868 to 1872.[40]

The United States attorney labored under tremendous pressure. Corbin had spent weeks in York County hearing testimony and gathering evidence for the trials. To him fell the task of indicting the hundreds of Klan members who had been arrested and had surrendered. Preparing indictments was no easy job; Corbin was feeling his way in uncharted constitutional territory. He sought the advice of Attorney General Akerman and hoped that his superior would be on hand for the South Carolina trials as he had been for the first major Ku Klux Klan trials in Raleigh, North Carolina, where Akerman and Corbin had both assisted. Encouraged, perhaps, by federal district attorney Darius H. Starbuck's successful prosecution of the North Carolina Klan and pressed by the work he had to do in Washington, Akerman declined to attend the opening of the South Carolina trials in November 1871. Even the news that the defense had secured some of the most formidable legal talent in the nation did not convince Akerman that Corbin needed him in court. "Skillful lawyers residing on the spot can generally match men of eminence from a distance," he wrote, "the very fact of sending off for celebrated counsel often striking the jury as evidence of a cause inherently weak."[41]

Akerman did not attend the South Carolina trials because he trusted Corbin's ability. Still he recognized the enormous pressure on the prosecuting attorney and arranged for him to have the assistance of Daniel H. Chamberlain, attorney general of South Carolina, and Major Lewis Merrill.[42] It was impossible for Corbin simultaneously to manage the witnesses, supervise the grand jury, and conduct the prosecution. Thus the assistance of Chamberlain and Merrill (who knew more than any other man about the Ku Klux Klan and worked hard to prepare the evidence and inform the grand jury) would prove invaluable to the government's efforts. Akerman also hired a stenographer to record verbatim the Klan trials in Columbia.

The United States Circuit Court opened in Columbia, South Carolina, on 28 November 1871 amid great excitement. Both sides recognized the enormous implications of the constitutional questions that would be argued in the Fourth Circuit Court. "The Constitution of the United States is on trial," the *Charleston Daily Courier* put it. "In the history of this country no questions more important have ever arisen or been presented to a judicial tribunal for adjudication than are those which will arise in the trials now about to take place." Members of the bar and state judges crowded into the state capital to observe the proceedings. Newspaper reporters from around the nation flocked to the city. Black witnesses, both male and female, also traveled to the capital city. Democratic newspapers complained loudly about the "lazy and idle looking negroes who were paid and clothed at government expense" and would be paraded as the "mangled victims of the murderous Klan." According to the newspapers, these were "witnesses ready to swear to anything" for the $2 per day they were paid to be in Columbia.[43]

When the court opened, the first order of business was choosing the jury. Internal Revenue agents throughout the state had previously submitted a list of one hundred potential jurors per district from which names were drawn. The clerk called the roll of jurors, black and white, from all over the state, but white South Carolinians were slow to answer the summons. Neither grand nor petit jurors showed up in a number sufficient to conduct the trials, undoubtedly because the Ku Klux Klan Act of 1871 required all jurors on Enforcement Act cases to swear an oath that they had never participated in the Klan. Perjuring themselves in federal court was a risk that few were willing to take.[44]

Corbin rose immediately to challenge the entire array. His action was no surprise. Judge Bond had written his wife on 26 November that "the jury has been drawn all wrong, I shall have to quash the array & there for [sic] a howl all over the country about packed juries." The judge was correct. Word had leaked out about the proposed challenge. The *Charleston Daily Courier* speculated that the government attorney planned to get rid of the jurors who had been called so as to make one up of bystanders "who would convict."[45]

Corbin made his challenge on grounds that the jury had been drawn irregularly. The law required that the jury be drawn in the presence of the clerk and the marshal, but the clerk had allowed a small child to draw the names from the jury box when the marshal was not present. Judge Bryan and the bailiff had been in the courtroom when the names were chosen, however. Reverdy Johnson opposed the challenge and wondered what Corbin hoped to accomplish by the delay. Corbin feared that an irregularly chosen jury could be used by the Supreme Court as reason to set aside the venire and order a new trial in any case that might proceed to the Supreme Court. Johnson offered to waive all objections to the manner in which the jury had been chosen, an offer that was accepted the following day, when Corbin withdrew his challenge.[46]

There still remained the problem, however, of finding enough people to fill the grand and trial juries. Both sides agreed that a jury made up of bystanders was unacceptable, that the jury would have to be drawn from the entire district. Exactly what constituted the district was the next problem. Reverdy Johnson argued that the jury must be drawn from the western district, where the Klan had been most active. Clearly the defense hoped to impanel jurors who would be intimidated by the prospect of convicting their neighbors. The prosecution insisted, however, that the entire state was one district so far as the circuit court was concerned. It was divided into eastern and western districts only for district court purposes. Judge Bond agreed, a decision favorable to the prosecution. He ordered the United States marshal to summon more jurors from the entire state.[47]

Bond's order resulted in a majority of black Republicans on both the grand and petit juries. Many of the whites summoned for jury duty again defaulted. Thus fifteen of the twenty-one-member grand jury were black; the foreman, Benjamin K. Jackson, was a white Republican. Over two-thirds of the petit jurors who answered the summons were black. Each of the cases in this group of trials would be tried by a jury with a black majority.[48]

The black majorities on the juries increased the white population's animosity toward federal efforts to stop the Klan's activities. Administration of justice in the pre–Civil War South had been the exclusive prerogative of white males. The law forbade blacks to sit on juries or testify against whites in court. That they could do so now was still unthinkable to most white South Carolinians. The specter of white defendants being hauled before black juries offered visible proof that theirs was a world turned upside down. Local attorneys considered it humiliating to have to address black jurors, and whites considered it beneath their dignity to have to sit on the jury with blacks. Southern newspapers sneered at juries and witnesses alike and labeled the trials a "farce which is now being acted in the United States Court under the name of a trial." Judge Bond wrote, "I fear that we will not be able to control the court, tempers run very high, and the populace is unsettled."[49]

The nation turned its attention to South Carolina as the courtroom drama began. Democrats and Republicans across the country understood that it was not only the Ku Klux Klan that was on trial. The meaning and scope of the Reconstruction Amendments and Enforcement Acts were also before the court. Decisions made in South Carolina would carry important implications for the future of four million freedmen. It was up to federal judges to breathe life and meaning into the ambiguous words and phrases of the Fourteenth Amendment and laws of Congress. The prosecution and defense squared off to present their opposing constitutional views. The black citizens of South Carolina, meanwhile, looked to Judge Bond for protection.

4

The Constitution and the Klan on Trial

The South Carolina Ku Klux Klan trials provided a unique opportunity to explore the meaning of Republican Reconstruction measures. The Fourth Circuit Court became a forum for constitutional interpretation as prosecution and defense attorneys struggled to define the meaning of the protean phrases of the Fourteenth and Fifteenth Amendments, the Enforcement Act of 1870, and the Ku Klux Klan Act of 1871.[1] Both sides recognized that the decisions of the judges on the constitutional issues were more important than the fate of the individual Klansmen.

The goal of the prosecution was not only to gain convictions, a relatively simple matter under the conspiracy provisions of the Enforcement Acts, but to establish a broad nationalization of black civil and political rights. The United States attorneys framed long indictments with counts designed to extend the meaning of the Reconstruction Amendments, stretch the limits of the state-action concept, and nationalize the Second and Fourth Amendments through the Fourteenth to secure for blacks the right to bear arms and to be safe in their homes from illegal search and seizure. These fundamental freedoms were essential if blacks were to maintain their political rights. Nationalization of the Bill of Rights also offered the best hope of extending federal protection to black women, who were often the victims of Klan atrocities but totally unprotected by the conspiracy provisions of the Enforcement Acts, which were designed to protect political rights, which women did not enjoy. The prosecution needed to gain strong precedents at the trial level if the federal government was to secure black citizens in their civil and political rights, but the nationalistic goals of the federal attorneys were not the only ideas represented during the trials.[2]

The defense attorneys spoke for the multitude of Americans, North and South, who desired a quick return to traditional federal-state relations.

Henry Stanbery and Reverdy Johnson pressed for a conservative, states'-rights interpretation of the constitutional questions, while making clear that they abhorred the violence committed by their clients. The South Carolina Klan trials delineated the constitutional conflicts within a nation deeply divided over its responsibilities to four million freedmen and the limits of federal authority to protect them in the rights of citizenship. The fate of the hundreds of individual Klansmen awaiting trial was almost incidental to the larger issues to be considered in the federal court in Columbia, South Carolina. The defense attorneys, as Henry Stanbery put it, "came to the conclusion that the two laws of 1870 and 1871, under which these proceedings in your State had been going on for some time, were unconstitutional." Thus they undertook the defense of the Carolina night riders for the express purpose of sending a case to the Supreme Court so that the nation's high court would have the opportunity to interpret the Fourteenth Amendment and the Enforcement Acts. Federal law did not provide for appeal in criminal cases; therefore, the defense attorneys hoped to secure a division of opinion between the two judges which would certify a case to the Supreme Court. The Supreme Court could then decide the issues on which the judges had divided.[3]

Attorney General Akerman shaped the prosecution's strategy in deciding which Klansmen to try. Prosecuting all the individual night riders would have overwhelmed the federal judicial system for many years. Thus Akerman instructed Corbin confidentially to classify the Klansmen into three groups according to their moral guilt, social influence, and intelligence. Offenders of "deep criminality" and community leaders who should have used their influence to stop the Klan's outrages rather than encouraging them were to be tried first. But most of the influential and affluent leaders had fled when the government suspended habeas corpus. Still, the prosecution focused as much as possible on trying Klan leaders and those who perpetrated some of the more heinous crimes. The second group, whose "criminality was inferior" to that of the first class, was released on light bail with the instruction that "their cases need not be pressed to a speedy trial unless they should desire such trial." The third group consisted of the reluctant night riders, those who were coerced to join and took little or no part in the violence. Many of this group confessed voluntarily and appeared as witnesses for the prosecution. Akerman advised that they need never be prosecuted if "they bear themselves as good citizens henceforth." Corbin followed the attorney general's instructions, hoping that implicating community leaders would break the Klan permanently.[4]

The first case to come to trial, *U.S. v. Allen Crosby,*[5] involved a large Klan raid on the home of Amzi Rainey, a "most respectable mulatto," who had "always maintained an excellent character." Rainey's only offense was that he supported the Republican party. Klansmen broke into Rainey's home at night, fired on Rainey and other family members, beat his wife senseless though she held a young child in her arms, raped one daughter, then shot another in the head, wounding her slightly. The night riders then dragged Rainey from the house, beat him, and threatened to kill him. They ultimately allowed Rainey to run for his life after he promised never again to vote the Radical ticket. The same night the Klan continued its rampage, intimidating and whipping other blacks in the neighborhood.[6]

District Attorney Corbin framed a long indictment designed to secure an expansion of black rights under the Fourteenth and Fifteenth Amendments and the Enforcement Acts. The federal attorney's commitment to black rights emerges clearly from his letters to Attorney General Akerman. Corbin studied the Constitution and Enforcement Acts carefully, wrestling with the problem of intent. He recognized the novelty of "setting up Constitutional rights in an indictment" but concluded that the purpose of the recent amendments to the Constitution was to secure positive civil and political rights for black citizens and to protect them in those rights from both state action and individual discrimination: "The more I study it the more I am convinced that the citizens of the Country generally may appeal to it under the legislation of Congress, and many a poor man in the South will rejoice that it is so." Corbin recognized, however, that his expansive view of the Fourteenth and Fifteenth Amendments was not universal, that many people believed the Constitution operated on the people only as they were represented by their state governments. He was "satisfied," however, "that this ought not, and never was intended to be its full scope."[7]

Corbin's nationalistic view of the Reconstruction Amendments held that the Fourteenth and Fifteenth Amendments, although stated negatively, conferred positive rights. The Fourteenth Amendment, in Corbin's mind, had radically altered the nature of the federal system. Through the "privileges and immunities" clause, the first eight amendments became federally enforceable rights. If a state did not protect its citizens in the exercise of those rights, the federal government could place itself squarely between the citizen and the state.[8] The sixth section of the first Enforcement Act, which made it a felony to "conspire together or go in disguise upon the public highway, or upon the premises of another with intent . . . to prevent or hinder . . . free exercise and enjoyment of any right or privilege granted or secured . . . by the Constitution," was the vehicle through which the federal government could enforce this broad interpretation of federal rights against individual action as well as official state action.[9]

Corbin recognized that charging a conspiracy to deny the right to vote under the first Enforcement Act was inadequate to protect black citizens from Klan brutality. Although the Klan was largely political in its purposes and the typical outrage consisted of breaking into a black Republican's home, stealing or destroying his gun, dragging him outside and whipping him unmercifully, then warning him never again to vote the Republican ticket, many of the Klan's most brutal atrocities were crimes against women and children, who could not vote.

Corbin sought a method by which he could bring women and children under the protection of the federal government. He had already experimented with the problem of protecting women during the August 1871 term of the Western District Court of South Carolina. There he had charged several persons with "going in disguise for the purpose of depriving one Harriet Martin of the equal privileges and immunities under the laws, to wit, the privileges and immunities of life, liberty, and property." The grand jury found a true bill, but the case was never tried. The indictment indicated, nonetheless, that Corbin was searching for a way to protect female victims of the Klan. He continued that process during the November 1871 circuit court. He framed an indictment that charged several Ku Klux Klansmen with committing an assault and battery on two black women, Lucretia Adams and Phoebe Smith, in the act of "hindering, preventing, and restraining" some black males from exercising their right to vote. Attaching the assault and battery charge to the charge of interfering with Fifteenth Amendment rights demonstrated the difficulty of extending the federal law to women. The Klan outraged the two women at the request of Adams's husband, who was apparently a favorite of the whites. When the wife left her husband for "keeping another woman," the husband beat her himself, then sent the Klan to whip both the wife and her aunt to punctuate his demand that she come home. This crime clearly had nothing to do with voting rights, but Corbin could not charge an ordinary assault and battery in federal court unless it was connected with a federal violation.[10]

Corbin's best hope for securing the rights of all citizens from the Klan's outrages lay in his assumption that the Fourteenth Amendment nationalized the Bill of Rights. Because many of the Klan's outrages included breaking into the homes of black state militia members to seize their guns, Corbin planned his strategy to secure for these South Carolina citizens the Fourth Amendment right to be free from illegal search and seizure and the Second Amendment right to keep and bear arms. If he could establish these basic constitutional rights in federal court, the United States would have the means to protect all citizens, male and female, black and white.[11]

Corbin consulted with Akerman before the November trials began, seeking his advice on the question of securing these Bill of Rights guarantees in an indictment. The attorney general had previously given the problem much thought. Because the field of civil rights enforcement was so new, Akerman had written a United States attorney in Mississippi a few months earlier, it was impossible to determine without some experimentation exactly "what should be the theory of the prosecution" or exactly how indictments should be framed. He had advised a variety of different forms and charges to "see how they will stand the scrutiny of a trial" and "where the dangers are." Akerman wanted to convict. He was perfectly willing to press for a broad interpretation of federal rights under the Fourteenth Amendment, but he wanted to make sure that all the bases were covered. Akerman's reply to Corbin demonstrated that he shared the federal attorney's expansive view of federal power. "Upon the right to bear arms," he wrote, "I think you are impregnable." He doubted, however, that a Fourth Amendment charge would stand. Akerman thought the amendment provided protection from unreasonable search and seizure made "under color of official authority" rather than those that were "irregular and unofficial." He was not certain that his interpretation was correct, however, and he encouraged Corbin to "make the point."[12]

Corbin made his points in an eleven-count indictment that promoted a nationalistic construction of the Fourteenth and Fifteenth Amendments and the Enforcement Acts. Two of the counts, the first and eleventh, were similar to those with which U.S. Attorney D. H. Starbuck had already won convictions under Judge Bond in the first major Ku Klux Klan trials in Raleigh, North Carolina, where both Corbin and Attorney General Akerman had assisted.[13] The first count charged, under section six of the first Enforcement Act of 31 May 1870, a general conspiracy to violate the first section of the act by interfering with black voters. The eleventh charged numerous Klansmen with conspiring specifically against Amzi Rainey on 21 April 1871 for having supported the election of Republican Congressman A. S. Wallace. The date is significant; Corbin drew the eleventh count on the Ku Klux Klan Act of 20 April 1871, even though the outrage occurred in March 1871. Corbin initially planned to rest his entire case on the 1870 act, as he wrote Akerman, but changed his mind and included the Ku Klux Klan Act to make the point that the conspiracy continued after its passage.[14] Two other counts, the ninth and tenth, also depended on the 1871 act. They charged a conspiracy to deprive Rainey of equal protection of the laws and equal privileges and immunities. These counts demonstrated the difficulty of establishing constitutional rights in an indictment; they were so general as to be virtually meaningless. It was impossible, as Judge Bond stated, to judge what crime had been committed or which privilege violated.[15]

The second through seventh counts evinced Corbin's understanding that the Fifteenth Amendment conferred a positive right to vote. Each charged some offense against the "right and privilege . . . of suffrage." Ordinary crimes such as burglary, assault, and breaking and entering were attached to these charges. Here Corbin was testing the controversial section seven of the 1870 law, which stated that if an ordinary crime was committed in the act of violating the Enforcement Act, the offender could be punished in the same manner as if he were convicted for the crime in a state court. The federal government did not, as Corbin stated in court, intend to try the defendants for offenses "against the laws of the state." Rather, the ordinary crimes were attached to the civil rights charges "simply to inform the Court how this man should be punished for committing this conspiracy." Corbin entertained some doubts about the efficacy of this manner of determining punishment for the guilty, but he determined to fight out these "exceedingly embarrassing" questions in court if necessary. He later complained that the method had caused him great inconvenience.[16]

The eighth count, brought under the sixth section of the first Enforcement Act, charged a conspiracy to deny the Fourth Amendment right to be secure against unreasonable search and seizure. Here Corbin was asserting his notion that the Fourteenth Amendment nationalized the Bill of

Rights and that the federal government could protect individuals in their rights when the state failed to act in their behalf. Thus he stretched the state-action concept in the amendment to include a state's lack of action.[17]

Taken as a whole, the indictment promoted an enlarged sphere of authority for the federal government and a broad nationalization of black civil and political rights. The Fourth Amendment count—if it stood—would afford federal protection for women and children. The expansive version of federal authority promoted in this indictment would not only enhance black rights and protect women and children, it would also secure the future of the Republican party in the South. Corbin recognized that the defense would launch a furious attack on the constitutional rights he had attempted to set up in his indictment, but he confidently labeled it "an amusement I trust we shall live through."[18] The government attorney expected the full support of Republican circuit judge Hugh Bond, who had already overruled a motion to quash an indictment against the Ku Klux Klan in North Carolina.

Stanbery and Johnson did indeed attack furiously, moving to quash the entire eleven-count indictment. The arguments on the pretrial motion took three long days. The defense's most important arguments centered around the broad interpretation of the Enforcement Acts and Reconstruction Amendments which informed the indictment. They argued, predictably, for a narrow states'-rights interpretation of federal authority. The Fourteenth and Fifteenth Amendments, in this view, were framed entirely as prohibitions upon state action. Individual acts of discrimination or violence were beyond the reach of the federal government. Stanbery insisted first that the Fifteenth Amendment did not confer a positive right to vote; it merely limited the states' authority in regulating the suffrage for federal elections. In state and local elections, according to Stanbery, the amendment offered no protection whatsoever. Thus the counts that described voting as a right granted by the Constitution were invalid.[19]

Stanbery objected to the Fourth Amendment charge because the Bill of Rights was a restriction against federal authority. The defense refused to consider the possibility that the Fourteenth Amendment had altered "well-established doctrine"[20] regarding federal-state relations; only the states were competent to protect individual rights. Although the United States Constitution declared "these sacred rights," it was still the states that guaranteed "all the rights, immunities and privileges secured to the citizen of the United States by the Constitution." Federal jurisdiction was limited. "Great God," Stanbery asked, "Have we forgotten altogether that we are citizens of States and that we have States to protect us?" He vowed to "fight to the last ditch, against Federal usurpation" of those "personal, sacred immunities that attach to us as individuals, and are protected by the domestic [i.e., state] law."[21] In more technical, legal terms, Stanbery objected to the language of the indictment and its lack of specificity. And in a disingenuous argument, Stanbery claimed that a conspiracy against the rights of voters could be effected only on election day.[22]

Stanbery reserved some of his most intense arguments to castigate Republican efforts to bring ordinary crimes under the purview of the federal courts. His reasoning demonstrated the difficulty of charging common law crimes as a measure of punishment for civil rights violations. Noting that the federal courts had no authority to try or punish ordinary crimes, Stanbery insisted that "you must try him first and find him guilty before you can apply the punishment." Thus in Stanbery's mind it was impossible for the federal government to *avoid* trying ordinary criminal cases if state law was used to determine the punishment to be used in federal courts. The seventh section of the first Enforcement Act, according to the defense attorney, was clearly unconstitutional. Hoping for a division of opinion between the two judges, the defense attorney suggested that the judges should "refer this question to the Supreme Court."[23]

Reverdy Johnson reiterated Stanbery's narrow interpretation of national powers under the Reconstruction Amendments. The Thirteenth, he argued, "does nothing but abolish slavery." In no way did it allow Congress to regulate suffrage.[24] The Fourteenth Amendment, according to Johnson, granted citizenship to the freedmen, but it, too, stopped short of conferring on the national government the right to interfere with the suffrage. The proof was in the fourth section, a "persuasive measure," which provided for a reduction in congressional representation if a state made restrictions on the grounds of race or color. Even the Fifteenth Amendment, Johnson maintained, did not "clothe the Congress of the United States with the whole authority to regulate" the suffrage. It merely restricted the states in their power to interfere with existing rights. If the Fifteenth Amendment had "clearly and unambiguously" taken from the states "the right to regulate the suffrage," Johnson insisted, "it never would have been adopted by the people of the United States." Because the recent amendments to the Constitution did not allow national regulation of the voting laws, he continued, the Enforcement Acts clearly lacked constitutional authority. To the extent, therefore, that the Enforcement Act of 1870 and the Ku Klux Klan Act of 1871 assumed that the Fourteenth and Fifteenth Amendments granted a positive right of suffrage their "provisions are void."[25]

Like his fellow defense attorney, Johnson launched some of his most strenuous objections against the charges that included the common law crime of burglary. Charging burglary in federal court, he insisted, was an unwarranted usurpation of state authority; the federal government had no jurisdiction in such cases. Johnson maintained, "with great confidence, that Congress had no power whatever to pass that seventh section."[26]

All these questions, Johnson concluded, were serious matters of constitutional interpretation involving the relative powers of the federal government, the states, and their respective judiciaries. He urged upon the judges a traditional evaluation of dual federalism: "May our political planets be suffered also to revolve in their respective orbits, and may God, in His mercy, so guide and instruct them as not to subject them also to the peril of a collision, which may involve all in ruin."[27] The defense had raised important questions for the bench to consider. If the judges agreed with the defense attorneys' interpretation, the broadly conceived enforcement effort of the government was in jeopardy. No Southern Republican could rest in the knowledge that the federal government would be able to protect him. And the Republican party in the South was likely to be short-lived if federal protection of individual rights was not forthcoming.

Daniel Chamberlain, attorney general of South Carolina and special assistant prosecutor, countered the defense's narrow interpretation of federal power with support for the government's broad construction. He conceded that the Fifteenth Amendment did not grant an absolute right to vote. Practically speaking, however, it did secure citizens of African descent in the suffrage. This "great public fact" was understood "throughout the length and breadth of the Union." The language of the first Enforcement Act, Chamberlain continued, demonstrated Congress's understanding of the Fifteenth Amendment when it referred to citizens "to whom the right of suffrage is secured or guaranteed by the Fifteenth Amendment." The defense's objections were "too nice."[28]

Chamberlain's remarks on the Fourth Amendment count demonstrate his understanding that the Fourteenth Amendment authorized Congress to protect citizens in the privileges and immunities guaranteed by the Bill of Rights. He agreed with defense counsel that personal rights were generally secured to citizens by state laws. When the Southern states failed to protect black citizens, however, Congress had said, "we will protect you." With the Enforcement Acts Congress had undertaken "directly and without leaving it any longer to state laws, to protect the citizen of the United States from unreasonable searches and seizures." The enforcement clauses of the Fourteenth and Fifteenth Amendments merely reiterated authority already reserved to the national Congress to enforce the rights "secured by the Constitution to the citizens of the United States." Thus Chamberlain would countenance no "constitutional objection" to the first Enforcement Act as "appropriate legislation" under the Fourteenth Amendment.[29]

On the charges that included burglary, Chamberlain noted sarcastically that the prosecution was "ready to grant the entire argument of the distinguished counsel . . . and to agree . . . that the United States Courts cannot take jurisdiction." He explained, however, that the government neither charged burglary as a separate offense nor claimed jurisdiction. Rather, the prosecution, under the authority of the seventh section of the Enforcement Act of 1870, had attached these ordinary crimes to the federal crime of conspiracy so as to determine the appropriate measure of punishment. The statute authorized the government to "enquire . . . whether an additional crime or felony against the laws of the State has been committed; and, if so, to make that the measure of its punishment of the offense against the laws of the United States." Chamberlain reminded the court that a conspiracy is complete the moment two or more persons plan to do some unlawful act, whether or not the act was ever accomplished. Thus, he argued, many of the details Stanbery had insisted should be included in the indictment were "surplusage." The charges were sufficient, moreover, because they followed the language of the statute.[30]

District Attorney Corbin made the final arguments for the government against the motion to quash. Like Chamberlain, Corbin insisted that the federal government was not attempting to try ordinary crimes. Charging a burglary committed in the act of carrying out a conspiracy against the rights of voters was "simply a measure of punishment—nothing more, nothing less." Corbin admitted that he personally did not like the method Congress had chosen of alleging ordinary crimes committed against state law in connection with offenses tried in federal court: "I do not like the policy of the Act. I do not like the method. It has given me an exceedingly great amount of annoyance; but still it is there, and I am here to enforce the policy of the law."[31] Corbin's doubts echoed those he had already expressed to Akerman on the subject; like the defense attorneys, he may well have doubted the constitutionality of the seventh section of the first Enforcement Act.

Corbin held stronger convictions on the Bill of Rights charge. Making a direct case for the nationalization of the Fourth Amendment through the Fourteenth, Corbin recognized that the Bill of Rights was originally intended as a restriction on the United States. Now, however, the danger was that the states would "encroach upon the rights of the newly enfranchised citizens." The Fourteenth Amendment secured individual rights against the state governments and empowered Congress to pass appropriate legislation to enforce those rights. Rather than attempting to punish the state, Congress chose a method that would punish individuals who conspired to violate the rights of citizens. If Congress deemed this method appropriate, Corbin argued, then it was appropriate. Corbin's remarks both adhered to and stretched the limits of the state-action concept, the idea that the Fourteenth Amendment empowered the national government to legislate only against *state* action that denied civil rights. Corbin's remarks indicate that he considered a state's failure to protect its citizens a form of state action.[32]

Corbin's rejoinders were more conservative than the policy he had set out in the indictment and the ideas he had expressed in his letters to Akerman. The indictment conveyed a bold, forthright nationalistic strategy. Now Corbin tempered these ideas with a more conservative reading of the Reconstruction Amendments, which suggests how fully he appreciated the novelty of his efforts to enhance civil rights for blacks. He maintained that the Fourteenth Amendment enabled the federal government to protect the rights of citizens against infringements of the privileges and immunities secured by the Bill of Rights but bound himself by the state-action concept rather than arguing forcefully that the federal government could act directly on individuals who violated the rights of citizens. He adopted a similar stragegy on the Fifteenth Amendment, admitting that it secured the right to vote only "in some particulars." He insisted nonetheless that the amendment secured blacks in the suffrage sufficiently to state it as a right in the indictment. Corbin was likely influenced as much by political reality as by the reasoning of Reverdy Johnson and Henry Stanbery. He complained of the vagueness of the Ku Klux

Klan Act and the difficulty of charging offenses under it; he regretted "exceedingly that Congress should use these indefinite terms, and leave the Court, the attorney, and the people to grope around to find out what they mean."[33]

Corbin's exasperation demonstrated the enormous pressure under which the government attorney had labored, the hundreds of indictments he had written—all of which were now under attack—and the seemingly interminable legal haggling. Corbin personally thought that the Fourteenth Amendment and Enforcement Acts secured the citizen "in all the rights which the Constitution grants and secures to a citizen against any combination of persons that undertakes to deprive me of those rights." But he closed his remarks with an appeal to the court for an interpretation of the Fourteenth Amendment and Enforcement Acts.[34]

The opinion of the court on the pretrial motion effectively curbed all the broader aims of the government attorneys before the first Klansman was ever tried. As the ranking judge, Bond wrote and delivered the opinion, but the two-headed structure of the circuit court required him to consider the ideas of District Judge Bryan if any of the night riders were to be brought to justice. Recognizing the political differences between the two judges, Stanbery and Johnson had focused their strategy toward dividing the court in order to send the case to the Supreme Court.[35] Bond was determined to punish the Klan, but his commitment to justice was tempered by an honest concern that the indictment exceeded constitutional authority.[36]

Bond upheld the first count, a ruling that enabled federal attorneys to convict a Klansman by proving a conspiracy existed to prevent black citizens from voting and demonstrating that the defendant belonged to the organization. He rejected Stanbery's argument that such a conspiracy could operate only on election day. Voters could be intimidated, Bond observed, long before the election actually took place. "The usefulness of the Act of Congress would be entirely frustrated by such requirement," he stated. Neither did he accept the idea that the law applied only to federal elections. Bond adhered to the position that conspiracy did not depend upon any overt act but was complete the moment the conspirators made their initial compact.[37]

The judge's rulings both endorsed the state-action theory of federal power and strained to make it fit the situation in South Carolina. Clearly he understood that a discriminatory state voting statute was not the problem: "Congress may have found it difficult to punish a state which by law made such distinction, and may have thought that legislation most likely to secure the end in view, which punished the individual citizen who acted by virtue of a State law, or upon his individual responsibility."[38] Bond's interpretation of state action indicated that he considered the state responsible under the Fourteenth Amendment when the rights of citizens were denied, whether by state law or individual action. In this view, state and local officials who failed to protect black rights were involved in a kind of state action that could be punished by the federal government. Bond was willing to go to the outside limit of the state-action concept but not one step beyond. Thus he decided that the federal government could stand in the place of a state when that state refused to protect a citizen's constitutional rights. If the state did not punish the individual conspirators of the Ku Klux Klan, the national government would do so. Bond did not personally appraise the constitutionality of the Enforcement Act; rather he deemed Congress the "sole judge of its appropriateness."[39]

The bench divided on the burglary charge. Given Judge Bryan's states'-rights philosophy, it is evident that Judge Bond was willing to allow the federal courts to take cognizance of ordinary crimes committed as a part of the Ku Klux conspiracy. This assumption fits Bond's decision to let Congress determine the appropriateness of punishing individuals. It also demonstrates his desire to convict Klansmen, but it does not square with the conservatism Bond demonstrated in interpreting the Fifteenth Amendment and the Enforcement Acts. The case that was actually certified to the Supreme Court involved murder rather than burglary, so it is possible that Bond divided because of an inclination to test the law rather than from the conviction that the federal government could inquire into the facts of ordinary crimes as a measure of punishment for civil rights offenses. "Whether this case ought to be tried in the U.S. Courts or the State tribunals is a legitimate matter for arguments," Judge Bond had written his wife from the North Carolina Klan trials.[40] This evidence suggests that Bond doubted the federal government's authority to supersede the state's traditional role in the administration of criminal justice.

Bond insisted that the states retained responsibility for protecting and defining civil rights. Therefore, he quashed the second count of the indictment, which declared the vote to be a right granted by the Constitution. The Fifteenth Amendment did not grant suffrage, Bond noted; that power was reserved to the states. The purpose of the Fifteenth Amendment was to prevent voter restriction based on race. He was equally cool to the Bill of Rights charge. Bond insisted that the right to be secure from unreasonable search and seizure preexisted the Constitution as a part of common law. The Fourth Amendment did not confer a right but acted as a restriction on the United States.[41] Thus the judge rejected the notion that the Fourteenth Amendment transformed the first eight amendments into federally enforceable rights. Bond did not mention the Fourteenth Amendment in his remarks on the Fourth Amendment charge.

Judge Bond's estimation of the Fourteenth and Fifteenth Amendments in his decision was consistent with strict construction constitutional theory. He believed that Congress framed the Reconstruction Amendments in a narrow, negative fashion so as to disturb traditional federal-state relationships as little as possible. The amendments, in this view, limited the ability of the states to pass discriminatory laws or to execute laws unequally, but they did not directly confer additional powers on the national government.[42] Federal interference was limited to cases of state action or a state's failure to act, as discussed above. Paradoxically, then, Bond's constitutional views paralleled those of conservatives and Democrats, while his commitment to black rights equaled that of the more Radical Republicans. Bond did not stand alone among Republicans in his determination both to preserve state-centered federalism and to provide equal rights of citizenship for the former slaves. Even the congressmen who shaped the laws shared these conflicting goals. Judge Bond's personal dilemma was symptomatic of the forces that shaped the federal judiciary's overall reaction to federal Reconstruction policy.[43]

Despite his conservatism, Bond found a way to reach the Ku Klux Klan in the federal courts. He upheld two counts of the indictment: the first, which charged a general conspiracy, and the eleventh, which charged a conspiracy to injure Rainey for voting in a congressional election. Bond did not look to the recent amendments for his authority. Instead, he maintained that Congress possessed the power to protect voters in federal elections even before the Reconstruction Amendments and federal laws were passed: "It is a power necessary to the existence of Congress."[44] Although the preliminary legal arguments lasted over a week, the decision Bond made in the first case simplified the indictment process for the following trials so that the federal attorneys could attend to the prosecution.

Despite the extended pretrial arguments, the *Crosby* case for the Klan raid on Amzi Rainey was never tried. Both prosecution and defense wanted a case that would be appropriate for certification to the Supreme

Court. If this case were certified, Corbin pointed out, "nothing of value goes up" because the opinion on the motion to quash had ruled the counts to which Corbin had attached the burglary charges defective. Corbin wanted to drop the burglary charges and try the defendants without them. The defense refused. There followed a lengthy argument on jury selection. The defense claimed the right of ten peremptory challenges and claimed severance, meaning that each defendant would have ten challenges, quickly exhausting the panel of available jurors and wasting valuable time in the voir dire process. Corbin immediately announced that he, too, would sever, meaning that he would separate individual defendants from the group on each indictment and try them one at a time. Thus Corbin selected Sherod Childers from the Crosby indictment to be tried alone.[45]

Eventually a workable compromise was reached. Judge Bond agreed to go along with the peremptory challenges rather than dividing with Judge Bryan on an issue that would hold up the prosecutions without deciding the substantive constitutional issues. The defense then exchanged guilty pleas on the two counts the judges had left standing in *Crosby* for a division of opinion on a murder case, *U.S. v. James W. Avery*, which was then certified to the Supreme Court. Both sides wanted the Supreme Court to rule on the constitutionally novel issue of determining in federal court whether ordinary crimes had been committed as a means of deciding the appropriate punishment for civil rights violations. The *Avery* case was selected because murder was a capital offense. Corbin prepared an indictment for *Avery* which attached the murder charge to the first count of the *Crosby* case, which Judge Bond had held to be good. He charged James W. Avery and others with a general conspiracy to deny the franchise to black voters under the first and sixth sections of the First Enforcement Act. He then attached the murder count, testing the seventh section of the same act, to the conspiracy charge. *U.S. v. James W. Avery* went up to the Supreme Court on a division of opinion on the preliminary motion to quash the indictment. The case was not tried in circuit court. Thus there was no verdict and no conviction. Rather, answers were sought from the Supreme Court on two questions: that of using ordinary crimes as the measure of punishment in civil rights cases and a Second Amendment question.[46]

The first case to be tried, *U.S. v. Robert Hayes Mitchell*,[47] involved the same Klan raid and murder as *U.S. v. Avery*. The original indictment had contained approximately thirty names. With the approval of the bench,

Corbin separated the names into two separate indictments charging the Avery group with murder and leaving the murder count out of the second indictment. Corbin entered a *nolle prosequi* to remove the first indictment from the docket, and the grand jury returned true bills for the two separate indictments. The judges divided on the first indictment, the *Avery* case. On the second indictment, the *Mitchell* case, there was no division of opinion. Mitchell was then separated from the second group and tried alone because of the defense's right of peremptory challenge. *Mitchell* seems to have been chosen for trial simply because his name appeared first on the indictment.[48]

In *Mitchell* District Attorney Corbin attempted a second time to convince Bond that the Fourteenth Amendment had altered the traditional relationship between the federal government and the states. Corbin was sorely disappointed by the opinion of the Republican judge on whom he had counted to uphold his efforts in behalf of black rights. Corbin insisted specifically that the Fourteenth Amendment guaranteed the Second Amendment right to keep and bear arms. The Fourteenth Amendment, he said, "lays the same restrictions upon the States that before lay upon the Congress of the United States." Following Judge Bond's line of reasoning on the Fourth Amendment charge, Corbin argued that the right to bear arms did not exist under the common law but was guaranteed by the United States Constitution for the first time in history. Thus the Second Amendment, according to Corbin, was one of the privileges and immunities which the Fourteenth Amendment secured to the citizens against the state. Because many of the Klan's outrages had focused on taking the guns that had been issued to black militia members, Corbin considered the Second Amendment right vital to the prosecution. "We will never abandon it," he insisted, "until we are obliged to." Without their weapons, these men had no way to protect themselves, their homes, or their families from the marauding night riders. Acceptance of the charge would enable government attorneys to bring black families under the protection of the federal government.[49] Again, however, Corbin's efforts were frustrated.

Although the district attorney pressed him hard, Judge Bond refused several times to address the Second Amendment issue. He allowed the district attorney to *nolle prosse* the count in *U.S. v. Robert Hayes Mitchell*, however, so that the case could proceed to trial. Eventually the judges divided on the Second Amendment issue and certified it to the Supreme Court along with the murder charge in *U.S. v. Avery*.[50] Judge Bond's silence on the right to bear arms makes it difficult to determine whether he changed his mind upon reflection or endorsed the idea that the Fourteenth Amendment authorized the federal government to enforce at least some part of the Bill of Rights. Bond was not generally disinclined to state his opinions. If he had accepted the idea that the Fourteenth Amendment nationalized some part of the Bill of Rights, he probably would have given his reasons. It therefore seems likely that he rejected the entire notion of federally enforceable rights under the Fourteenth Amendment, divided so the Supreme Court could consider the problem, and failed to write a decision on the matter to avoid the appearance of intellectual inconsistency. Thwarted by the court's silence, the government attorney eliminated the charge from all the cases that were actually tried during this session of the circuit court.[51]

In seven days of pretrial arguments the prosecuting attorneys saw their major constitutional aims defeated before the first Ku Klux Klan trial ever began. The conspiracy charges accepted by the court would enable Corbin and Chamberlain to prosecute successfully in case after case, but the defense had already attained its goals on the most important constitutional issues involved in the cases. The actual trials, in this sense, were epilogue. But the federal prosecution efforts had stopped Klan violence in the upcountry. And the government attorneys used the trials wisely, not only to bring criminals to justice but also to make the extent and nature of the South Carolina Ku Klux Klan a matter of public record.

The initial pretrial proceedings simplified the indictment and trial process for the trials that followed. In the remainder of the 1871 Ku Klux Klan trials, the government relied on the conspiracy charges left standing by Judge Bond's opinion on the motion to quash. Robert Hayes Mitchell was indicted on two counts of conspiracy under the First Enforcement Act of May 1870: a general conspiracy under section one unlawfully to hinder or restrain citizens from voting at future elections on account of race, color, or previous condition, and a conspiracy under section six specifically to injure and oppress James Williams for having previously exercised the right to vote.[52]

Williams, also known as Jim Rainey, was a captain of the black militia in York County.[53] He had served in General William T. Sherman's forces and had been instrumental in training the militia. Williams had been outspoken in his determination to protect his race and party. Reluctant to return the arms that had been issued to his men when Governor Scott disarmed the militia, he had insisted that the freedmen first have guarantees that black citizens would be safe. Rumor got out among the whites that Williams had made threats to "kill from the cradle to the grave." Witnesses for the prosecution, however, insisted that Williams was a peaceable, law-abiding citizen. None of these witnesses had heard about any threats until after Williams was murdered by the Ku Klux Klan. They maintained, in fact, that "Jim Williams said he was opposed to anything like retaliation" even though the Klan was committing outrages against members of the Republican party. Defense witnesses, however, insisted that Williams had endangered the entire white community. Williams's greatest offense was that he was, as District Attorney Corbin put it, "a pretty independent negro" who "stood up for his rights" and was considered "consequently, a pretty bad boy." Abhorring the Klan's secret, nighttime oppression of the black community, Williams had, according to one witness, suggested that the "way to decide between the blacks and the whites is to go into the old field and fight it out" like men.[54]

Leaders of the Ku Klux Klan had decided to silence this outspoken proponent of black rights. Approximately seventy Klansmen in disguise, under the leadership of Dr. J. Rufus Bratton, a prominent citizen of York County, assembled on the night of 6 March 1871. The night riders made several calls on their way to Williams's home, delivering whippings at every stop. A smaller party of about a dozen, personally led by the doctor, abducted Williams from his home, took him to a pine thicket, and hung him from a tree. On his chest the Klansmen pinned a sign that read "Jim Williams on his big muster." The brothers of the Ku Klux Klan then returned to the plantation yard of John S. Bratton, where their host provided food and plenty of whiskey. Defendant Robert Hayes Mitchell was one of the night riders who participated in the raid on Williams, although he had remained with the horses while the murder took place.[55]

Because all members of the Klan were technically guilty of any of the offenses carried out by the conspiracy, all the prosecution had to do to convict Mitchell on the first count of the indictment was to prove that a Ku Klux Klan conspiracy existed, that the accused was a member of the Klan, and that the organization's purpose was to hinder blacks from voting. The second count required proof that the Klan conspired specifically to punish Jim Williams for having voted in a previous election.

A copy of the obligation, constitution, and by-laws of the Ku Klux Klan served as the basis of proof that such a conspiracy existed. During the course of the investigations in York County, Major Merrill had located the constitution in the possession of "Squire" Samuel G. Brown, a prominent citizen of the county. This document stated that the Klan rejected the principles of the Radical party and supported "justice, humanity, and constitutional liberty, as bequeathed to us in its purity by our forefathers." The Klan constitution went on to pledge mutual aid in the event of sickness or distress; females were to be the "special objects of our regard and protection." Blacks were barred from membership. The penalty prescribed by the oath for any member who divulged information pertaining to the organization was the "traitor's doom, which is Death! Death! Death!"[56] Several Klan members identified the constitution as the one they had promised to uphold. As further proof of conspiracy, the witnesses described the disguises worn by the night riders and revealed secret signs and signals by which they had recognized members of the Klan.

Throughout the trial the government attorneys focused attention on the political nature and purpose of the Klan. The meaning of the Klan obligation, with its dedication to constitutional purity, Corbin insisted, was that the organization supported the Constitution "*as it was*, not *as it is now*— not with the thirteenth, fourteenth and fifteenth amendments in it. . . . We reject the results of the late war. We trample upon these Amendments of the Constitution, and we intend to destroy and defeat them."[57] Kirkland Gunn, a former Klansman, stated that the goals of the Klan were to be accomplished by "killing off the white Radicals, and by whipping and intimidating the negroes, so as to keep them from voting for any men who held Radical offices." Charles Foster stated that the Klansmen rode to "put down Radicalism"; the method employed was "to whip them and make them change their politics." Dick Wilson, a Union League member and victim of the Klan, related that the night riders came to his house "because you damned niggers are ruining the country, voting for men who are breaking the treasury." After a brutal beating by the Klan, Wilson had promised, "I will vote any way you want me to vote; I don't care how you want me to vote, master, I will vote."[58]

Having established the political nature and purpose of the Klan, the prosecution next proceeded to demonstrate that the defendant was a member of the conspiracy and that he had participated in the raid on Jim Williams. Several witnesses testified that they had ridden with Mitchell on the night of the murder. Each witness insisted, however, that he had known nothing of the crime but had remained in a thicket with the horses while a group of about ten, led by Dr. Bratton, committed the offense. One of the witnesses related that he had not known a murder was intended until after it was over. When he asked Bratton if he had found Williams and where he was, he was surprised to hear him say, "He is in hell, I expect." The witnesses made clear also that Mitchell was not one of the Klansmen in the advance party who had dragged Williams out and killed him. Like the witnesses for the prosecution, Mitchell had stayed in the woods with the horses.[59]

While the prosecution focused attention on the political goals of the Ku Klux Klan, the defense attorneys sought to convince the jury that the Klan was a defense organization established solely to protect the white community from abuse by armed black soldiers. "We want to show," Henry Stanbery stated early in the trial proceedings, "that the overt act was connected, not with the voting matter, but with this arming matter and the danger apprehended." Jim Williams was murdered, according to the defense, not to prevent him from voting but because of the alarm he had raised among the whites. It was strictly a matter of self-defense. Julia Rainey, a white woman who testified for the defense, related that the "feeling in the country had become very alarming." Arson was common, and people were afraid of having their houses burned. The "disorderly conduct of the militia" caused people to dread an attack by the blacks. Clearly, her testimony suggested, the whites had to organize to defend hearth and home.[60] James Long testified that the armed blacks had created a state of alarm in his part of the county: "Folks were pretty much scared." Several witnesses insisted that Jim Williams was a dangerous man who had threatened to murder the white population "from the cradle up." William Bratton, for example, maintained that he had personally heard Williams make threats "that he would rule the country, and if he could do it in no other way, he intended to Ku Klux the white ladies and children, gin houses and barns." Minor McConnell reported that Williams had told him that "the people and me myself would see mighty work when he took his company and went to Ku Kluxing." Stanbery summed up the testimony by arguing that although the Klan and the raid on Jim Williams were not "absolutely legal . . . it was such a duty as no man would shrink from who felt the fears felt in that neighborhood from the danger of leaving those arms in the hands of those men." Because the governor had "armed the blacks and left the whites defenseless," the whites were forced to take matters into their own hands. The outrages of the Ku Klux Klan, according to the defense interpretation, were the natural result of the governor's folly.[61]

The defense did not attempt to deny that the defendant had participated in the raid on Jim Williams. Stanbery made clear, however, that Mitchell had not been directly involved in the murder. He argued, moreover, that Mitchell had been charged with one offense, conspiracy against the franchise, and tried for another, murder. The defense attorney deplored the outrage that had been committed against the militia captain but nonetheless maintained that the defendant should not be punished. He had known nothing of the plan to hang Jim Williams. Mitchell had understood the purpose of the raid—his first and last—was "to disarm Jim Williams and his colored company." He had no intention of taking away Williams's vote or of punishing him for having voted the Radical ticket, the offenses for which he was indicted. "This young man," Stanbery argued, "supposed he was going for what he considered a proper purpose, and what I would consider a proper purpose if I had lived in that neighborhood."[62]

Stanbery admitted that someone ought to be punished for the crime, but that someone, according to the defense attorney, was not his client. "When you get Dr. Bratton," he continued, "deal with him. But for God's sake, don't make this young man his scape-goat. . . . Have the man who committed the crime before you, and then mete out the punishment."[63] Stanbery implored the black jurors to honor their race by demonstrating that they could acquit a white man. If they were determined to have a victim when the right man was not on trial, he said, "I do not want to see one of your race on a jury again." He seriously questioned whether the jurors could rise above their racial prejudice and consider the case on its merits. The defense attorney was surprised, in fact, that the jury had listened to the case so attentively.[64]

Stanbery's condescending remarks to the predominantly black jury demonstrated that the defense attorney shared local values as well as local white constitutional principles. Like the South Carolina Democrats he represented, Stanbery seemed to assume that the black quest for equality would lead inevitably to a quest for superiority. "I warn you colored men of South Carolina," he cautioned the jury, "if you attempt to make a step in advance of the white man, your doom is sealed." Throughout the trial Stanbery exhibited the same fear of armed blacks which he attributed to the white population of upcountry South Carolina. Jim Williams would not have drilled his men so thoroughly, he suggested, if he had not had some "secret motive" in mind, "a mission to fulfill." Clearly the defense attorney considered the black militia a grave danger to the white population. "I hope you of the colored race will not expect or desire to rule white men," he warned again in a closing argument. If the blacks were to have arms and the whites have none, "your triumph will be short and your doom inevitable."[65]

Reverdy Johnson, like Stanbery, addressed black jurors for the first time in the Ku Klux Klan trials. He insisted, however, that he held no prejudiced view of the jury: "We are all children of the same Father." Johnson's attitude, nonetheless, betrayed his personal conviction that armed blacks were not to be tolerated. "In the name of justice and humanity," he declared, "in the name of those rights for which our fathers fought, you cannot subject the white man to the absolute and uncontrolled dominion of an armed force of a colored race." The defense attorney's expressed fear of the black militia spoke for whites throughout the state. Pushing the fear issue hard, he insisted that "each poor lady, as she laid down in her bed at night," had reason to believe the blacks would set her house on fire or rise up against her. "What is the husband to do," Johnson asked; "band themselves together as a defense," of course. Who could possibly blame the Ku Klux Klan for its determination to defend hearth and home against the threat of angry, armed blacks?[66]

It is difficult to determine what the defense attorneys hoped to accomplish by their remarks against the black jurors. Clearly they were suffering from culture shock as they addressed the black men who composed the jury. Of the twelve-man jury, only two in the *Mitchell* case were white. Even the foreman, Joseph Taylor of Richland County, was a person of African descent. The jurors were about equally divided geographically between those who came from Georgetown and Charleston in the low country and those who came from Columbia and Richland County in the center of the state. Only one juror came from the upcountry, Franklin McMakin, a white man from Newberry County. Defense counsel may have wanted to appeal to the race prejudice of the white jurors in hope of obtaining a mistrial. It seems more likely, however, that their harangues were an attempt to browbeat and intimidate black jurors who must have felt already the enormous white prejudice against the entire prosecution effort.[67]

Johnson's closing arguments reiterated the notion that the government was attempting to convict Mitchell without "the least particle of evidence" that he had known the object of the raid on Jim Williams. "It is not proved," according to the defense, "that he made any attempt to do anything wrong, but upon him the wrongs done by others are to be visited, in the view of the prosecuting counsel, upon some notion of the law."[68]

Corbin, in his closing arguments for the government, made clear to the jurors that the defendant was not being tried for murder, as the defense had suggested, but for conspiracy. The defense had clouded the issue by maintaining that Mitchell should not be punished because he was not guilty of the murder. If the facts demonstrated that Mitchell was a member of the Ku Klux Klan, then he was guilty under the law of conspiracy for all the works of the Klan. The United States government, Corbin argued, is a government of law. When a conspiracy exists "to rob our colored citizens of African descent of their newly acquired rights," then it is the duty of the government to intervene.[69]

The prosecutor reiterated his insistence that the Klan rode for political purposes; it was not a defense organization. The Klan constitution demonstrated in writing that its purpose was to "oppose and reject the principles of the Radical party." The night riders had committed such heinous crimes on those who dared to support the Radical ticket that the world will "shudder as it reads the testimony of this trial." It will be said "that the dark ages have come again, and the crimes of savages . . . present no parallel to these." It was the black militia, according to Corbin, that was created in self-defense. The Klan was organized in 1868, the militia in 1870.[70]

Corbin castigated the defense attorneys for their unwarranted remarks to the predominantly black jury. The freedmen, according to Corbin, had never aspired to or claimed "more than is conceded to white men." Rather they were attempting to elevate themselves "to become what the Constitution says they shall be—clothed in all the rights of American citizens." However much the whites of South Carolina and their "distinguished counsel" protested, "the laws of this state are equal and just. . . . The colored man in South Carolina is raised by the fundamental law of this State, and that law is supported by the Constitution of the United States, and by the conscience of the great American people, that the colored man shall be a citizen, and he shall be protected in all the rights of an American freeman."[71]

The prosecution's closing remarks stressed the historical importance of the Klan trials. Many former Confederate soldiers who had laid down their arms and promised to behave henceforth as good citizens had conspired instead to undermine the results of the war. The verdict in this trial, according to Corbin, would "mark an era in the history of the administration of justice in South Carolina" and demonstrate to the people of the state and the entire South *"that the rights of the newly enfranchised citizens shall be protected.*" The government was determined, Corbin insisted, "that this organization to defeat the rights of our colored fellow-citizens, *must and shall be put down.*" The district attorney thanked the jurors for their patience throughout the week-long trial and anticipated the verdict with confidence.[72]

As the ranking member of the two-headed circuit court, Judge Bond charged the jury. His remarks emphasized that the defendant was being tried for conspiracy, "not the particular acts done in pursuance of it." The purpose of the Ku Klux Klan, according to the judge, did not have to be single. If one of its purposes was set forth in either count of the indictment, then the person engaged in it could be punished. Each member of the conspiracy, Bond emphasized, "is responsible, personally, for every act of the conspiracy and for the acts of each member thereof." It made no difference in the law of conspiracy whether the defendant was actually present when a crime was committed. It was up to the jury to decide whether a conspiracy did in fact exist to deprive the freedmen of their right to vote. If it did, and Mitchell was a member, then he was guilty of all the overt acts committed by the Klan. Similarly, if the Klan had conspired to injure Jim Williams for having previously voted, and Mitchell was a member of the Klan, then Mitchell was guilty of the second count whether or not he had actually harmed Williams. It was up to the jury, however, to determine the actual reason for the violence.[73]

The jurors had little regard for the arguments of the defense lawyers. They found the defendant "guilty of the general conspiracy" after less than an hour of deliberation. Judge Bond explained, however, that they must find the prisoner guilty or not guilty on one or both of the counts. After further deliberation, the jurors returned a verdict of "guilty on the second count, not guilty on the first."[74]

Although Judge Bond had insisted that each member of the Ku Klux Klan was responsible for all the deeds of the organization, he sentenced Mitchell with a keen regard for the fact that he had not actually participated in the murder of Jim Williams. If the court had "any intimation that you had countenanced" the murder, he said, we "would exhaust the full penalty of the law and then consider that you had been very mercifully dealt with." Because Mitchell had confessed and "dealt candidly with the Court," his punishment was light—eighteen months' imprisonment and a fine of $100. Judge Bond was firm but fair; clearly he recognized that Mitchell was not one of the leading members of the Klan.

Thus ended the first of the South Carolina Ku Klux Klan trials. Three weeks of intense effort by the opposing sides had resulted in the conviction of one rather insignificant Klan member, Robert Hayes Mitchell.[75] Hundreds more awaited trial. The most wanted Klansmen were still at large. Whether the government would ever be able to prosecute the leaders, who were responsible for the most heinous crimes, remained to be seen. Doubt remained, also, on the most significant constitutional questions that had been raised. The Fourth Federal Circuit Court had provided a forum for the opposing sides to air their interpretations of the Reconstruction Amendments as well as their conflicting views of the Klan's purposes. The prosecution had failed to convince the judges that the Fifteenth Amendment provided a positive right to vote or that the Fourteenth Amendment had radically altered the federal system, granting the national government authority to protect citizens in their individual rights. The institutional nature of the two-headed circuit court had doubtless contributed to the prosecution's difficulty in securing its nationalistic goals, but Judge Bond, the Republican circuit judge who had been expected to support the government's policy, had demonstrated a cool reception to the more novel constitutional goals of the prosecution. Bond, like so many federal judges during this period, was locked into a traditional notion of dual federalism which precluded his acceptance of a major change in federal-state relations. Although Bond was not convinced that the Fourteenth Amendment nationalized the Bill of Rights, he had nonetheless agreed to disagree on the Second Amendment question and the issue of trying common law crimes in federal court. The highest court in the land would thus have the opportunity to consider the problems. If the government attorneys had failed to secure their more novel constitutional goals, they had nonetheless managed to convict, despite the best efforts of some of the finest and most expensive legal talent in the nation. The guilty verdict signaled that the South Carolina night riders must yield to the rule of law. And the prosecution had successfully developed a strategy that could be used in the succeeding trials.

5

The Ku Klux Klan in Court

Although the United States attorneys had secured a conviction in *U.S. v. Robert Hayes Mitchell*, the trial had largely been a failure regarding constitutional goals. So novel were the prosecution's constitutional arguments that they had not even convinced the reportedly Radical Republican judge Hugh Bond. Subsequent efforts by the government proved similarly disappointing. Despite their success in winning convictions time after time on conspiracy charges, the government attorneys were unable to prosecute the most wanted Klansmen, most of whom had fled. Those who stood trial were generally not the influential members of the community responsible for spearheading the Klan's activities, although some of them were among the more affluent Klan members who were available for trial. Further efforts to secure a Supreme Court ruling on the constitutional issues were no more successful. The Republican government achieved an enviable conviction rate, but the long-term goal of changing the social and political structure of South Carolina was a failure.

The trial strategy developed by the government attorneys in *Mitchell* nevertheless assured a perfect conviction record in the subsequent Ku Klux Klan trials during the November 1871 session of the Fourth Circuit Court. In each case the prosecution followed the same approach that had brought a guilty verdict in the first. Witnesses identified the constitution and oath of the Klan as that which they had promised to uphold. Then they described the disguises worn by the night riders and demonstrated secret signs and signals by which they had identified themselves as members of the Klan. Numerous witnesses in each trial testified that the Klan's overriding purpose was political. Having established the nature and purpose of the Klan, the prosecution next proceeded to establish the connection between the defendants and the conspiracy. Black citizens related the details of outrages committed against them and sometimes identified the accused as among those who had perpetrated the crimes. Klan members who had become government witnesses identified the defendants as members of the Klan with whom they had ridden. In three out of the four cases that followed *Mitchell*, this strategy was simple, straightforward, and successful, although two of the trials were long. Corbin directed testimony toward the political nature of the Klan to prove the outrages resulted from a conspiracy to obstruct voting rights.[1]

The prosecution went beyond this initial strategy, however, in the second case to be tried, *U.S. v. John W. Mitchell and Thomas B. Whitesides.* As prominent members of their community in York County, Mitchell and Whitesides were precisely the sort of men Attorney General Akerman had advised Corbin to prosecute first. If men of their position and influence had united against the Klan, the Enforcement Acts would have been unnecessary. Instead, Mitchell was a Klan chief, and Whitesides, a physician, had participated in at least one raid. The government attorneys massed their evidence against the Klan in this trial to demonstrate the extent of Klan atrocities and put the responsibility for these outrages squarely on the shoulders of those members of the community in places of leadership. The first count of the four-count indictment charged a general conspiracy to obstruct the voting rights of black citizens. The second, third, and fourth, respectively, charged a special conspiracy to injure Charles Leach, the victim of a Klan raid in which both Mitchell and Whitesides had participated, for having voted in 1870, to prevent him from voting in the future, and for voting for a particular person for Congress. Leach, a black Republican and Union League member, testified that thirty to forty Klan members broke into his home, demanded his guns (he had none), dragged him outdoors, then administered some fifty to seventy-five lashes with hickories as wide as his thumb. Wounded from his waist to his shoulders, the freedman was unable to work for a week.[2]

Corbin initially proceeded as he had in the preceding trial, proving that the Klan was a conspiracy to deny the political rights of Republicans, particularly blacks. Kirkland Gunn, a former Ku Klux member, testified, for example, that the purpose of the Klan was "to put down the Radical party and rule negro suffrage." A freedman stated that the Klan had vowed to "make me a good old Democrat." Corbin next produced witnesses who testified that they had participated in Klan raids with the defendants. Charles Foster stated that he had ridden with both Whitesides and Mitchell on 9 January 1871, when the Klan had committed outrages against several Republicans, including Charles Leach. Black victims of the Klan's actions then identified the accused as among those who had terrorized them.[3]

The prosecution could doubtless have closed its case at this point and obtained convictions from the predominantly black jury. Instead, the government presented a veritable parade of atrocities for the record. While reporters from across the nation were gathered in South Carolina, the government seized the opportunity to release the ugly truth about the Ku Klux Klan. The defendants, Mitchell and Whitesides, had not participated in most of the crimes detailed in this trial, and the connection between some of these outrages and the political rights of black males was tenuous at best. Clearly the government had purposes in mind which went beyond the guilt or innocence of the accused. An interesting aspect of this trial is the number of female witnesses who took the stand to testify in a case concerning Fifteenth Amendment rights. One black woman testified, for example, that several Klansmen who had previously visited her home "came back" a second time "after my ole man." Failing to find the Republican husband at home, the frustrated night riders broke into the house, stole food from her kitchen, then dragged her outside and raped her. The Klan returned yet another time and burned her home to the ground. Another woman reported that Klansmen whipped her severely when they did not find her husband at home. Her steadfast refusal to "lie down" for the men who attacked her probably saved her from being raped. Several other women testified as witnesses for the prosecution relating their treatment at the hands of the Klan and their lack of security in their own homes. A male witness, a former Klan member, described a raid in which the night riders poured tar into the "privates" of a white woman who concealed two black men in her home. Several other witnesses recounted at length the Klan's attack on Thomas Roundtree, brutally murdered by the night riders—shot for daring to defend himself against the Klan, then his throat cut from ear to ear—but not by either of the defendants.[4]

The prosecution developed this strategy to reveal the extent of Klan brutality in upcountry South Carolina. Democratic papers had scoffed at the government's efforts to stop the Klan, insisting that it was not serious or that its purpose was self-defense. They had sneered at the humble black citizens who came to testify and complained of the "packed juries" who would not give the night riders a fair hearing.[5] Now the courtroom drama reached its peak. The government attorneys had the attention of the entire nation, and they proceeded to portray the Ku Klux Klan in all its horror. If the prosecution had failed to gain its major constitutional goals, it would nonetheless demonstrate the seriousness of the Klan. Judge Bond fully concurred with this object . He pressed the witnesses for more of the gory details, insisting that the full truth be revealed. "Let the witness detail all the circumstances," he told the prosecutor. "Tell me, exactly, how they did it," he encouraged a witness. The presiding judge insisted on knowing the extent of the victims' wounds and whether they were able to walk after they had been whipped. Several times during this trial Bond insisted that the black victims of the Klan should be allowed to "tell the story" in their own way without being interrupted by the attorney's questions. Clearly he deemed it important, as he put it, to "let the people hear and let the jury know what things exist about us."[6]

Because the prosecution's efforts to nationalize the Second and Fourth Amendments had failed to convince the judges, leaving the national government without the constitutional means to protect the families of the freedmen, the government attempted to connect outrages committed against women and children with the conspiracy to defeat the Radical party. When the Klansmen whipped and ravished women, according to the government attorneys, it was not only "to gratify their lusts" but also "to punish them" because they would not reveal the whereabouts of their Radical husbands. By injuring the families of Republicans, the Ku Klux Klan forced Republican voters to pay "the penalty for their radicalism" and "deterred them from voting at future elections."[7] Thus the government in this trial spread a net of responsibility for the atrocities committed by the Klan which stretched far beyond the charges in the indictment.

Chamberlain's closing arguments emphasized that men of substance, standing, and education like Whitesides and Mitchell, whether or not they had actually perpetrated acts of violence, bore heavy moral responsibility for all the crimes the Klan had committed. These defendants were "nobody's dupes." Unlike Robert Hayes Mitchell and many of the other Klansmen who had been indicted, they could not claim "any exemption from the full responsibility of what they have done, and what they intended, on the ground that they occupied a humble position in society." Nor could they insist that they were swept along against their better judgment. These were men who were accustomed to leading their community. Others looked to men like Mitchell and Whitesides for guidance. Thus "the full responsibility for acts done and purposes planned is to be visited upon such defendants." As co-conspirators, moreover, they were legally responsible for all the atrocities committed by the Klan.[8]

Democratic papers quickly expressed their horror that the federal government would attempt to implicate men of such excellent reputation in these heinous crimes. "Even the seductive allurements of a city courtesan would appeal in vain," they insisted, to the "gentlemen of wealth and refinement, having charming families" who were on trial. That they would even touch such a "filthy-looking fright of a negress" was unthinkable. If such crimes had been committed, and allowance had to be made "for the exaggerations of the witnesses who are mostly ignorant negroes," then they were obviously perpetrated only by lower-class whites.[9]

While the prosecution focused the attention of both the jury and the nation on the full extent of Klan atrocities, the defense demonstrated that the two men on trial were innocent of the Klan's more heinous crimes. Whitesides and Mitchell relied on their personal, local counsel. Stanbery and Johnson remained in South Carolina but no longer conducted the day-to-day defense of the Klan. Whitesides's attorney, W. B. Wilson, insisted his client was completely innocent, that he had never even joined the Klan. A witness for the prosecution, on cross-examination, testified that he, too, had reason to believe Whitesides was not a Klansman. The witness had given the defendant the secret signs of the Klan, but Whitesides had failed to return them. Another government witness testified in rebuttal, however, that he had personally helped Whitesides to secure his disguise and borrow a saddle so that he could ride with the Klan. The witness then rode alongside the defendant. A second former Klansman, also a government witness, stated that he thought Whitesides had participated in only one raid. The witness had a conversation with the defendant shortly after that "one time," during which Whitesides said that he "was opposed to it." The Klan was "running all his hands off, and he would be obliged to suffer if they didn't stop it." Charles Leach, the victim of the Ku Klux raid for which Whitesides was charged, testified that the doctor had been kind to the freedmen. Leach had personally received a bushel of free corn from Whitesides in a time of need. He refused to say, however, that he had heard of the doctor giving free medical attention to the blacks. Nonetheless, Leach had "never heard anything against Dr. Whitesides, no way."[10]

Mitchell's attorney, C. D. Melton, could hardly insist that his client had never participated in the Ku Klux Klan. Several government witnesses had testified that they knew Mitchell to be a Klan chief. The defense attorney insisted instead that his client was not guilty because the Klan was never "designed or intended to interfere with African citizens as a class" or to "prevent them from exercising the right of citizens to vote." He produced black witnesses who made the point that Mitchell was "kindly disposed towards the colored people." Mitchell wanted the freedmen "to live and do well; if they were responsible people and wanted help . . . they were to go to him about it."[11]

The defense directed its primary efforts toward demonstrating that Mitchell had not participated in the raid on Charles Leach. Mitchell and Whitesides, with the cooperation of their attorneys and a "host of witnesses," including another physician, family, and friends, constructed an elaborate alibi which seemed at first guaranteed to succeed. On 9 January, numerous witnesses testified, Mitchell's elderly mother had suddenly taken sick with "epilepsy and a fit." Mitchell went to fetch Dr. Whitesides and another physician, Dr. Dawson. The old lady was so ill that the two doctors and the entire family, including the defendant, had sat up with her all night. Witness after witness recounted the event—family members and the other physician, who was certain of the date because he had written it in his log. Each defense witness recalled the date, and each testified that he or she had heard about the raid on Charles Leach the following day when Mitchell's young son had brought the news from the post office.[12]

The alibi obviously depended on the precise date of the raid. The date, however, was not as definite as the defense attorney attempted to make it. Although an important government witness, Charles Foster, had fixed the date on 9 January others had placed it variously as the Monday after Christmas, a Monday shortly after Christmas, and a Monday sometime in January. Neither Charles Leach nor his wife could recall the exact date on which they had been outraged. The prosecution, in rebuttal, was able to produce a witness who could demonstrate that the date on which the alibi depended was wrong. The Klan had visited William Wilson, a white Republican, one week before the raid on Charles Leach. On the night of the raid, Mrs. Wilson had been confined to her bed following the birth of a child. Naturally, the parents knew the exact birth date of their child. Through their testimony and that of Amos Howell, who stated with certainty that he had been whipped during the week of 25 January, the government was able to destroy the defense alibi. Numerous participants had already testified that both Leach and Howell were outraged on the same night.[13]

The trial of Mitchell and Whitesides, as the stenographer on the job reported to Attorney General Akerman, "afforded a good illustration of the necessity of a verbatim report of the testimony." The government attorneys were able to examine the trial records to determine that Charles Foster was the only witness who had fixed the date of the outrage on the same date of the alibi. Evidence suggested that Foster had been led to fix the date by "rumors started by the defense." Foster in rebuttal admitted he was not positive of the date. Without a stenographer's record, the government "would certainly have been worsted."[14]

The careful trial record enabled the government to gain two more convictions. The jury returned guilty verdicts for both Whitesides and Mitchell, finding the defendants guilty on two counts: a general conspiracy to obstruct the voting rights of black citizens and a special conspiracy to injure Charles Leach to prevent his future voting, respectively. Although this trial was relatively unimportant regarding constitutional argument and experimentation, it nonetheless advanced the government's goal of prosecuting first those Klansmen of property and authority who were in a position to persuade their neighbors to live peaceably with the new political order—the very people who white Southerners complained were excluded from power under the Republican state government. The successful prosecution of influential members of the white community signaled to the entire South that the government was seriously committed to protecting the civil and political rights of the freedmen regardless of the opposition. And the trial accomplished another purpose which the government considered important. The record of atrocities that had been "repeated in this Court" would "go forth to the world in the public prints." The world, or at least the nation, would recognize the suffering of the Klan's innocent victims, both male and female, and rise to support the more radical goals of the Republican party.[15]

The prosecution continued its policy of implicating prominent members of the community and publishing the gory details of the Klan outrages in the next trial, that of John S. Millar.[16] In this case, however, the government was perhaps overzealous in its desire to prosecute men of substance. Millar was a plantation owner who "had a great many hands to work for him." His wealth and availability probably prompted the government attorneys to choose him for prosecution. Millar was indicted under the first section of the Enforcement Act of 31 May 1870 on a single count of conspiracy to prevent male citizens of African descent from voting. Proceeding in the usual manner, the government established the political nature and purpose of the Klan. One witness testified, for example, that "the general purpose of the Ku Klux Klan order was to keep the Radical Party from voting . . . by raiding amongst them in the night time." The intention of the Klan, according to a former member, was "to tear down the party in power and build up the other party." This goal was to be accomplished by "whipping and Killing." Witnesses identified the constitution and oath of the Klan and demonstrated secret signs and signals by which the members identified themselves.[17]

If the government attorneys were successful in demonstrating, once again, the odious nature of the Klan, they were less so in connecting the defendant to the Klan's outrages. The prosecution established only that Millar had attended two meetings of the Klan. Former Klansmen testified that they had seen Millar at an election at which the Klan chief, grand Turk, and Cyclops were chosen. According to these witnesses, Millar had voted along with all the other members. They insisted, moreover, that people who were not Klan members were not allowed to attend meetings "unless they wish to go into it." Members were initiated the first time they attended, thus there was "never any person present only those sworn in." Although Millar had definitely attended Klan meetings, there was no evidence that he had ever ridden with the Klan. Even the witnesses for the prosecution insisted that he had returned to his home rather than going on a raid because he had no disguise "or may be naturally [he] didn't want to go."[18]

The defense attempted to establish doubt as to whether Millar was actually a Klan member or whether he had merely attended the meetings with his cousin "out of curiosity." No one had ever seen Millar wearing a disguise. No one had seen him take the oath. The government witnesses, on cross-examination, admitted they were not certain that Millar had actually voted at the Klan election.[19]

Like the other defendants in the Klan trials, Millar was not allowed to testify during his trial.[20] This common law custom, which seems strange in light of modern criminal procedure, was imported from England and remained the norm in America until reform began during the 1860s. Felony defendants were excluded from the witness stand on the grounds that their interest in the case made their testimony unreliable. They were, however, allowed to make a final statement to the bench. The common law rule fell first in 1864 in Maine; several other states followed in the next two decades. Not until 1878, however, did Congress adopt the rule that defendants could take the stand in federal trials.[21]

Because Millar had appeared as a witness for the defense in the previous trial (that of Mitchell and Whitesides), his testimony is included in the records. Millar maintained that he had never been a member of the Ku Klux Klan. He had attended only two meetings, he insisted, because the Klan had threatened to visit him. "I thought I would like to know when they would be riding around," he said, "so I might watch for them." His cousin had encouraged him to attend the meetings to determine if he wanted to join: "He knew I would just keep it safe." Millar's connection with the Klan, it seemed, was tenuous.[22]

The trial of John S. Millar demonstrated more than anything else the pressure on the white population in upcountry South Carolina to join the Ku Klux Klan and the difficulty of remaining outside the organization. Testimony demonstrated that Millar himself had been visited by the Klan on at least one occasion. Some of the freedmen had taken their guns to Millar's place to prevent the Klan from "getting them and breaking them to pieces." The Klan wanted the guns, and it wanted Millar. The defendant hid in a back room while his mother swore that "there was nobody there but an old woman, and for God's sake they were not to scare her." Daniel McClure, the black captain of road work in the area, "by the influence of Mr. Millar," lived with Millar and testified that he did not think Millar "was in favor of the Ku Klux organization" but rather "was scared of them." A freedman who lived on Millar's plantation swore that Millar never "interfered in any way with the voting of colored people." He remembered that Millar was not planning to vote in the election of 1870, "but if he was he did not know but that he would vote the radical ticket."[23]

Daniel Carroll, a white neighbor of Millar's, testified that Millar had attended the Klan meeting only to learn the purposes of the organization. Carroll thought Millar had "kindly feelings toward the Radical Party." Pressure from the white community, however, had made it difficult for whites to remain aloof from the Klan. White Republicans all over the upcountry, having received visitors in the night, were announcing in the papers their withdrawal from the party. Carroll had voted Republican, but he was eventually "obliged to join the [Klan] organization." He admitted that he had joined the Ku Klux Klan and taken the oath, but "it was to protect myself and my colored hands." According to Carroll, Millar had similarly attended the meeting "to save his hands."[24]

Like the testimony of the defense witnesses, that of witnesses for the prosecution demonstrated the enormous pressure on the white community to conform to Klan values and aspirations. Reluctant night riders were summoned to join the organization and then to participate in the outrages that terrorized the freedmen. The owner of a country store and drinking establishment testified, for example, that the Klan had come to his place at night, threatening him with violence, demanding a good part of his whiskey, and insisting that he close his place of business. He had joined the Klan for safety's sake even though he "didn't care anything about going into it." Klan members coerced the witness into the organization stating that he would have been shot if they had not saved him, and he "had better go into it." He did.[25]

Testimony regarding a murder committed by the Klan demonstrated another way it established control over reluctant members of the white community. Government testimony revealed that Klan members who declined to participate in the crimes were ordered by their superiors in the organization to help dispose of the body of Charley Good, a freedman who had been killed for his "rather defiant" support of the Radical party and its principles. Both Thomas Berry and Lawson Davis testified that they were summoned to participate in the "burial," where Good was thrown into the river and anchored with plowshares. The Klan's intention, according to Davis, "was to get all the white men in the community to assist in removing the body." The murderers "didn't want anybody left behind, so that no information could leak out in reference to Good." If all the members of the white community were implicated in the crime, no one could be free to oppose the Klan or reveal the truth. Opposition to the Klan was dangerous for white people in upcountry South Carolina.[26]

In his closing arguments, Millar's attorney stressed that Millar was "both alarmed and fearful of this organization." Millar was not a member of the Klan, according to the defense, but had attended meetings only "to protect himself and to protect the colored men in his employment." District Attorney Corbin insisted, however, that Millar's attendance at the meetings proved his membership in the Klan. "Do you suppose for one moment," he argued, "that band of conspirators, who had been present at murders . . . would have permitted this man to be present if he had not been a member of the organization, and if he was not known to be a member?" Corbin reminded the jury, moreover, that Millar was being tried for conspiracy. Under the law of conspiracy, Millar was guilty of the offense if he was a member of the Klan whether or not he had actually participated in its outrages. "A man is known," the district attorney stated, "by the company he keeps." The jury—all black with the exception of its white foreman—agreed. As in the previous Klan trials, the jury quickly returned a guilty verdict.[27]

The Millar case, in retrospect, seems a poor choice for prosecution. Attorney General Akerman had advised Corbin to proceed first with persons in places of influence who had committed serious crimes. Millar was apparently innocent of committing outrages; the government did not even attempt to prove that he had done anything more serious than attend Klan meetings. With hundreds of indictments prepared and many other Klansmen who had committed more serious offenses awaiting trial, the case of John S. Millar seems trivial and downright mean-spirited by comparison. Perhaps Millar was chosen because he owned a large plantation and employed many laborers; Akerman's guidelines had established wealth and community position as criteria for prosecution.

The fourth and final trial of the November 1871 term of the Fourth Circuit Court began on 29 December 1871, the twenty-third day of proceedings. Edward T. Avery, the defendant, was exactly the kind of man the government had hoped to prosecute successfully as a signal that the elite could no longer persecute the freedmen or coerce their white neighbors to follow their political lead. Avery was a prominent physician who lived in the Ebenezer community near Rock Hill. He was indicted on four counts, one charging a general conspiracy against the suffrage, the others charging threats, intimidation, and interference with Samuel Sturgis in his right to vote.[28]

The prosecution proceeded initially as it had done in the previous trials, demonstrating first the existence of the Ku Klux Klan and its political purpose. Witnesses revealed that Klan members were willing to go as far as murder to carry out the purposes of the organization. The bulk of the testimony, however, concentrated on the outrages allegedly committed by the defendant.[29]

Testimony indicated that several Klan members with Dr. Avery at the lead had visited Sturgis one night at the home of Abram Brumfield. Both Brumfield and Sturgis were known to be Radicals. When Brumfield managed to escape, the Klan concentrated its wrath on Sturgis. They knocked him down, kicked him repeatedly, damaged his wrist permanently, then put a buggy line around his neck and dragged him around. They lifted him by the line until his toes did not touch the floor. This "hanging" left the old man with a swollen neck for weeks. Brumfield, Mrs. Brumfield, and Sturgis had all recognized Avery as one of the assailants. They lived in the neighborhood with Avery and knew his voice and appearance well. Each testified that despite the Klan disguise he or she recognized the defendant by his mustache, his voice, and his crippled left hand, which had been injured in the war.[30]

On the night they outraged Sturgis, the night riders had also visited the home of a black preacher, Isaac Postle, known in the community as Isaac the Apostle. The Postles, like Sturgis and the Brumfields, testified that they had recognized Dr. Avery. Mrs. Postle had hidden her husband under the floor when they heard the Klan members approaching. When the pregnant woman, "some seven or eight months gone in travail," with another baby in her arms, refused to reveal her husband's whereabouts, Avery, himself the father of a young family, had knocked her to the floor, then pinned her baby down with his foot while another Klan member stepped on Mrs. Postle. Then they "beat my head against the side of the house till I had no sense hardly left." Avery allegedly put a line around the woman's neck as the night riders had done with Sturgis. Reaching up to remove the line, she felt his crippled hand. "I knows you," she thought.[31]

Finding the preacher under the floor, the Klan members took him away from the house and demanded to know if he had "been preaching up burning and corruption." Postle assured them that he "never preached nothing but peace and harmony." Unconvinced, the night riders hung him from a tree so that only his toes touched the ground and he was "choked and could not tell them anything." They repeated this process over and over, Postle testified, even though he insisted "ever so many times" that he did not "advise or instruct anything that was wrong." Although his reassurances did not "seem to have any impression," the Klan members eventually released Postle.[32]

While her husband was locked up in the York County jail for the crimes against Brumfield and Postle, Mrs. Avery set about to free him. In this mission she enlisted the assistance of her minister, the Reverend Robert E. Cooper. Cooper visited Postle and insisted that he accompany him the next day to see Mrs. Avery, at which time she insisted that she had "lawful evidence" that her husband had not committed the crimes.

She demanded that Postle sign an affidavit stating that the charges were false. Postle doubted that she could produce such evidence, but the woman, assisted by the white minister and two household servants, continued to wear him down "for a considerable time." Postle "felt very small," he testified, "being with a lady like her—of her ability and position—and I felt it was almost wrong not to submit to her." Finally, Mrs. Avery threatened that Postle would be arrested for perjury if he would not yield. She would have him "cropped and branded and penitentiaried for ten years and perhaps for your lifetime." Still unconvinced, Postle finally agreed to withdraw charges "on their oath" but "not on my oath."[33]

The defense attorneys, Wilson and Colonel F. W. McMaster, produced in court an affidavit signed by the black preacher stating that "according to the evidence now appearing" the charges against Dr. Avery were false. Postle insisted in court, however, that he had never believed Mrs. Avery, Rev. Cooper, or the two black women, servants of the Avery family, who insisted that Avery had been in his own bed the night of the Klan raids. Postle understood the paper he signed to mean that *if* their story was accurate, then Avery had not outraged him. He remained certain throughout, however, that the defense's alibi was false.[34] The federal district attorney agreed. Corbin brought charges of conspiracy by force, intimidation, and threats to prevent Postle from testifying in the case against Mrs. Avery, Rev. Cooper, and the two servant women. The grand jury found a true bill, but the conspirators were never tried. The charges were discontinued in April 1873.[35]

Having failed in their efforts to establish an alibi, Avery's attorneys produced an expert witness to testify in his behalf. Dr. Tally was a physician, former Confederate surgeon, and expert on gunshot wounds by virtue of his experience in the Confederate army. Tally testified that the nature of Avery's wound rendered him unable to raise his arm in the manner necessary to tie a buggy line around the neck of the witness. If someone with a wounded hand had committed such an outrage, according to his story, it could not have been Avery. Tally exhibited the injured hand to the jurors, demonstrating that Avery had limited use of his hand. The testimony of the doctor, however, did not affect the legitimacy of the charges against Dr. Avery. Mrs. Postle had testified that Avery put the line around her neck, but Sam Sturgis, against whom Avery was charged, stated that a black man who accompanied Avery had actually tied the line around his neck.[36]

Avery clearly decided that the case against him was strong enough to convict, despite the efforts of his attorneys. As the closing arguments began on Monday morning, Corbin suddenly realized that the defendant was not in court. He demanded to know Avery's whereabouts. F. W. McMaster, Avery's attorney, stated that was for Corbin "to find out." When McMaster again refused to answer, Judge Bond was furious. He angrily instructed the clerk to "lay a rule on Mr. McMaster to answer the question or show cause why he should not be thrown over the bar." Avery had disappeared, forfeiting his $3,000 bail. After arguments from both sides to determine how to proceed, the judges allowed the attorneys to continue their final arguments. The jury, predictably, was unimpressed with the defense's claims of innocence. After a lapse of only fifteen minutes, the jurors returned with a guilty verdict. Sentencing, however, would have to wait until Avery could be located.[37]

Two days later, Colonel McMaster was tried for contempt. His defense attorneys argued that "it was not his duty to become an informer against his client." Instead, they insisted, had the defense attorney "attempted to betray the confidence of his client, he would have deserved the reprimand of the Court." They even suggested that forfeiture of the bond represented full payment for the disappearance of their client. Corbin and Chamberlain submitted authorities stating that attorneys could be struck from the roll for ill practice, fraud, or dishonesty against the obvious rules of justice. Allowing the defendant to escape was not a matter of privileged communication but "a palpable and direct attempt not to act as an officer of the Court, but to act in defiance of the Court." By no means, they argued, did the bail set a price for the worth of the defendant but served as a guarantee that he would appear "to stand his defense and meet his verdict." The U.S. attorneys recommended disbarring McMasters "to protect the integrity of the bar" and prevent others from assisting criminals "in escaping from the meshes of the law."[38]

The *Charleston Daily Courier* labeled the hearing the "dying struggle of the tribunal which has been working in the interest of the Grant dynasty for the past six weeks." McMasters's case was held under advisement, according to the Democratic newspaper, "the plain English of which is that the Court (meaning Judge Bond) upon reflection has found that his personal temper got the best of his judicial prerogative." The newspaper predicted that "a decision will never be pronounced." The *Courier*'s assessment of the outcome appears to have been correct. Neither the verbatim court

records nor the Sessions Index and Minute Book of the Criminal Court indicate the outcome of McMasters's trial. McMasters continued as a prominent and influential member of the South Carolina bar. His client remained
at large, his case carried on the docket from term to term.[39]

Judge Bond's anger with McMasters and his client, Edward T. Avery,
continued unabated. The judge had no sympathy or respect for an influential member of the community who jumped bail and disappeared after
the government had expended so much time and effort on his trial. As the
political climate changed and interest in enforcement of civil rights
waned, Mrs. Avery appealed to Attorney General George H. Williams
to allow her husband and father of her six children to return home.[40]
McMasters submitted affidavits from two former Ku Klux members who
admitted being on the raid when Sam Sturgis and Isaac the Apostle were
outraged. Both men swore that Avery had no part in the attack. Williams
instructed Corbin (despite the strong recommendation of the district attorney to the contrary) to allow the doctor to return to his family. When Judge
Bond received the document that would have discontinued the case
against Avery in April 1873, he refused to sign the closing orders of the
court session until he had deliberately struck through the part excepting
Avery from arrest. Clearly Bond considered Avery guilty and wanted to
see him serve his term. McMasters, however, claimed that the "verdict
was unrighteous & the jury which tried him a disgrace to civilization."
The opinion of the defense lawyer captured the feelings of most of the
white community in South Carolina as the trials had proceeded. Avery remained at large until his case—along with several hundred other Klan
cases still pending—was discontinued during the April term of 1874.[41]

Throughout the trials the two sides had displayed sharply contrasting
attitudes toward the humble black people who took the witness stand and
filled the jury box. The presence of so many black people in the jury box
and on the witness stand demonstrated to white Southerners that their
world had turned upside down. Blatant racism worked against the public
credibility of the black participants. Editorial comment in the Charleston
paper constantly berated both the witnesses and the jurors. The presiding
judge, however, found it easier to bear the ignorance and inexperience of
the freedmen than the condescending attitudes and constant interruptions
of the defense attorneys. Weary of the interminable legal haggling, Bond
complained to his wife that Reverdy Johnson had used the trials as a
political showcase. "I will not hear Stanbery's harangues longer," Bond

wrote his wife. "I believe now their speeches are more for delay and with the hope that I have to go home. I shall stick them out." Although he grew tired of the defense arguments, the presiding judge listened with patience to the witnesses and treated the jurors with respect. Bond's charge to the grand jury demonstrated his belief that blacks were able to exercise good judgment and to assume the responsibilities placed on them by the law. He urged them to do their duty "with impartiality and fairness, but with firmness." Recommending the pattern that he followed personally, Bond counseled the grand jurors that witnesses were under unusual strain and it was necessary to "bear with them patiently." The judge instructed the petit jurors on the law of conspiracy, confident in their ability to decide intelligently.[42]

U.S. v. Edward T. Avery, concluded on 2 January 1872, was the final trial of the November 1871 term of the Fourth Circuit. The Ku Klux Klan cases had consumed the entire six-week court session, yet only five persons had been tried in four trials. The cases tried had scarcely made a dent in the load. Some 278 Enforcement Act cases were carried over to the next term of the court. If the number of persons tried was small, the government had nonetheless obtained a perfect conviction record. Forty-nine guilty pleas added to the government's success rate. Attorney General Akerman wrote Corbin from Washington that he was pleased with the results of the trials: "As far as I can learn, the prosecuting lawyers have answered every reasonable expectation, and have managed the business ably." Corbin and Chamberlain had "done excellently well." When Akerman resigned his position at the end of 1871, he found it "comforting to believe that I have born some part in the exposure and destruction of that terrible conspiracy."[43]

If the government had successfully prosecuted the Ku Klux night riders, the cost had been tremendous in time, effort, money, and constitutional goals. As determined as Judge Bond was to see justice done, he had been reluctant to accept the most constitutionally novel goals of the prosecution. Confusion remained on the two issues the judges had certified to the Supreme Court in *U.S. v. James W. Avery*: the Second Amendment question and the problem of using ordinary crimes as the measure of punishment for civil rights violations.[44] Both the prosecution and defense wanted a definitive answer to the question of whether the Fourteenth Amendment secured to the freedmen the right to bear arms. The *Avery* case was chosen to certify to the high court because it involved a murder.[45] If the Court decided that the federal courts had jurisdiction to determine whether a common law crime had been committed so as to ascertain the measure of punishment for interfering with the franchise, a Klansman could potentially be put to death for interfering with the rights of the freedmen. Many people throughout the United States doubted that the Fourteenth Amendment was meant to bring such a radical change in the federal system.[46] With hundreds of Klan cases pending, federal attorneys throughout the South looked to the Supreme Court to clarify the confusion. So, too, did the opposition, certain the nation's high court would find that the Enforcement Acts exceeded constitutional authority.

Reverdy Johnson pressed for an early hearing, a goal with which Corbin and Chamberlain heartily agreed because the next circuit court in South Carolina was set for April 1872. Arguments began in mid-March. But the new attorney general of the United States, George H. Williams, deliberately blocked a thorough review of the case by the Supreme Court.

President Grant appointed Williams attorney general upon Akerman's resignation at the close of 1871. Akerman was asked to resign for reasons that are unclear. "The reasons for this step," Akerman wrote Corbin, "I would not detail fully without saying what, perhaps, ought not to be said." Akerman took comfort in the knowledge that he had helped to break up the Klan and assured Major Merrill that his successor was "an able and experienced man" who could carry on the work "free from some of the hostilities that have obstructed me." Historians have traditionally held that Akerman was forced out of the cabinet because of his lack of popularity with the railroad magnates. William McFeely has suggested, however, that it was Akerman's devotion to the concept of equality that shortened his tenure in office: "Men from the North as well as the South came to recognize, uneasily, that if he was not halted, his concept of equality before the law was likely to lead to total equality."[47] If McFeely is correct, then Grant may have deliberately chosen an attorney general who was not so dedicated to the task of securing civil rights for the nation's black citizens.

A former Republican senator from Oregon, Akerman's successor, George H. Williams, had written the Tenure of Office Act, served on the Joint Committee of Fifteen on Reconstruction, and become one of Grant's "chief flatterers and hangers-on." For his efforts, Williams was rewarded with a place in the cabinet even though he was considered a "third-rate lawyer." It was Williams's responsibility to guide the South Carolina Klan case through the Supreme Court. Williams's behavior on the *Avery* case seems downright obstructionist at first glance. He insisted that the Supreme Court lacked jurisdiction in *U.S. v. James W. Avery*. The Klan case had gone up to the high court on a certificate of division on a preliminary motion to quash the indictment without ever proceeding to trial. Thus there was no conviction in the case but simply a request for direction. The government had not yet tried in South Carolina any Klan case with an ordinary crime attached. The Fourth Circuit Court was waiting for the Supreme Court to rule on section seven of the 1870 Enforcement Act. Two years earlier, however, the high court had declined to rule on a matter involving a preliminary motion over which the lower court had broad discretion.[48] Now Williams insisted that the Supreme Court must follow precedent. Reverdy Johnson, who was certainly a finer constitutional lawyer than Williams, argued against dismissal. Because the question involved the jurisdiction of the circuit court, Johnson insisted, "the case cannot proceed until the question is decided." Williams replied, however, that the trial could have proceeded. The circuit court did not doubt its jurisdiction to try the defendants for conspiracy. The same question could have been raised later when the prosecutor offered evidence to prove murder. If the decision of the high court, announced on 21 March 1872, pleased the new attorney general, it proved disappointing to both sides of the constitutional issues at stake. Following precedent, the Supreme Court justices refused to address the issues involved in the Ku Klux Klan cases because *Avery* went up on a preliminary motion over which the circuit court had broad discretion. The decision left the government attorneys without the direction they needed for future trials.[49] As Williams may have understood, however, the lack of a Supreme Court ruling on the constitutional issues at this time may have postponed the Court's decision against the prosecution, thus enabling the government to obtain many more guilty pleas in succeeding Klan cases.

The defense tried yet another device to bring a case before the Supreme Court in *Ex parte T. Jefferson Greer*. After Judge Bond left South Carolina in January 1871, defense attorney W. W. Fickling petitioned Judge Bryan for a writ of habeas corpus for Greer and two others on the grounds that they were held on authority of indictments that were unconstitutional. Bryan initially understood that the defense attorney was protesting his client's being arrested and held without the customary procedures. By the time of the hearing, however, Greer had been indicted and was held on a bench warrant. Fickling sought the writ, he clarified, not because his client was improperly confined but rather "on the ground that the law under which he is indicted and under which the warrant was issued against him, is unconstitutional." To have the nation's high court apprise the Enforcement Act, the defense sought habeas corpus relief, "habeas corpus being the only mode known to the law by which a criminal matter can be taken to the Supreme Court without a division and certificate of the Judges of the Court."[50]

Bryan decided to cooperate with the defense effort. Although he considered the law constitutional "so far as the enforcement and protection of the right of suffrage is concerned," he granted the writ. After inquiring into the cause of detention, he remanded the prisoner to custody. The defense then appealed to the Supreme Court.[51] Congress had provided for appeal on habeas corpus proceedings in 1867, a law that was hastily withdrawn to deny the Supreme Court jurisdiction in *Ex parte McCardle* in 1868.[52] The revocation of the statute left the Supreme Court's authority to use habeas corpus where it had been originally under the Judiciary Act of 1789. Habeas corpus could be used in conjunction with certiorari, the Supreme Court had indicated in *Ex parte Yerger*, and it was the combination of the two procedures which brought *Ex parte Greer* before the Court now. Certiorari enabled the Supreme Court to review the lower court record and arguments of counsel which the justices would use to determine whether to grant Greer's release on habeas corpus.[53]

Henry Stanbery submitted a brief for petitioner which made the familiar argument that the federal courts lacked jurisdiction over ordinary crimes. Greer was indicted (under section six of the first Enforcement Act) on several counts of committing murder while denying the voting rights of a freedman. Because murder was a common law crime, Stanbery argued, only state courts were authorized to try such cases. Stanbery further challenged the entire law as unconstitutional on the grounds that it prohibited all interference with the franchise, not just that on account of race as provided by the Fifteenth Amendment.[54]

The government's brief prepared by Solicitor General Benjamin Bristow made three primary points. First, it denied that the Court had jurisdiction. Habeas corpus had never been used to discharge a prisoner held on indictment by a U.S. circuit court and should not be so used now. The brief defended congressional authority to pass the Enforcement Act under the Fourteenth and Fifteenth Amendments. The framers intended the right to act "on the people individually," not merely to provide remedies against state action. Finally, the government claimed that when the states deprived the freedmen of their rights they had failed to provide a republican form of government, thus violating the guarantee clause and authorizing Congress to act.[55] The law was clearly constitutional, and the Supreme Court should not release Greer on habeas corpus.

Judge Bond hoped that the Supreme Court would not grant the writ. "I am very anxious to know what the Supreme Court is going to do in the case now being argued before them," he wrote, "for upon that depends the safety of all our witnesses formerly examined and also the future suppression of the Klans. I would not live in this state 24 hours if I was a Republican if they grant that writ."[56]

The Supreme Court may have followed Bond's logic. A divided Court refused Greer's petition for reasons that are unclear. A vote to deny the writ could mean that the justice thought the Court lacked jurisdiction to accept a habeas corpus appeal, that the justice considered the law constitutional—in which case the prisoner should remain in custody—or even that the justice deemed it improper to preempt the circuit court's authority to rule on the Enforcement Act.[57] Whatever the individual reasons for denying relief may have been, the Court's refusal to address the issues in *Greer* preserved the integrity of the government prosecution efforts and the safety of the witnesses. Like the insistence on following precedent in *Avery*, however, *Ex parte Greer* left both sides without clear directions for future trials. The government attorneys had developed a successful method of prosecution, but the meaning and scope of the Reconstruction Amendments and the Enforcement Acts were still unclear.

Preparing for the next round of trials, Corbin warned both Akerman and his successor, George Williams, that the successful prosecution of a few Klan members had not yet changed the minds and hearts of white South Carolinians. Things were quiet, he admitted, but it was understood among the Klansmen that "when the *storm blew over*, and *before the next election* they were to be allowed to resume operations." Because "nothing creditable [had] been done toward getting at the leading responsible men in the Ku Klux organization," it was mandatory that the government should not seem to vacillate. Ku Kluxers would "naturally construe their immunity from prosecution and punishment into license to do the like again."[58]

Like Corbin, Major Merrill advised Williams that the national government should avoid any signs of weakness; the policy of clemency the new attorney general was inclined to follow was premature. Without government protection, the citizens of upcountry South Carolina has no "assurance of safety." The "blind, unreasoning, bigoted hostility to the results of the war" that had given birth to the Klan were "still potent for evil." Indeed, Merrill reported, an important government witness in the Klan trials had recently "had his throat cut almost from ear to ear . . . the act prompted solely by hostility to him" because he had dared to testify. Corbin expressed dissatisfaction with the government's progress in arresting Klan members outside York County. The large number of cases pending came primarily from York County. Other counties in upcountry South Carolina, "when properly worked up," would yield a similar "catalogue of crime." Thus Corbin insisted that the government should continue its efforts to capture leading Klan members who had escaped when habeas corpus was suspended.[59]

Capturing the criminals proved an elusive task. Some of the Klansmen were able to remain in the vicinity, trusting their family and neighbors to warn them when federal troops approached. Hundreds of other night riders had escaped to parts unknown when President Grant suspended habeas corpus. Extradition procedures proved difficult. Corbin complained to the attorney general of "bad faith" on the part of a federal marshal in Arkansas, for example, who refused to serve warrants on several fugitive Klan chiefs who were "covered all over with blood." It was disheartening to the federal attorney to know where the criminals were and not be able to get his hands on them.[60]

Government investigators traced two of the most wanted Klan leaders, Major James W. Avery and Dr. J. Rufus Bratton, to London, Ontario. Both men were indicted on several counts of conspiracy and wanted by the federal government for the murder of black militia captain Jim Williams. Major Avery had helped to organize the York County Klan in 1868 and was allegedly the top man in the county. Avery had ordered the raid and murder of Williams. J. Rufus Bratton had commanded the murder party. Both men were named in *U.S. v. James W. Avery*, which had been certified to the Supreme Court. John Bratton, brother of Rufus, "entertained and fed the Klans" in his plantation yard immediately after the grisly deed was accomplished.[61]

The United States attempted to arrange extradition for the South Carolinians who had fled to Canada. The Canadian government, however, refused to cooperate. Rather than recognize the runaway Klansmen as fugitives from justice covered by treaty, the Canadians considered them political refugees worthy of protection.[62]

When extradition failed, the United States sent secret service agents to bring these leaders to justice. The agents kidnapped Dr. Bratton near his lodging in London and forcibly returned him to South Carolina. The Canadian government sharply protested, however, and the United States returned the suspect. Evidence indicates that the agents kidnapped the wrong man, having mistaken Bratton for Avery. They arrested Bratton on a warrant for Major J. W. Avery. The United States would have been delighted to keep Bratton, however, because both men were among the most wanted suspects.[63] The prosecution intended to focus more intently on Klan leaders and those who had committed the most serious crimes in the upcoming session of the Fourth Circuit Court.

The April 1872 circuit court session in Charleston opened amid great controversy. Six weeks of testimony exposing the heinous nature of Klan atrocities in the previous court session had failed to convince the white community that the trials were anything but a travesty of justice. "There can be no question," the *Charleston Daily Courier* had announced at the close of the November term, "that the Councils of Safety called elsewhere Ku Klux, were not political organizations, had no political purpose, no hostility either to the Government or Constitution of the United States, or any intention to interfere with the right of suffrage." The government had been able to obtain convictions, according to the paper, only because of "a packed jury and witnesses willing to swear to anything." The court was worse than a star chamber; the "old court law maxim that every man is to be regarded as innocent until his guilt be proven is reversed."[64]

Now the Charleston paper scornfully announced the new circuit court session: "The so-called Ku Klux Crusade has been reopened. The days of the Star Chamber have been renewed. . . . In this state there has been inaugurated a reign of terror, which dethrones the Constitution, and puts an end to all law and liberty." The paper was particularly indignant that the accused had been incarcerated without the usual procedures whereas the Constitution "declares the right of every citizen to be secure" in his home. White citizens complained privately of "packed juries" and predicted "no chance of acquittal" for any of those who were being persecuted so unmercifully by the federal government. Black citizens, meanwhile, crowded into the city, some to testify, others to attend the court sessions as spectators "taking every available inch of sitting and standing room." The crowd was so great that the ceiling underneath the courtroom "cracked in several places and showed signs of falling in." The freedmen looked to the federal government to protect their right to be secure in their persons and homes.[65]

Several days of the court session passed before any Klansman was actually put to trial. "They all plead guilty," Judge Bond wrote his wife, "if you only won't hang them." The judge hoped the trend would continue, thus cutting short the time before he could return home. The Klansmen had good reason to plead guilty. The government, represented this time by Major Merrill, District Attorney Corbin, and his assistants William Stone and William E. Earle, offered to drop the murder charges in a large number of cases in exchange for guilty pleas. Because the Supreme Court had not yet ruled on the constitutionality of inquiring whether common law crimes had been committed in the process of interfering with the franchise, the deal was too good for many of the night riders to refuse. The prosecution was determined to include murder counts in the cases that came to trial during this term.[66]

Doubtless disappointed by the Supreme Court's refusal to decide the issues, District Attorney Corbin during the South Carolina Klan trials in April 1872 resurrected both the question of trying common law crimes in federal court and the Second Amendment charge, which he hoped would protect the civil rights of black citizens independent of their political rights. He brought indictments deliberately formed to test the issues on which Judge Bond and Judge Bryan had previously disagreed. The prosecution, local defense attorneys—Stanbery and Johnson did not attend this session—and judges all agreed to accept the charges so as to send up a case to the Supreme Court.[67] Elijah Ross Sapaugh was chosen from among the many who were indicted for the murder of freedman Thomas Roundtree.

The murder of Thomas Roundtree was a particularly heinous affair. Approximately eighty night riders raided his home expecting to find guns that were reportedly stored on the property. When they broke into the house, Roundtree shot into the crowd from a loft, injuring Sapaugh. Roundtree then dropped from the loft to the outside, attempting to escape. Someone yelled that Sapaugh had been shot. For daring to defend himself, Roundtree received the full force of Klan fury. A witness related that he had counted some thirty-five bullet holes in the freedman. In the event that that was not enough to kill him, Henry Sapaugh, brother of the accused, had drawn his knife and slit Roundtree's throat from ear to ear.[68]

Elijah Ross Sapaugh was tried on a six-count indictment carefully constructed to test the extent of federal power. Two counts charged murder
committed in the process of denying Thomas Roundtree's political rights,
one by shooting, the other by slitting Roundtree's throat. Another charged
conspiracy against Roundtree's Second Amendment right to keep and
bear arms. Other counts charged conspiracy against Roundtree for voting
previously and planning to vote in the future. Three other Klan cases tried
at this session of the circuit court similarly charged murder "against the
peace and dignity of South Carolina" in a deliberate attempt to test the
constitutionality of the seventh section of the Enforcement Act of 1870,
which allowed the federal court to take cognizance of ordinary crimes
committed in the process of denying civil rights. Judge Bond insisted,
however, that the defendants were not being tried for murder. They were
being tried for conspiracy "and that in the execution of that conspiracy a
murder was committed."[69]

The trial proceeded quickly, requiring only one day. In the Sapaugh
case, unlike the Klan cases in the previous session of the court, the jury
was racially balanced—six blacks and six whites. Still the Charleston
paper complained of fixed juries. When the prosecuting attorneys questioned white jurors carefully to ascertain that they had not been connected
with the Klan in any way, the newspaper labeled the process "pumping."
The district attorney, according to the *Courier*, ordered "every white man
of respectable looks to stand aside, whom he suspected of being other than
Radicals." Once the jury was impaneled, Judge Bond allowed the defense
attorney, John F. Ficken, to enter a plea that the circuit court lacked jurisdiction because murder is a common law offense. Then the trial proceeded. First, the prosecution proved the existence of the Klan, as in all
the previous cases. Next, the government demonstrated the Klan's political nature. The bulk of the testimony, however, concentrated on the murder of Roundtree and the issue of taking the guns. The defense attorney
deplored the crime against Roundtree, "as foul and deliberate a murder as
he had ever heard of," but insisted that Sapaugh was not the one who
should be tried. He was only one of many in the crowd; there was no evidence "to show that the prisoner took part in the murder." Indeed, according to the defense, there was no evidence that the murder was a result of
conspiracy.[70]

Corbin's closing arguments indicated that he was willing to seek the
death penalty in Enforcement Act cases. He felt sympathy for Sapaugh,

he said, but he could not shrink from his duty. He felt even more for the one who had been so viciously murdered. The demands of society required that the guilty must pay. He emphasized primarily the facts of the murder. "If the facts alleged in the indictment had been proven," he insisted, it was the responsibility of the jury to "bring in a verdict of guilty, and leave the law to fix upon the prisoner the punishment that he had incurred." The law, as Corbin had previously stated, "says that when men commit murder they shall die, and we have no right to complain of it."[71] Thus the trial of Elijah Ross Sapaugh highlighted the objections the defense had made throughout the Klan trials. Using the state penalties for common law crimes could result in people being put to death for violating the political and civil rights of their fellow citizens. Such a dramatic departure from traditional state-based federalism was too much to concede. And the law of conspiracy made plain that anyone involved in the Ku Klux organization was guilty of all the crimes committed to carry out its purposes.

Although Judge Bond had stated that the defendant was being tried for conspiracy rather than murder, his jury charge carefully defined the crime of murder and the nature of malice which constituted the felony. To find the prisoner guilty, he said, the jury must first find that a conspiracy existed and that the people involved in it "had in view the commission of the felony." In other words, the crime must be premeditated. Then the jury must determine that "in carrying out the conspiracy the felony was actually committed." It was not necessary for a conspirator "actually to strike the blow" to be guilty. Rather, "all persons were principals who go out for the purpose of doing an unlawful act, and who are ready and willing to assist in it." Consent was the key. The jury apparently had no compunction about finding the defendant guilty of charges involving murder. It returned a guilty verdict in only one hour, recommending Sapaugh to the mercy of the court. Defense attorney John F. Ficken quickly moved in arrest of judgment.[72]

Despite the complaints about "packed juries" and witnesses "willing to swear to anything," the government did not achieve the success rate in the April 1872 session in Charleston that it had enjoyed in the previous session in Columbia. Eighteen persons were tried and convicted for conspiracy; of this number two cases included murder charges. Elijah Ross Sapaugh was found guilty of murder. Robert Riggins was found guilty of conspiracy, not guilty of murder. A third murder case against Thomas

Zimmerman ended in acquittal. A fourth, *U.S. v. Wesley Smith and Leander Spencer*, resulted in a mistrial. Corbin announced that he was satisfied, however, because the testimony had conflicted. The government then dropped the murder charges in the case for guilty pleas on the conspiracy counts. The severity of the charges perhaps contributed to the jury's reluctance to convict in these cases, although the jury in the Sapaugh case certainly demonstrated no hesitation. Eighteen guilty pleas added to the government's success rate.[73]

Corbin was more determined than either the attorney general of the United States or Judge Bond to continue to prosecute vigorously. He requested a special session of the court in August 1872. "The K.K.'s are becoming very much emboldened" in the upcountry, he had reported to Williams. There was once again a "general feeling of alarm among the colored people," especially those who had testified against their neighbors. A strong federal presence was necessary to protect the freedmen. Corbin recognized, however, that the court system as it stood was "utterly inadequate" to handle the press of business. Corbin recommended that those "worst and leading characters" who had been instrumental in committing the "most shocking murders" be held for trial. Those suspected of lesser offenses could remain at home on their own recognizance subject to appear when called. Their cases would be continued on the docket from term to term to encourage their good behavior. Major Merrill reiterated Corbin's plea for a court session in August. "Affairs are getting into a very bad condition by reason of hopes excited by refusal of Congress to extend suspension of Habeas Corpus," he reported to the adjutant general. If there was any "relaxation or appearance of it," he predicted, "there will most certainly be renewal of serious trouble before the election." Thus it was "vital to the interests of peace" that the government continue to prosecute vigorously.[74]

Judge Bond declined to come for a special session. "There are a great many reasons why somebody should come," he wrote his wife, "but I don't want to. . . . The South in August is not particularly agreeable & trying Ku Klux less so. Besides," he continued, "it is extremely expensive & we are economizing." The judge had done his part "to suppress this revolt for it amounts to that, and I can do no more." Thus the judge who had earlier pledged "if all the defence they have is my want of patience I shall see that it don't avail" had run out of patience for trying the Klan.[75] A few more Klan cases were heard during the November 1872 session of the circuit court in Columbia, but the government had tired of the effort. Clearing the docket had become more important than continuing the cases to persuade the accused to conduct themselves as good citizens. Corbin began at this session to *nolle pros* all but the most serious cases. Some 1,188 Enforcement Act cases in South Carolina remained pending at the end of 1872, a number that would have overwhelmed the federal courts for many years to come.[76]

The Sapaugh case was certified to the Supreme Court on a division of opinion on the court's "jurisdiction to find whether the crime of murder has been committed . . . in order to ascertain the measure of punishment to be affixed." Ficken unfortunately failed to include the Second Amendment count in his motion so the issue did not go up to the Court a second time.[77] It is clear, nonetheless, that the bench upheld the count only to test the issue because no later indictments for a Ku Klux Klan case tried in South Carolina charged a conspiracy against the right to keep and bear arms.

The Supreme Court never heard the *Sapaugh* case despite the importance of the constitutional question. Reverdy Johnson expected to present the case for the defense; government attorneys and judges in South Carolina and throughout the South agreed on the need for a decision. Once again Attorney General Williams sabotaged efforts to obtain a ruling. Williams directed Corbin to enter a *nolle prosequi* to remove the case from the Supreme Court docket. His reasons are unclear. He wanted the case terminated, he wrote, "not for the sake of Sapaugh, but for the sake of the public good." Despite his personal desire to have the constitutional question resolved, Corbin obviously followed the order of his superior. The government attorney protested "on general principles" but dropped the murder count nonetheless. The conspiracy conviction still stood. Sapaugh was sentenced to pay a $100 fine and serve one year in the Albany penitentiary, a far cry from the sentence he would have received if the murder count had stuck.[78]

Thus ended the great South Carolina Ku Klux Klan trials—"not with a bang but a whimper." Thanks to the efforts of the attorney general, the Supreme Court did not have the opportunity to rule on the issue of charging common law crimes in conjunction with the abuse of voting rights. The federal government's most sustained effort to provide positive civil and political rights for black citizens ended with no substantial constitutional gains. The goal of bringing all black citizens of South Carolina, women as well as men, under the protection of the federal government through the

Second Amendment died with the *Sapaugh* case; confusion remained on the federal government's authority to enforce the Bill of Rights. Federal attorneys in South Carolina made no further attempts to attach ordinary crimes to voting rights violations.

On the positive side, the prosecuting attorneys won numerous convictions and confessions restoring—for the time being—an uneasy peace. But the attempt to punish the leading citizens who had spearheaded the Ku Klux Klan was, by and large, also a failure. The most wanted Klansmen had the wherewithal to disappear indefinitely. Thus the brunt of the government's prosecution efforts fell on those who were guilty of lesser crimes. If the letter of the law made clear that all the people involved in a conspiracy are responsible for all its deeds, the sentencing disparities nonetheless would indicate that Judge Bond recognized the difference between the educated and influential members accustomed to dominating society and the reluctant night riders who followed them into the Ku Klux Klan.

Radical members of the South Carolina Legislature. Courtesy South Caroliniana Library, University of South Carolina, Columbia.

Robert K. Scott, Republican governor of South Carolina.
Courtesy South Caroliniana Library, University of South
Carolina, Columbia.

George S. Bryan, federal district judge for South Carolina. Courtesy South Caroliniana Library, University of South Carolina, Columbia.

Daniel H. Chamberlain, South Carolina attorney general and special federal prosecuting attorney. Courtesy South Caroliniana Library, University of South Carolina, Columbia.

Defense attorney Reverdy Johnson of Maryland. By permission of
Maryland State Archives, Special Collections (Albert P. Close Collection),
Annapolis.

Federal Circuit Judge Hugh Lennox Bond. By
permission of Maryland Historical Society, Baltimore.

Defense attorney Henry Stanbery of Ohio. By permission of Ohio Historical Society, Columbus.

U. S. Attorney General Amos T. Akerman. Courtesy Georgia Department of
Archives and History, Atlanta.

6

Sentencing and
the End of Reconstruction

The great South Carolina Ku Klux Klan trials of 1871 and 1872 were the federal government's most sustained effort to enforce civil and political rights for its black citizens. The executive and judicial branches set out to implement the tough new laws passed by Congress to safeguard the rights of the freedmen. "I am contemplating a sort of pronouncement to the Grand Jury," Judge Bond had written his wife, Anna, before the trials began, "which will indicate to these night shirted scoundrels that they have now engaged in a war with the U.S. Courts & that I don't mean to be whipped."[1] Bond was true to his word. His firm direction of the trials enabled the federal prosecutors to attain an enviable conviction record. Federal effort broke the back of the Ku Klux Klan in South Carolina, and order was restored. In the final analysis, however, the federal officials who fought for justice, equality, and a new social order in the South were defeated by Southern intransigence, which refused to yield to the forces of the national government. White South Carolinians had insisted in 1868 that they would "never quietly submit to negro rule" but would "keep up this contest until we have regained the heritage of political control handed down to us by honored ancestry."[2] Their determination outlasted the central government's will to impose a standard of equality which was completely unacceptable to white southerners. The fight for justice and equality was also defeated by an administration that lost interest in its black constituents and tired of dealing with the "annual autumnal outbursts" of violence. And it was defeated by a constitutional vision which failed to recognize that the Thirteenth, Fourteenth, and Fifteenth Amendments to the United States Constitution could have effected a nationalization of government powers broad enough to establish a "Second American Constitution."[3]

The federal government's entire prosecution effort was replete with paradox. The Justice Department had ordered the federal attorneys to focus on prosecuting those Klan members who had status and influence in the community: "The higher the social standing and character of the convicted party, the more important is a vigorous prosecution and prompt execution of judgment." But the leaders had fled the upcountry "like rats from a burning house, excepting a few old and infirm men."[4]

Their followers were left to bear the brunt of federal enforcement efforts. With some important exceptions, the men who stood trial, confessed, or pleaded guilty were poor, young, illiterate, unimportant, and guilty of lesser offenses. These Klansmen thought it unfair that they should be "severely punished while the leaders are suffered to escape." At least one of them, however, confessed his willingness to "suffer an imprisonment if afterward he might be allowed to cultivate his farm in quietness with neither Ku Klux nor soldiers to trouble him." These were men, according to a Northern newspaper correspondent, "whose condition of social subordination is unknown" in the North: "For generations they have been led by the 'gentlemen' of their section, and have never been used to consider political acts from a moral stand-point, or think of a personal responsibility in such matters."[5]

The same issues troubled Judge Bond as he examined the Klansmen who made guilty pleas. Again and again the men who came before the court to make their statements testified that they had joined the Klan out of fear. "There were two chances for me," William Robbins recollected, "one was to join the order; the other was to be abused by them." W. P. Burnett agreed: "They pushed the poor people into it, and made them go . . . they came to my house and told me if I didn't I'd have to pay five dollars and take fifty lashes." When Thomas J. Price similarly claimed that he had "joined the Klan because I thought I was obliged to," Judge Bond noted that there "ought to be another proclamation of emancipation"—one to free the poor whites of the South from their more educated and influential neighbors.[6]

These poor, ignorant, unlettered night riders lacked the "manliness," as Judge Bond put it, and self-sufficiency to defy the wishes of their neighbors. "The reason I joined the order," John Moore testified, "was, I suppose, because I hadn't sense to do any better; nobody that know'd any better didn't tell me." William Ramsey told the same tale: "We did not unite and resist them because we did not have sense enough; but I know a good many didn't join voluntarily; it seems to me that men who had good learning and knowledge ought to have teached us better." District Attorney Corbin agreed. Responsibility for the Klan's outrages, he said, rested on its leaders, many of them men of property, who had "led and controlled these others." The leaders had fled the country, leaving their reluctant followers to take their punishment. Although he thought that no member of the conspiracy should be held guiltless, Corbin desired a "wise and merciful discrimination . . . in favor of those who have been led, seduced, or forced into an organization guilty of such inhuman atrocities."[7]

Judge Bond grappled with these issues when he sentenced the Klansmen who pleaded guilty. He recognized that most of these men had been "brought up in the most deplorable ignorance." It was their custom to look to men of substance and education for guidance. Yet those who "establish and control public opinion" were themselves "participants in the conspiracy." The judge insisted, nonetheless, that even the reluctant were responsible for their crimes. The facts may "palliate in some degree" the offenses committed, but they "cannot justify you." Bond sentenced the Klansmen so "that you may learn that no amount of threats or fear of punishment will justify a man in unprovoked violence to another." The Ku Klux Klan and the laws of the United States cannot exist together, Bond continued, "and it only needs a little manliness and courage, on the part of you ignorant dupes of designing men, to give supremacy to the law."[8]

Judge Bond was firm but fair in determining the punishment for the Klansmen. Although the law of conspiracy deemed each participant guilty of all the crimes committed in pursuance of the conspiracy, the judges clearly considered some of the criminals more guilty than others. Section six of the Enforcement Act of 31 May 1870 provided for fines up to $5,000 and sentences up to ten years for conspiracy.[9] Bond imposed sentences ranging from one month and a fine of $10 to ten years and $2,000 for those Klansmen who were convicted or pleaded guilty. Five years and $1,000 was the maximum sentence imposed during the first group of Klan trials, the November 1871 term of the circuit court. Eight- and ten-year sentences were set during the April 1872 session when the government attorneys concentrated on prosecuting Klansmen who were implicated in murders. These sentences were far more lenient, however, than those that could have been imposed if the state penalties for ordinary crimes had been used as the measure of punishment under section seven of the Enforcement Act.[10]

This wide disparity in sentencing reflected the crimes actually committed by the defendant, the amount of repentance displayed, the social class standing and potential to influence the community, and the amount of time already spent in jail. It undoubtedly reflected plea bargaining as well, but the legal records are silent on the deals that were struck. For those who confessed, many of whom had "staid with the horses" allegedly ignorant of the atrocities that were being committed, Bond generally set a light sentence between three and eighteen months and a fine of $50 to $100, depending on the number of raids in which the guilty party had participated.[11]

Judge Bond, assisted by Judge Bryan, tempered justice with mercy in determining the sentences for the individual Klansmen. In the case of James Wall, who could read and write and had the advantage of having been out of the state of South Carolina during the war and thus "should have had better sense than this," the judges agreed on a sentence of three months. The sentence should have been eighteen months, Bond said, but he wanted to "allow you to put in your crop next Spring." The judges acted out of consideration for Wall's wife and children, even though "you had no consideration" for the families of others. "The Court has been very much puzzled to reconcile justice with humanity," Judge Bryan announced. "It is an extreme exercise of mercy to you that they announce this judgment."[12]

Bond threw the book at "Squire" Samuel G. Brown, a white-haired gentleman who came to court to confess. Brown was a man of education and influence in York County. He had been a magistrate until 1868. Yet it was from Brown's desk that the prosecution had obtained the copy of the Ku Klux Klan constitution and by-laws which was used to prove the existence of the conspiracy and its political purposes. Brown's connection with the Klan is clouded. He claimed that he had attended meetings only to dissuade the younger men from "committing excesses, but that he had never been on a raid." He had obtained the constitution in 1868, he said, out of curiosity, merely to learn the purpose of the organization. His sons, Chambers Brown and Amos Alonzo Brown, were Klan leaders, one of them a chief. The government claimed that the elder Brown was also a prominent member. The *New York Tribune* reported that although the old man appeared "genial and benevolent," the case against him was "quite black." Neither the *Tribune* nor the Ku Klux Klan reports, however, clarify the exact nature of Brown's alleged crime. During the course of the Klan trials, however, witnesses had testified that Brown attended several meetings and even that he was the person who had initiated them into the order. No one had seen Brown on a raid; the implication was that he was a power behind the order.[13]

Judge Bond was determined that Squire Brown make a "candid statement of all your connection with this Klan, and all the other people in your community who have connection with it" if there was to be any mitigation of his sentence. Had Brown chosen to make full confession, the evidence seems to indicate that he would have received a lighter sentence. Bond allowed Brown extra time to prepare affidavits to support his case. The documents were a disappointment, however, and Brown refused to talk. He proclaimed his own innocence and refused to implicate any other Klan members.[14]

Because Brown refused to cooperate, he received the full force of the judge's wrath. Brown was an educated man, "advanced in years," from whom those "who were young and ignorant had a right to look . . . for direction and advice." He had used his influence in favor of the Klan. Bond was especially perturbed that a former magistrate, "a man who had been appointed to protect the innocent and the helpless," had instead taken a "prominent part" in the Ku Klux Klan. He had violated the trust put in him by the state when he refused to protect the local freedmen. Bond professed to allow Brown the benefit of one instance of a "return to manhood" when he claimed to have prevented a raid the Ku Klux had planned. Whatever advantage that attempt to stop the violence gave the old man, he still received a stiff sentence—five years in prison and a $1,000 fine. "You evidently don't propose to tell all you know," Bond stated impatiently, "and I don't, therefore, propose to hear you further."[15] Brown's punishment was as harsh as that received by any of the Klansmen who had stood trial during the November 1871 court session.

Randolph Abbott Shotwell, an embittered North Carolina journalist sentenced to Albany prison for Ku Klux offenses, reported in his prison journal that the government accused Brown falsely, then cheated him out of the deal he made in a plea bargain. Shotwell obviously had a biased view; in his estimation, the old man had "no more business here than Judge Bond who sent" him. Brown had been dragged unmercifully from the comforts of home by a detachment of cavalry, Shotwell said, locked up in jail for weeks, then released on $5,000 bond to appear in court in Columbia. Recognizing that he stood no chance of a fair trial when the government "wanted victims," Brown's lawyers urged him to plead guilty. According to Shotwell, Judge Bond had indicated that those who made confession and pleaded guilty would receive nominal sentences whereas those who demanded a trial would be punished more severely. Major Merrill was reported to have promised Brown he would be at home within a few weeks. "Such a pressure was hard to resist," Shotwell noted; Brown yielded.[16]

Whether the government broke faith in Squire Brown's case is difficult to determine. Shotwell insisted that the evidence against Brown was "utterly unworthy of belief." Thus the "villains had designed" an evil plot to put Brown behind bars at hard labor. If there was a deal that depended on Brown's full confession and disclosure of all the details he knew concerning the Klan, he clearly had not fulfilled his part of the bargain. Brown may well have been the real leader of the Klan; it is impossible to judge from the record. Even if it was true that he had attended only one Klan meeting, as he alleged in his affidavit, he obviously had not revealed all the details to which he was privy. In either case, Judge Bond was harder on Brown than on the others who made guilty pleas because of Brown's position in the community and because he had formerly held a position of trust as a magistrate.[17] The judge clearly expected those in positions of influence in the South's social structure to exercise their power in a manner that would benefit the community. When they failed to earn the trust of the people beneath them, in Bond's estimation, they should expect to pay a higher price for their error.

Public opinion, North and South, condemned Brown's sentence as excessive. South Carolinians wrote their friends in other states, who made appeals in Brown's behalf. The abolitionist Gerrit Smith visited the Ku Klux prisoners at Albany and recommended clemency in the case of Brown, who was reported to be in poor health. Even the governor of New York and his wife traveled to the prison to investigate Brown's condition. Friends and family kept up a steady barrage of mail to the president and attorney general in hope of obtaining a pardon. The federal officials refused to yield to the pressure, however, evidently convinced there was a valid reason why Judge Bond had imposed so stiff a sentence.[18]

As he listened to confessions and set the punishment for each Klansman, Judge Bond wrestled with what he considered to be a serious moral defect among Southern whites. As serious as the crimes committed, in the judge's estimation, was the lack among those who had confessed "of any sense or feeling, that you have done anything very wrong in your confessed participation in outrages which are unexampled outside of the Indian territory." The humblest men in the other sections of the United States, Bond insisted, would have been wounded in their spirits by participation in the Ku Klux outrages. In the South, however, there was not "the slightest idea of, or respect for, the sacredness of the human person." Grasping for "some features of humanity" in the confessed Klansmen, Bond recognized that the South's peculiar institution was responsible for the lack of moral outrage.[19]

Slavery and racial oppression, according to Judge Bond, had caused a sickness that pervaded the entire social structure of South Carolina. Poor whites deferred to people with wealth and education, the same individuals from whom they had learned to despise blacks as inferior creatures. The "whipping post was a standing institution" in South Carolina, Bond noted; "to see blacks flagellated was no unusual occurrence." The prevalence of violence had desensitized whites long before emancipation. Because whites had no sense of the sacredness of the black man's life, they had ceased to respect themselves. Thus the white man had been enslaved along with the black.[20]

Judge Bond deplored the lack of Christian principles he found in South Carolina. "If anyone wants to see a reason for the war, why it ought to have occurred & why our Heavenly Father made it result the way he did," he wrote his wife from South Carolina, "he has only to come here. . . . I do not believe that any province in China has less to do with Christian civilization than many parts of this state." Bond could not understand why local preachers had not spoken out against the Klan. Over and over again during the course of the trials he asked the witnesses whether the white ministers of the gospel had opposed the Klan. Invariably he found they had not. People generally went to church in the upcountry, however, and the members of the churches "pretty much" all belonged to the Klan. In Bond's mind, it would take a combination of genuine Christian concern and Republican party principles to complete the Reconstruction process; the freedmen would never achieve equal rights until "we have added to the power of our political truth the energy of religious fervor."[21]

Although the Klansmen who stood trial were not allowed to testify during the course of their trials, they were allowed to make a statement before they were sentenced. Judge Bond questioned these men as he had those who came to court to plead guilty. Once again the judge was looking for repentance. And again the punishment fit both the crime and the social status of the perpetrator. Robert Hayes Mitchell, the first Klansman tried during the November 1871 session of the circuit court, had been a member of the Klan since 1868. Mitchell was a tenant farmer or renter. He rode with the Klan the night Jim Williams was hung, but he had been unaware of the purpose of the raid. While the advance party murdered the militia captain, Mitchell had remained with the group who held the horses. He turned himself in to the authorities, making confession to Major Merrill. He had planned to plead guilty, he stated, but the defense lawyers had encouraged him to stand trial instead. Judge Bond fixed Mitchell's sentence at eighteen months and a $100 fine. Mitchell's manner had impressed the court. We "believe that you have dealt candidly with the Court," Judge Bryan stated, "and that you have told the truth." Had it been otherwise, the court would "exhaust the full penalty of the law, and then consider that you had been very mercifully dealt with."[22]

The court was harder on the two men convicted in the second trial. John W. Mitchell—a Klan chief whose Klan unit was allegedly responsible for several murders—was an educated and influential member of the white community. Although he claimed to have been beside the bed of his ailing mother when he was supposedly outraging the black community, the jury found him guilty on two counts of conspiracy. "All these young and ignorant people had a right to look to you for direction," Bond instructed Mitchell. Thus he had failed the entire community. Instead of fulfilling his position of leadership for good, he had led the Ku Klux Klan. Mitchell received the stiffest sentence of any of the Klansmen tried during the November 1871 session of the circuit court, five years' imprisonment and a $1,000 fine. The penalty fit both the crime and the perpetrator's social status. To Thomas B. Whitesides, the physician who had been tried with Mitchell, Bond assigned a lighter sentence, one year in prison and a $100 fine. The prosecution had not proved, as Judge Bond recognized, that Whitesides had ever been on a raid or played an active role in the Klan. A person of his position was nonetheless responsible for communicating his knowledge of the Klan to the authorities. Instead, he had acquiesced to the values of the Ku Klux Klan. The Enforcement Acts would have never been necessary, Bond insisted, "if gentlemen in your position in York County, having found out what was going on, had united to put it down."[23] It is important to reconcile Whitesides's light punishment with that of Squire Brown. Both were influential community members. Neither had been proved to have been on any Klan raids. Still the constitution and by-laws of the Klan had been found in Brown's possession. And his sons, both of whom had fled from justice, were known to be leaders of the Klan. Bond evidently believed the conventional wisdom that Brown was one of the influential behind-the-scenes leaders of the Klan. And the judge was clearly angry that Brown refused to divulge the information he wanted.

Judge Bond gave a light sentence to John S. Millar, who was a poor choice for prosecution in the first place. Millar was a plantation owner who employed many black laborers. He had been tried and found guilty on only one count of conspiracy to prevent the freedmen from voting. Although he had attended two meetings of the Klan, allegedly to protect his hands, the witnesses for both the prosecution and defense agreed that he had never ridden with the Klan. Indeed, the Klan had come twice looking for Millar before he started to attend its meetings. "The Court is of opinion that you are the least guilty of the parties brought here," Judge Bond said to Millar. He required him to serve only three months and pay a $20 fine.[24]

Judge Bond never had the opportunity to sentence Edward T. Avery, the defendant who fled during the course of his trial. If he had, he doubtless would have imposed a stiff sentence. Avery was an educated and influential member of the white community, the kind the judge held most responsible for the outrages of the Ku Klux Klan. Bond refused to drop the charges against Avery when Attorney General Williams ordered Corbin to do so in 1873 and "with his own hand struck out the portions" of the end of session order pertaining to the runaway. Avery's jumping bail and disappearing had made the judge very angry.[25]

The bench continued during the subsequent court sessions to impose sentences that differed widely according to the crimes actually committed and the social position of the criminal. The prosecution made a concentrated effort during the later trials to try those involved in crimes of a heinous nature. Thus during the April 1872 session of the Fourth Circuit Court, the bench imposed harder sentences on those who pleaded guilty upon arraignment as well as those who stood trial. Sentences during this session of the court ranged from one month for two men who had already spent considerable time in jail awaiting trial to ten years and a $1,000 fine for several men whose indictments included murder counts. Leander Spencer, for example, had been tried for conspiracy and murder. When the case resulted in a hung jury, the prosecution had dropped the murder

charges for a guilty plea rather that trying Spencer again. Spencer nevertheless was sentenced to ten years and $1,000, the maximum imposed on
any night rider, but still a good deal considering that the Supreme Court
had not yet ruled on the seventh section of the first Enforcement Act.
Hanging was still a possibility for Klan members guilty of murder. Several
others who pleaded guilty received sentences of eight to ten years. Each
was charged with conspiracy and murder; the murder counts were
dropped for guilty pleas on the conspiracy charges. Robert Riggins chose
to stand trial on the same charges. The jury found him guilty of conspiracy, not guilty of murder. He received a lighter sentence, three years
and a $100 fine, even though he was known to be a Klan chief. Because
there is no verbatim trial record, it is impossible to know why his punishment was less severe.[26]

Bond insisted when pronouncing sentence on shaping the punishment
to fit the community status of the Klansman as well as the crime. That he
held community leaders more responsible than others for Klan activities
demonstrates, ironically, that he shared the laissez-faire constitutional
values that informed white South Carolinians. Like so many other Americans, Bond believed that the propertied, educated classes should govern
and lead. Leadership carried with it an obligation to exercise an uplifting,
civilizing influence on the community. When community leaders failed to
live up to their obligations and pursued a destructive, criminal course,
they deserved the harshest punishment.

The prosecution—even after it had failed in its goal of securing a broad
nationalization of fundamental rights for the freedmen—had two important goals in mind throughout the Klan trials. First was to make the guilty
pay for their crimes. The second goal was perhaps more important—to
convince the white South that the federal government would no longer tol-
erate the counterrevolution the Ku Klux Klan represented. In this purpose
the federal government was initially successful. Guilty Klansmen fled the
area by the hundreds. The violence abated. But white Southerners kept
their eyes peeled for any signs of vacillation on the part of the government. Their watchfulness was soon rewarded. Preservation of equal rights
for the freedmen required a strong federal presence, which the Republican government was unwilling to maintain over a long period of time.

Most of the South Carolina Ku Klux Klan cases were never put to trial,
which is not surprising in light of the sheer numbers involved. It took almost six weeks during the initial court session in Columbia to try only five

men in four trials. Forty-nine guilty pleas added to the prosecution's success rate, but some 278 cases were carried over to the next term. Another 18 cases were tried during the April term of 1872, but the backlog swelled as the federal grand juries continued their work. Although 96 cases were terminated in South Carolina during 1872, more than 1,200 cases were still pending at the end of the year. Such a caseload could have overwhelmed the federal courts in the South for many years to come. The press of business on the criminal docket made it difficult, if not impossible, for the courts to attend to civil matters. Something clearly had to be done. Attorney General Williams decided as early as December 1872 to back away from enforcement of black rights: "My desire is that the pending prosecutions be pushed only as far as may appear to be necessary to preserve the public peace and prevent further violations."[27]

Major Merrill disagreed. He strongly advised the attorney general that the white South would construe any retreat from a strong enforcement policy as weakness. Merrill emphasized that the policy of trying only those of high social status and those guilty of the most heinous crimes had already exempted some five or six hundred South Carolina Klansmen from prosecution, an amazing degree of clemency in Merrill's mind. Because of the "inadequacy of the machinery of the United States courts, and the utter worthlessness of the state courts in this section hundreds of participants in murder even will never be brought to justice." The causes that bred the Ku Klux Klan had not changed, Merrill continued: "The blind unreasoning, bigoted hostility to the results of the war is only smothered not appeased or destroyed. The only safety or assurance for safety for citizens is the protection of the general government." A policy of executive clemency, Merrill warned, would be interpreted as "a confession that wrong had been done." Justice for local Republicans, especially those who had dared to testify in court, demanded that the government stand firm.[28]

Williams determined, nonetheless, on a policy of clemency. Prosecutions under the Enforcement Acts were discontinued or postponed during the spring of 1873. Williams was evidently more concerned about public opinion and the cost of the prosecution effort than he was about justice. "These prosecutions as a general rule are carried on to enforce an observance of the laws of the United States and protect the rights of citizens," he wrote a federal attorney in Texas; "when those ends are accomplished, it is not desirable to multiply suits of this description as they tend to keep up an excited state of feeling, and are a great expense to the United States."[29]

Williams hoped that his appeasement policy would serve as a deterrent for further Klan crime; in his mind suspension of the prosecution effort would "produce obedience to the law, and quiet and peace among the People." He instructed the district attorneys in the Carolinas to *nolle prosequi* all but the worst cases. "The Government has reason to believe that its general intentions in prosecuting these offenses . . . have been accomplished, that the particular disorder has ceased, and that there are good grounds for hoping that it will not return," he wrote. "At all events it affords the Government pleasure to make an experiment based upon these views."[30]

This policy seems singularly shortsighted in light of the South's continued hostility to Reconstruction. Peace had been attained, as Major Merrill had stressed, only because of a strong federal presence. As the Northern electorate tired of the interminable Southern problem, the Grant administration in general and the attorney general in particular lost interest in maintaining the rights of their black constituency. Appeasing Southern Democrats and pinching pennies seemed more important than the rights of the freedmen. Williams was forced to economize by a Congress that had armed the federal government with strong enforcement laws without providing the money to enforce them. The Klan trials had dramatically increased federal expenses in the South. The Justice Department was broke. Williams warned his local attorneys in an increasingly menacing tone that they must practice the most "rigid economy."[31]

Even more important to the administration and the attorney general was the desire to win public approval. Indeed, the expressed justification for canceling the enforcement effort masked the real reason: "Expediency was the primary consideration," as Everette Swinney put it. Williams had become one of the most unpopular men in the country. A congressional committee had investigated his alleged excesses in the use of federal troops. Newspapers ridiculed him as the "Secretary of State for Southern Affairs." When Grant nominated Williams for chief justice in 1873, the attorney general quickly became the focus of a huge public outcry against his appointment. The bar opposed him on the grounds that he was "wanting in those qualifications of intellect, experience and reputation which are indispensable to uphold the dignity of the National court, and to maintain respect for the law in the person of the officer who presides over the administration." The national press uncovered scandals concerning his private use of Justice Department funds.[32] Williams could ill afford any further negative publicity.

The attorney general and indeed the entire scandal-ridden Grant administration became scrupulously sensitive to public opinion. Many Northerners were concerned about "bayonet rule" in the South and with what they perceived as excessive federal interference in local affairs. Thus Williams lent a willing ear to Southerners who complained about the excesses of the enforcement efforts. He sent a steady barrage of letters to Corbin in South Carolina inquiring about the particulars in various cases. Williams's tone indicated he assumed that the complaints were valid. President Grant responded similarly to the requests of white Southerners who came to call on him at his vacation house in Long Branch, New Jersey. During the summer of 1873 the president announced a policy of clemency for those Klansmen who had not yet been tried and pardon for those who had.[33]

The wisdom of Grant's policy is questionable, although it is doubtful that further prosecutions would have convinced the white population to respect the rights of black citizens. The enforcement efforts of the national government had failed to change the minds and hearts of white South Carolinians. Coercion does not automatically bring consent. Inbred racism among white South Carolinians convinced them that blacks were inferior creatures suited only for the lowest place in society. Laissez-faire constitutional principles persuaded them that their state government was unauthorized, and traditional notions of dual federalism satisfied them that the federal government had overstepped its bounds. "There is a fixed determination on the part of these bad men," a local white Republican complained, "never to acknowledge the results of the war."[34] The Grant administration's appeasement policy failed to pursuade the whites to do good and may have even convinced them they could get away with murder. Pardoned Klansmen returned to the scene of their crimes once again to "broadcast over this section the seeds of rebellion, sedition, and murder." The Democrats quickly began to prepare for the election of 1874, when they planned to restore the state government to its rightful participants, the educated, propertied, taxpaying citizens. Rifle clubs, white leagues, and secret police, "organized ostensibly for 'social purposes,'" made a show of force in both town and countryside throughout the state. Rumor had it that Democrats from the Augusta, Georgia, area would help local whites take over the polling places. The Democrats insisted that the freedmen were responsible for starting all the problems, and once again the whites were forced to take up arms to defend themselves. Outrages occurred frequently. Republicans appealed to the federal government for more troops.[35]

Apparently recognizing the folly of expecting leniency to produce obedience to the law, Williams once again ordered vigorous efforts under the Enforcement Acts. "I consider it my duty," he wrote his field attorneys in September 1873, "to instruct you to proceed with all possible energy and dispatch to detect, expose, arrest, and punish the perpetrators of these crimes; and to that end you are to spare no effort or expenses." Troops were made available, and the election of 1874 proceeded relatively peacefully in South Carolina.[36]

Consistency was not a virtue of the Grant administration, however. Immediately after the election, Williams changed his tune. "I am not aware of anything that has transpired that should lead you to inquire whether or not you would be sustained by this department in taking vigorous and active measures," he wrote a district attorney, indicating that he was in favor of a strong enforcement policy. What Williams gave with one hand he took away with the other. "You should be careful," he cautioned, "and not involve the government in groundless or frivolous prosecutions, which are not only an annoyance and an invitation to the people, but are a matter of great expense to the United States." Pleasing the public and saving money were, once again, more important to the attorney general than the rights of the freedmen. Federal enforcement efforts were discontinued again in 1874.[37]

The government in the Ku Klux Klan trials had successfully prosecuted some of the night riders and temporarily stopped the outrages of the Ku Klux Klan. Perhaps a sustained effort to stamp out political terrorism would have effected real changes in the social and political structure of South Carolina but perhaps not. Government coercion had not convinced Southern whites that Republican policy was right; instead, it had united them in opposition. An ongoing dependence on federal muscle to keep Southerners in check was no substitute for the consent of the governed. Whatever the possibilities, a serious lack of consistency in the Grant administration hampered the entire effort. The political costs of enforcement had made the freedmen an impediment to the Republican administration. Northerners were weary of Reconstruction; public opinion would not sustain military intervention long enough and strong enough to stamp out Southern resistance. Thus the president and attorney general both chose to believe in the good faith of the enemy. White Southern Democrats soon realized that they had nothing to fear from a vacillating central government dedicated more to pleasing an impatient, unsympathetic Northern electorate than to providing substantive rights for the freedmen.[38] Recognizing that the Republican party had begun a general retreat from its commitment to the former slaves, white South Carolinians determined in 1876 to mount an all-out campaign to "redeem" the state from its oppressors and return it to those whom they had insisted all along should rightfully govern—the property-owning, tax-paying, educated citizens.

Following the lead established by the "Mississippi Plan" in 1875, South Carolina Democrats in 1876 campaigned on a forthright white supremacy platform. No longer would the party cooperate with reform-minded Republicans. Having captured control of the state Democratic party, the "straight-outs" campaigned exclusively on the issue of race. Framing the issues in black and white made it very clear to the white electorate what was at stake and went a long way to persuade apathetic whites to get out and vote.[39]

Confederate cavalry hero Wade Hampton was the straight-out choice for governor in 1876. Although the Democratic cooperationists considered him "insufficiently cautious and responsible," Hampton maintained a moderate, conciliatory tone on racial issues throughout his campaign. He pledged to "know no race, no party, no man, in the administration of the law." No rights enjoyed by the black people would be withdrawn, according to his campaign promises. "We propose to protect you and give you all your rights," he insisted, "but while we do this you cannot expect that we should discriminate in your favor, and say because you *are* a colored man, you have the right to rule the State." Their understanding of constitutional government convinced Hampton and men of his breed—men of rank and position—that they were the only ones suited to rise above the race and class interests that informed the Republican state government and work for the good of all South Carolinians. The Democratic program in 1876 was one of white supremacy which left room for only the talented few, if any, of the black race. If Hampton was a moderate on racial issues, however, he was still "the representative of the hot heads and reckless hearts which dictated his nomination." He was unable, perhaps even unwilling, to keep Negrophobes such as Martin W. Gary, Matthew C. Butler, and young Benjamin Tillman in line.[40]

While Hampton campaigned in conciliatory tones, his straight-out supporters pursued another course. Political violence and the threat thereof played a significant role in the redemption of South Carolina. Rifle and saber clubs previously organized all over the state for "social purposes" eagerly joined Hampton's gubernatorial campaign. The official Democratic policy in 1876 was "force without violence." Thousands of Redshirts—so called as a gesture of defiance toward the Republican tradition of "waving the bloody shirt"—rode with Hampton in a deliberate attempt to strike fear in the hearts of black voters. Torchlight parades, martial bands, booming cannons, and above all the bloodcurdling sound of rebel yells swelled the hopes of white South Carolinians and signaled to the black population that a new day was dawning. Redeemer sources indicate that this paramilitary force was so tightly organized that "aggressive intimidation" won the day for the Democrats. "There is an organized plan throughout the state of South Carolina not to have any violence committed on anybody," one black official was reported to have complained, "but the plan of intimidation was so thorough that there was no need to have any violence."[41]

If there was no need for violence, the straight-outs nevertheless embraced the tactic on several occasions to underscore their message of terrorism. Race riots replaced Klan raids as the preferred political statement. Not waiting for cover of darkness, Democratic paramilitary forces attacked black Republicans in the light of day. Traditional sources have insisted that the armed black militia once again provoked the whites to violence.[42] Justice Department records tell a different story, however, one with which Benjamin Tillman later concurred. Whites often preferred a fight to a peaceful settlement to provide a concrete example of the force behind the Redeemers' efforts. "Butler, Gary, and George Tillman had to my personal knowledge agreed on the policy of terrorizing the negroes at the first opportunity," Ben Tillman remembered, "by letting them provoke trouble and then having the whites demonstrate their superiority by killing as many of them as was justifiable." The riots, according to Tillman, "were most potent influences in shaping the conflict between the whites and blacks and producing the gratifying result which brought the white man again into control of his inheritance."[43] Edgefield and Aiken counties proved particularly susceptible to this campaign measure.

The Ellenton riot is the prime example of a small incident turned into a full-blown race riot. The trouble began when two black men allegedly broke into the home of Alonzo Harley, a white man, attacked his wife and son with sticks, then fled when the woman reached for a gun. White horsemen took off in pursuit. They caught and killed Peter Williams, whom Mrs. Harley identified as one of her assailants. While the other remained at large, white rifle clubs poured into the area, and blacks met to discuss a plan for defense. The ensuing violence lasted about a week. Federal troops arrived on 20 September in time to save a group of around 100 besieged blacks from almost certain massacre, but the death toll was still high. Several whites were killed, and the estimates run as high as 125 black deaths. Democrats insisted publicly that the blacks were entirely responsible for the bloodletting. Privately, however, it was another matter. "A correct and full account of the bloody affair will never be known to the public," a white resident of the area reported. Some 2,000 whites "determined to kill all the negroes they could find with arms" hunted the blacks down like animals and "dealt with [them] after the S.C. plan."[44] The South Carolina Plan worked as well as the Mississippi Plan. The physical and psychological terror established long before the election kept many black voters from the polls.

The election itself, according to a correspondent of the *Atlantic Monthly*, was "one of the greatest farces ever seen." Where terror failed to work, fraud prevailed. "The Democrats cheated and intimidated and bribed and bulldozed and repeated where they could," a Hamptonite admitted later, "and the Republicans did likewise." Threats and intimidation were common at the polls, but there was little violence.[45] There followed a period of confusion during which both political parties inaugurated their gubernatorial candidates, compounded by uncertainty over the presidential election. The presence of federal troops enabled the Republicans to maintain control of the state offices until April when the new president, Rutherford B. Hayes, announced his decision to withdraw the last of the federal troops from the South. Hayes, like the president and attorney general who preceded him, hoped that he could trust Southern whites to keep their promises to respect black rights. He was to be disappointed. After the midterm elections the president was forced to admit that "the experiment was a failure." By 1880 Hayes complained that a "practical nullification" of the Fifteenth Amendment had robbed the Republicans of a majority in both houses of Congress.[46]

South Carolina led the vanguard to nullify the voting rights of black citizens. Having reestablished home rule, the state legislature soon determined—despite the campaign promises of Governor Hampton—to institute state election laws which effectively disfranchised the freedmen. The state "promoted" Hampton to the United States Senate after a two-year term as governor, leaving his place to be filled by those less willing to allow limited political participation to the state's black citizens. The hard-won benefits of Reconstruction were in grave danger of disappearing at the hands of the state's Redeemers. The protection of the rights of black people across the United States depended upon decisions made in the Supreme Court.

7

Enforcement in the Supreme Court

While Democrats in South Carolina and throughout the South proceeded to disfranchise black citizens, the Supreme Court followed the lead of the executive branch in retreating from Reconstruction. The nation's high tribunal construed the Reconstruction Amendments in a manner that left traditional state-based federalism unaltered. This conservative reading of the Fourteenth and Fifteenth Amendments is not surprising in light of Judge Bond's similar reluctance to recognize any fundamental changes wrought by the Fourteenth and Fifteenth Amendments. That other possibilities existed, however, was clear.

Circuit Court judge William B. Woods in an Alabama case, *U.S. v. Hall*, decided in May 1871, had interpreted the Fourteenth Amendment in a manner that provided the broad nationalization of civil and political rights for which Corbin and Chamberlain had argued in the South Carolina Klan cases beginning in November 1871. Upholding the constitutionality of the first Enforcement Act and the indictments brought under it against private persons for interfering with the First Amendment rights of free speech and assembly, Woods declared that "the right of freedom of speech and the other rights enumerated in the first eight articles of the amendment" are the "privileges and immunities of citizens of the United States" as secured by the Fourteenth Amendment. The state-action concept posed no problem for Woods. The Fourteenth Amendment not only prohibited states from passing discriminatory laws, it also forbade them from denying equal protection of the laws. Denial of equal protection, in Woods's mind, "includes [state] inaction as well as action . . . omission to protect, as well as the omission to pass laws for protection."[1] This nationalistic interpretation of the Fourteenth Amendment provided an alternative to the conservative opinion of Judge Bond.

That the Fourteenth Amendment had made some changes in the rights of citizenship seemed clear. Exactly which rights were secured was more cloudy. Did the Fourteenth Amendment nationalize the Bill of Rights? What were the privileges and immunities of national citizenship? Was Congress authorized to protect the freedmen from private acts or only in cases of state action? The backlog of civil rights cases in the South demanded a decision by the high court, yet the justices had refused to address these issues as presented in *U.S. v. Avery*, and the attorney general had scotched federal efforts to secure answers to these problems in *U.S. v. Sapaugh*.[2]

For its initial interpretation of the rights of citizens under the Fourteenth Amendment, the Supreme Court heard, ironically, a case involving white butchers rather than black freedmen in which the United States was not even a party. Thus the Fourteenth Amendment was construed originally in an atmosphere that effectively depoliticized the explosive legal questions involved, enabling the high court to decide some of the controversial issues that had appeared in the Ku Klux Klan cases without hearing them. If the *Slaughter-House Cases* were about white butchers, they nevertheless presaged nothing but evil for the civil rights of the nation's blacks.[3]

The Republican state government of Louisiana had established in New Orleans a monopoly in the slaughtering trade which threatened to drive all other slaughterhouses out of business. Although the state justified the law as an exercise of its police powers, the other butchers brought suit on the grounds that their Thirteenth and Fourteenth Amendment rights had been violated. John A. Campbell, a former Supreme Court justice who had resigned to follow his state into the Confederacy, attacked the state law on the grounds that it was a form of servitude outlawed by the Thirteenth Amendment. Campbell particularly pressed the point that the monopoly violated the "privileges and immunities" guaranteed to citizens by the Fourteenth Amendment. Among these privileges was the right to follow the vocation of one's choice.[4]

The Court split five to four on the decision. Speaking for the majority, Justice Samuel Miller recognized that "no questions so far reaching and pervading in their consequences . . . have been before this court during the official life of any of its present members." Clearly the justices understood that accepting the butchers' argument would authorize federal protection of a wide range of individual rights, but the Court was not up to the job.

Miller quickly rejected the Thirteenth Amendment argument, then turned to the Fourteenth. The primary purpose of the Fourteenth Amendment, according to Miller, was to provide citizenship for blacks. He seemed genuinely surprised to think that the Reconstruction Amendments could be construed to uphold the rights of white citizens. If Miller interpreted the amendment to provide rights for the freedmen, however, his narrow reading of those rights gave them little reason to celebrate. National citizenship, according to Miller, was separate and distinct from state citizenship. *Slaughter-House* left the basic rights of citizens where they had always been, under the protection of the states. Miller listed several privileges and immunities that adhered to national citizenship; to his credit, some of them were important for African Americans: the right of assembly, petition, and habeas corpus. Most of the rights of U.S. citizens as interpreted by Justice Miller, however, would prove to be of little use to the freedmen. Basically Miller decided that the federal government could protect its citizens on the high seas or in foreign countries, but not in the states where they resided. That the Fourteenth Amendment was intended "to transfer the security and protection of all the civil rights . . . from the States to the Federal government" Miller emphatically denied. It was impossible, he decided, that the Congress meant to effect so drastic a change in the basic nature of the federal system.[5]

Miller's tortured construction aroused bitter dissent among four of his judicial brethren. Invoking a scriptural analogy, Justice Noah Swayne asserted that the construction was "much too narrow"; Miller had so limited the intentions of the framers that he changed "what was meant for bread into a stone." Justice Stephen Field insisted that the fundamental rights of citizenship belong to citizens of the United States and are in no way dependent upon citizenship in a state. If the amendment meant no more than the majority said it did, he argued, "it was a vain and idle enactment, which accomplished nothing, and most unnecessarily excited Congress and the people on its passage." Joseph Bradley similarly argued that the Fourteenth Amendment had brought the basic rights of citizenship under direct national protection: "To say that these rights and immunities attach only to State citizenship, and not to citizenship of the United States appears to me to evince a very narrow and insufficient estimate of constitutional history and the rights of men." The dissenting opinions recognized what Miller feared, that the Fourteenth Amendment was meant to transform the federal system. Rights were no longer to be "separate and exclusive" but "complementary and concentric," allowing the long arm of the federal government to reach in to protect the rights of its citizens when the states failed to do so.[6]

The Supreme Court had failed to recognize the revolutionary changes in the federal system inherent in the Fourteenth Amendment. Instead the Court left federal-state relations virtually unchanged. According to this interpretation, the Fourteenth Amendment would not nationalize the Bill of Rights; except for petition and assembly, those fundamental liberties were not among the privileges and immunities Miller assigned to the national government. The decision placed the basic rights of citizenship beyond the nation's authority. The privileges and immunities clause was emasculated. If the majority of Americans missed the political implications of *Slaughter-House*, the justices of the Supreme Court undoubtedly recognized that the case dealing ostensibly with the rights of white butchers would serve as precedent for any subsequent attempts to enforce the civil rights of the former slaves. *Slaughter-House* marked a turning point in the federal quest for the civil and political rights of black Americans. The narrow interpretation of the Fourteenth Amendment circumscribed any further attempts to establish a broad interpretation of the rights inherent in national citizenship.[7]

U.S. v. Cruikshank demonstrated the limitations that the Supreme Court in *Slaughter-House* had placed on future interpretations of the Fourteenth Amendment in cases concerning the civil and political rights of blacks. The case involved a massacre of around one hundred blacks in Colfax, Louisiana, following the disputed election of 1872. Both parties claimed the offices of sheriff and judge. A black posse, commissioned by the carpetbag governor, occupied the local courthouse on behalf of the Republican government. Whites attacked, set fire to the meeting place, then shot the freedmen in cold blood as they attempted to escape the burning building. These atrocities were so heinous that Attorney General Williams was forced to abandon his appeasement policy and order a vigorous prosecution under the Enforcement Act. Williams's stinginess and lack of regard for black rights ruled the day, however, when he decided to try only six to twelve of the criminals as a deterrent to future lawlessness. Of the approximately one hundred whites who were indicted, William Cruikshank and two others were convicted in federal circuit court under the sixth section of the Enforcement Act of 1870, which made it a felony to conspire to deprive blacks of their rights as citizens. The case was certified to the Supreme Court on a division of opinion concerning a motion in arrest of judgment between Circuit Judge William B. Woods, who found both the law and the indictment sufficient, and Supreme Court justice Joseph Bradley (on circuit), who considered the law and all counts of the indictment deficient.[8]

Cruikshank was tried on a thirty-two-count indictment designed, like that in the South Carolina Ku Klux Klan trials, to provide national protection for fundamental rights under the Fourteenth and Fifteenth Amendments. Indeed, it was in *Cruikshank* that the Supreme Court finally resolved many of the questions that had come before the court in South Carolina. Under the sixth section of the Enforcement Act of 1870 the defendants were charged with conspiracy to "hinder and prevent" black citizens from enjoying their First and Second Amendment rights to assemble peaceably and to keep and bear arms. These counts assumed, like those in the South Carolina Klan trials, that the Fourteenth Amendment had made the Bill of Rights applicable to the states. Other counts charged conspiracy to deprive African-Americans of their lives and liberty without due process of law. Still others averred interference with the right to vote and the denial of equal protection of the laws and equal privileges and immunities. Another charged the intent to hinder the "free exercise and enjoyment of every, each, all, and singular the several rights and privileges granted and secured" by the United States Constitution and laws. Sixteen of the thirty-two counts also charged under the controversial section seven of the first Enforcement Act that murder was committed in the process of denying these other civil and political rights. The defendants were acquitted on the murder counts, however.[9]

Bradley's circuit court opinion demonstrated a reversal of his original ideas concerning federal authority to uphold the rights of the freedmen under the Fourteenth Amendment. William Woods had sought Bradley's advice in 1871 before writing the decision in *U.S. v. Hall*. Bradley had counseled Woods that the privileges and immunities clause secured "by *direct* federal intervention" all the fundamental rights of citizenship "either as against the action of the Federal government or the State governments."[10] Bradley's dissenting opinion in *Slaughter-House* similarly contended that the Fourteenth Amendment had radically altered the federal system. "In my judgment," he said, "it was the intention of the people of this country in adopting that amendment to provide National security against violation by the states of the fundamental rights of citizens."

Bradley's ideas were not chiseled in granite, however: "My own mind is rather in the condition of seeking the truth, than of dogmatically laying down opinions," he wrote two years later.[11]

Bradley's circuit-level opinion in *Cruikshank* was obviously constrained by Miller's majority opinion in *Slaughter-House*. Bradley's reasoning in *Cruikshank* adhered closely to the state-action concept of the Fourteenth Amendment. He considered the rights and privileges of citizenship a birthright of Americans, a part of their "political inheritance derived from the mother country." The Fourteenth Amendment guaranteed these rights—Bradley never made it clear exactly which rights he had in mind—against state interference, but it did not charge the United States with the duty to enforce the rights of citizenship. "The affirmative enforcement of the rights and privileges themselves," he stated, "unless something more is expressed, does not devolve upon it [the United States], but belongs to the state government as a part of its residual sovereignty." The Fourteenth Amendment had not made any fundamental change in the federal system. When the amendment stated that "no state shall deprive any person of life, liberty, or property," it established protection "against arbitrary and unjust legislation." It was never meant to protect the individual from ordinary crimes; that remained a part of the police powers of the state.[12] Bradley found more room for the federal government to maneuver on behalf of African Americans in the Thirteenth and Fifteenth Amendments, which had not yet been interpreted—and thus constrained—by the Supreme Court, than in the Fourteenth. Not only did the Thirteenth Amendment free the slaves, he argued, it also empowered Congress "to give full effect to this bestowment of liberty on these millions of people." When blacks were not allowed to "enjoy equal rights" as citizens, Bradley continued, it was a "badge of servitude" cognizable under the Thirteenth Amendment. The key was race. Although Congress could not pass laws to punish ordinary crimes, the Thirteenth Amendment brought "offenses which aim at the deprivation of the colored citizen's enjoyment and exercise of his rights of citizenship and of equal protection of the laws because of race, color, or previous condition of servitude" under the purview of the federal government. Thus Bradley found all counts of the indictment defective not so much because the federal government lacked authority as because the charges did not aver discrimination on account of race. Turning to the Fifteenth Amendment, Bradley followed Judge Bond's reasoning in the South Carolina trials. The amendment did not confer a positive right to vote, he observed, but simply prevented any discrimination on the grounds of race. Because the Enforcement Act prohibited interference with the franchise for any reason, it "extends far beyond the scope of the amendment." Once again, the key was race. Although the opinion was bad news for black citizens and the federal attorneys in the South who hoped to protect them, Bradley left a broad scope of federal authority under the Thirteenth and Fifteenth Amendments. It was plain, however, that the laws and indictments made under them would have to demonstrate more clearly that discrimination was based on race.[13]

The Supreme Court opinion in *Cruikshank* closely followed Bradley's circuit-level reasoning on the Fourteenth Amendment without reiterating his expansive reading of the Thirteenth. That it should do so is not surprising in light of *Slaughter-House*. Indeed, the brief prepared by Attorney General George Williams and Solicitor General S. F. Phillips left the Supreme Court little option but to follow precedent. Rather than providing the Court with a constitutional theory broad enough to support the nationalization of civil and political rights, the legal representatives of the United States abdicated any responsibility to uphold the constitutionally novel aspects of the case. Williams conceded defeat on all but two counts of the indictment, the fourteenth and the sixteenth. The fourteenth charged conspiracy to "prevent and hinder" two citizens of African descent from voting in future elections. The sixteenth charged the defendants with conspiring to deprive the same black citizens of "their several and respective free exercise and enjoyment of each, every, all and singular the several rights and privileges granted or secured . . . by the Constitution and laws of the United States." Thus the nation's top legal spokesmen chose never to argue the First and Second Amendment issues before the nation's high tribunal. All efforts to provide a nationalistic interpretation of the privileges and immunities and equal protection clauses were similarly abandoned. Williams's refusal to provide the Supreme Court a nationalistic interpretation of the Fourteenth Amendment helped ensure a states'-rights interpretation. But the attorney general did attempt to demonstrate that the Constitution and the Fifteenth Amendment granted ample authority to protect all citizens in their right to vote. He maintained, moreover, that the Enforcement Act was authorized under the amendment.[14]

While the United States seemed to invite a decision that would relieve the government of any further responsibility to enforce civil rights, the defense mounted an effective campaign to secure the same goal. The Louisiana terrorists were represented by such eminent counsel as David Dudley Field, brother of the Supreme Court justice, Reverdy Johnson, reiterating his ideas from the South Carolina Klan trials, and John Archibald Campbell, who had completely switched his arguments since he had represented the butchers in *Slaughter-House*. The defense attorneys argued, predictably, for a narrow, states'-rights interpretation of the Fourteenth Amendment. The fundamental rights of citizens, they insisted, remained where they had always been—under the protection of the states. *Barron v. Baltimore*[15] had established in 1833 that the Bill of Rights applied only to the national government; nothing had happened in the intervening years to change that fact. The rights of national citizenship were limited to the few listed in *Slaughter-House*. The national government, the defense continued, was bound to respect the state-action concept established in the Fourteenth Amendment. Because the state of Louisiana had not passed a law that denied the rights of the citizens, the federal government was absolutely powerless to intervene. The defense denied the constitutionality of the first Enforcement Act because the law extended to the individuals who abridged the rights of the freedmen instead of to the state. Indeed, because there was no state action, there was no need for any enforcement act. A state's failure to protect its citizens did not authorize federal intervention. Although there was no conviction under the seventh section of the Enforcement Act, the defense attorneys nevertheless protested that portion of the law. Congress had no authority, they insisted, to legislate in the area of ordinary common law crimes: "Congress in this legislation attempts to do *indirectly* what it cannot do *directly*," punishing such crimes "under the guise of some trivial matter over which it claims jurisdiction." The defense argued, moreover, that the indictment was too vague. It violated the defendants' constitutional right to know exactly the charges against him.[16]

Chief Justice Morrison Waite, speaking for the Court, seized the ammunition the defense had provided. The decision rested on the constitutional doctrines of dual federalism, dual citizenship, and state action. The Court did not limit its interpretation of the Fourteenth Amendment and the Enforcement Act to the two counts the prosecution had argued but instead addressed the entire scope of the indictment. Waite defined a federal system, citing *Slaughter-House*, of national and state governments which are separate and distinct. The rights adhering to national citizenship were different from those of state citizenship. Following *Barron v. Baltimore*, Waite announced that the First and Second Amendment counts were defective on the grounds that the Bill of Rights applied only to the national government. For protection of their individual rights the people must "look to the states. The power for that purpose was originally placed there, and it has never been surrendered to the United States."[17] Thus Waite rejected the notion that the Fourteenth Amendment was intended specifically to effect revolutionary changes in the relations between the national government and the states. So far as the chief justice was concerned, nothing had changed since the days of the Founding Fathers.

Waite declared the counts charging deprivation of life and liberty without due process of law "even more objectionable." They amounted to "nothing else than alleging a conspiracy to falsely imprison or murder." Such meddling in the police powers of the state could not be sanctioned: "It is no more the duty or within the power of the United States to punish for a conspiracy to falsely imprison or murder within a state, than it would be to punish for false imprisonment or murder itself." Because the law applied to individuals rather than to the state, Waite found it objectionable. The Fourteenth Amendment provided that no state should deprive a person of liberty; it added "nothing to the rights of one citizen as against another." Waite refrained from declaring the Enforcement Act unconstitutional, but he significantly narrowed the scope of the law, making it more difficult to prosecute private acts of violence against black citizens.[18]

The chief justice voided all counts of the indictment, reversing the convictions of Cruikshank and the other two men who had been chosen from the ninety-seven indicted to discourage future atrocities against the civil and political rights of the freedmen. Approximately one hundred blacks had been brutally murdered in Louisiana, yet no one had to pay. The Supreme Court had allowed its interpretation of national citizenship in *Slaughter-House* to circumscribe the meaning of the amendment for those people for whom it was intended to bestow all the benefits of citizenship. The argument that the state had not failed to protect the rights of citizens was, as Loren Miller put it, "a sterile exercise in constitutional double-speak."[19] The states refused to defend the civil rights of the freedmen. Congress attempted through the Enforcement Act to remedy the defect. Now the Supreme Court would not allow the national government to protect them either. The chief justice spoke for eight members of the Court; Justice Nathan Clifford agreed that the judgment should be arrested but based his decision on technical problems with the indictment. The legal officers of the United States had not even exerted themselves to provide a constitutional theory broad enough to maintain the rights of all citizens.

The Court threw out the count that charged interference with the right to vote because it failed to allege that the conspiracy was predicated on race. "We may suspect that race was the cause of the hostility," Waite piously noted of this case in which one hundred white men viciously murdered one hundred blacks, "but it is not so averred." As with the indictment in *Cruikshank* so with the law itself in a companion case. Sections three and four of the first Enforcement Act fell on the same grounds in *U.S. v. Reese*, in which the Supreme Court construed for the first time the meaning of the Fifteenth Amendment for black citizens.[20]

Voting officials in Kentucky had attempted to disfranchise black citizens by refusing to accept their poll taxes and then declining their votes on the grounds that they had not paid the required fees. Kentucky Republicans went to court to protest. Hiram Reese, a local election official, was indicted on four counts of violating the Enforcement Act of 1870 for refusing to allow William Garner, a qualified voter of African descent, to vote because of his race and color.[21]

Chief Justice Waite once again spoke for the Court. The Fifteenth Amendment, he noted, echoing Judge Bond's observations in the Ku Klux Klan trials and Bradley's circuit court opinion in *Cruikshank*, did not confer a positive right to vote. The states retained the authority to decide who votes. The amendment had, nevertheless, invested the people with a new constitutional right: "That right is exemption from discrimination in the exercise of the elective franchise on account of race, color, or previous condition of servitude." Congress had the authority under the enabling clause to enforce that right by appropriate legislation. The question, then, was whether the first Enforcement Act was "appropriate legislation." Waite concluded that it was not. The problem, according to the chief justice, was overbreadth. Although the Fifteenth Amendment prohibited interference with the franchise only on the grounds of race, color, or previous condition, the Enforcement Act forbade "every wrongful refusal to receive the vote of a qualified elector at State elections." The Enforcement Act attempted to "set a net large enough to catch all possible offenders" rather than "manifesting any intention to confine its provisions to the terms of the Fifteenth Amendment." Sections three and four were struck down as unconstitutional.[22]

Justice Ward Hunt dissented. Because the Enforcement Act made clear in the first two sections that it forbade discrimination on the grounds of race and color, he insisted, the following sections did not have to repeat the formula. "By the words 'as aforesaid,'" he reasoned, "the provisions respecting race and color of the first and second sections of the statute are incorporated into and made a part of the third and fourth sections." For Hunt, the intentions of Congress were plain; the problem was with the Supreme Court. "Good sense," he concluded, "is sacrificed to technical nicety, and a sound conclusion to an extravagant extent."[23]

If Waite had sacrificed his good sense, he had not accepted defense counsel's argument that the Fifteenth Amendment could be applied only in cases of overt state action. He left standing the sections of the Enforcement Act which explicitly prohibited voter discrimination because of race. Thus the decision suggested that both private individuals and state officials could be punished for denying the franchise on racial grounds.[24] Within the next quarter century, however, the southern states developed other effective methods of disfranchising their black citizens.

In *Cruikshank* and *Reese* the Supreme Court had finally addressed most of the issues that had been pending at least since the great South Carolina Ku Klux Klan trials in 1871. The results were disappointing regarding rights for black citizens. The Court's narrow interpretation of the Fourteenth Amendment in *Slaughter-House* had circumscribed any future use of the amendment for the freedmen. The rights inherent in national citizenship were separate and distinct from those of state citizenship—and basically meaningless for black Americans. The Fourteenth Amendment did not nationalize the Bill of Rights. The national government could uphold the rights of its black citizens only in cases of state action; a state's failure to protect its citizens could not be construed as a reason for the federal government to intervene. If the Court did not specifically rule on the problem of charging ordinary crimes in conjunction with civil rights offenses, the allegation that conspiracy against life and liberty was nothing more than charges of murder and false imprisonment and therefore unacceptable in federal court made clear that the Court would not countenance any tampering with the traditional police powers of the states. The high court's interpretation of the Fifteenth Amendment left more room for the federal government to maneuver, but the lack of a positive right to vote—a clear call given the negative wording of the amendment—foreshadowed the eventual disfranchisement of most black citizens.

The government attempted in *U.S. v. Harris* to regain some of its losses from *Cruikshank*. An armed mob in Tennessee had taken some blacks from the custody of a sheriff, killed one of them, and beaten the others. The men were charged with conspiracy to hinder state authorities from providing equal protection of the laws and equal privileges and immunities. The case was designed to test the constitutionality of section two of the Ku Klux Klan Act of 1871.[25] Justice William B. Woods, now elevated to the Supreme Court bench, found that the Klan Act failed the examination.

Harris made more explicit the state-action concept implicit in *Cruikshank*. The decision demonstrates a remarkable change of heart since Woods wrote *U.S. v. Hall* in 1871, or perhaps more likely marks a bow to precedent. The provisions of the Fourteenth Amendment, Woods declared, "have reference to State action exclusively, and not to any action of private individuals." When the state "has not made or enforced any law abridging the privileges or immunities of citizens of the United States . . . the amendment imposes no duty and confers no power upon Congress." The Klan Act was bad law because it punished private wrongs without any reference to state laws or the administration of those laws by state officials. According to this interpretation, the Fourteenth Amendment allowed federal involvement only in cases of overt discriminatory state action. A state's "sins of omission," which allowed violation of black citizens' rights, were outside the purview of the amendment.[26]

The state-action concept once again was the determinant in the *Civil Rights Cases* of 1883. These five cases from across the United States went up through the courts simultaneously, demonstrating that although slavery had been a Southern problem, racism was national.[27] The issue was the constitutionality of the first two sections of the Civil Rights Act of 1875, an extremely controversial law even at the time it was passed. The law provided equal access for all patrons to privately owned accommodations open to the public—hotels, theaters, restaurants, and transportation—and made it a misdemeanor to deny the use of such facilities on the basis of race. Congress had proceeded with the law on two assumptions. The first was that segregation by race was a remnant of slavery which could be outlawed under the Thirteenth Amendment. The second was that such businesses were subject to federal law because they were licensed and regulated by state authority. When the states refused to uphold the rights of blacks, the federal government could assist. Blatant disregard for the law was widespread, however. Federal officers hesitated even to attempt enforcement of a law regulating the private sector.[28]

The Supreme Court ruled on the issue in 1883. Justice Bradley, for the majority, concluded that the Civil Rights Act was an unwarranted usurpation of state authority on the part of the federal government. The Fourteenth Amendment authorized national interference only in the case of state action: "It does not invest Congress with power to legislate upon subjects which are within the domain of State legislation; but to provide modes of relief against State legislation, or State action." Only "corrective legislation" was allowed. If there was no official state action that discriminated against the rights of blacks, then there was no federal remedy. "Individual invasion of individual rights," Bradley insisted, "is not the subject matter of the amendment." The law was clearly unconstitutional, according to this interpretation, and businesses could refuse to admit whomever they chose.[29]

Bradley also found the Thirteenth Amendment irrelevant. Although the amendment authorized the national government to make any laws necessary to "eradicate all forms and incidents of slavery," refusing service to a black person had "nothing to do with slavery or involuntary servitude." If such a wrong violated any right, redress should be sought under the laws of the state. Bradley ceremonially washed his hands of the freedmen's problems: "There must be some point in the elevation of the ex-slave, when he takes the rank of a mere citizen, and ceases to be the special favorite of the laws, and when his rights as a citizen, or a man, are to be protected in the ordinary modes by which other men's rights are protected."[30]

There was only one dissenting vote, that of John Marshall Harlan, a Kentuckian, who was ironically a former slave owner and the only Southerner on the high court. It was "scarcely just," he insisted, "to say that the colored race has been the special favorite of the laws." The idea was to "secure and protect" for blacks the rights that white men had always enjoyed. "The one underlying purpose of congressional legislation," he found, "has been to enable the black race to take the rank of mere citizens." Harlan found authority for the Civil Rights Act in both the Thirteenth and Fourteenth Amendments. Discrimination by individuals or corporations of a public or quasi-public nature was for Harlan "a badge of servitude the imposition of which Congress may prevent under its power, by appropriate legislation, to enforce the Thirteenth Amendment."[31]

Harlan read the Fourteenth Amendment as providing broad powers for the national government. Citizenship was a positive grant which clothed the former slaves with all the fundamental rights inherent in a free people.

That the amendment prohibited the states from making discriminatory law did not, for Harlan, mean that Congress was denied "the power, by general, primary, and direct legislation, of protecting citizens of the several States, being also citizens of the United States." Congress, in other words, was authorized to enforce all the provisions of the amendment, not just the prohibitions against the states. Thus Harlan found in the Fourteenth Amendment a nationalization of federal authority broad enough to protect not only the freedmen's civil and political rights but their social rights as well.[32]

If Harlan's judicial brethren did not join in his expansive reading of the Fourteenth Amendment, they had not entirely forgotten the needs of America's black citizens. The Supreme Court's decision in *Ex parte Yarbrough*, 1884, marked a resounding victory in the area of political rights. Jasper Yarbrough and several of his brothers and friends had been convicted in Georgia on two counts of conspiracy to deprive a black citizen of the free exercise of his voting privilege because of his race. One count was drawn under section six of the first Enforcement Act of 1870 (which had become section 5508 of the Revised Statutes in 1874). The other was drawn from section two of the Ku Klux Klan Act of 1871 (now section 5520 of the Revised Statutes) which made it a crime to go in disguise on the public highway. Neither of the laws made any specific reference to actions committed on account of race as stipulated in *Reese*. Whereas *Reese* was concerned with state elections, however, *Yarbrough* dealt with federal elections. Yarbrough appealed on the grounds that the federal government could not punish private citizens for civil rights violations.[33]

Justice Miller decided—as Judge Bond had stated in the South Carolina Klan cases—that neither the case nor the law depended on the Fifteenth Amendment, which forbade only those denials of the franchise which were based on race. Congressional authority to legislate in the area of national elections derived from Article one, section four. "If this government is anything more than a mere aggregation of delegated agents of other States and governments, each of which is superior to the general government," Miller ruled, "it must have the power to protect the elections on which its existence depends from violence and corruption." Thus the federal government had broad powers to protect blacks in federal elections against both private persons and state officials.[34]

Government success in *Yarbrough* encouraged the Justice Department to continue prosecuting voting rights offenders. Federal statutes dealing with intimidation and fraud at the polls remained on the books despite the sections of the first Enforcement Act that had fallen in *Reese*. Federal prosecutors throughout the South continued during the 1870s and 1880s to prosecute cases under the Enforcement Acts. Federal grand juries found true bills, and some of the offenders stood trial. It had become extremely difficult to convict, however. Juries were mixed racially, and very few whites were willing to put offenders behind bars merely for keeping blacks from the polls. Those who successfully denied the franchise to black citizens were often regarded as heroes worthy of respect. Thus these cases very often resulted in mistrials. The Supreme Court's favorable ruling in *Yarbrough*, like the successful convictions in the Ku Klux Klan trials, had failed to bring any lasting change in Southern values. White Southerners were determined, at all costs, to eliminate blacks from the political scene. The "annual autumnal outbursts" of violence remained a constant as long as the blacks continued to exercise the franchise.[35]

Initially cautious, the Democratic government of South Carolina moved within a few years after Redemption to solidify its electoral gains. Fraud was a constant; the stuffing of ballot boxes with tissue ballots sometimes swelled the number of ballots well beyond the number of eligible voters. In 1877 the Democrats passed a new election law which separated the box for national office from the box for state and local offices. The two boxes were kept in different places, effectively eliminating federal supervision of the state election. Another innovative election law in 1882 provided for an eight-box system in which state and federal ballots were separated, then each election further separated by office. Ballots that were put into the wrong box were eliminated from the count. Democratic election officials shifted the boxes frequently, confusing illiterate voters beyond measure. Voters could ask for assistance in reading the boxes, but the Democratic poll officials were of little help to the unlettered Republicans. The federal district attorney for South Carolina estimated that the law effectively disfranchised some 75 percent of the black voters. Violence and intimidation served to discourage many of the others until the official disfranchisement of blacks by the state constitutional convention of 1895 finished the task by stamping out the small remaining percentages of Republican voters.[36]

Thus Reconstruction failed in South Carolina to effect constitutional changes that would protect the freedmen over time in the fundamental rights of citizenship. Impelled by Southern intransigence, the Republican government had passed constitutional amendments so extraordinary they have been considered a second American Constitution. The Enforcement Acts granted unprecedented powers to the national government to intervene in behalf of the freedmen's rights. The federal government mounted a campaign in South Carolina designed to maintain by coercion what white South Carolinians refused to concede. The presence of federal troops, the suspension of habeas corpus, the appointment of a reputedly Radical Republican circuit judge, and the federal prosecution of Ku Klux Klan members were all designed to force white South Carolina to recognize the inevitable changes wrought by the Civil War. Yet when all was said and done local values did not budge.

The great South Carolina Ku Klux Klan trials are only one episode in the history of Reconstruction, but they demonstrate in microcosm the reasons why constitutional doctrines and a rule of law sufficient to protect the former slaves in all the rights of citizenship did not emerge. White Southerners had officially laid down their arms, but they had never changed their minds. Firmly convinced that slavery was the appropriate position for blacks to occupy in society, they determined that whatever freedom meant, it would not substantially alter the condition of the freedpeople. For blacks to rise socially and politically threatened the traditional honor of white South Carolinians and indicated that society itself was falling apart. Intense racism blended with deeply held laissez-faire constitutional principles to convince white South Carolinians that control had to be restored to the traditional governing class—white men of property and education.

The Republican Congress provided constitutional amendments and enforcement laws to secure the rights of those they had freed. But the negative wording and ambiguous phrases of the Reconstruction measures reflected Congress's deep reluctance to disturb traditional federal-state relations. A broad nationalistic construction was necessary if blacks had any chance to retain those rights. Yet interpretation devolved upon federal judges locked into traditional notions of dual federalism. However much these judges deplored the violence of Reconstruction, they could not bring themselves to declare that the Reconstruction Amendments had fundamentally altered the nature of the Union. As in the federal circuit court in South Carolina, so in the Supreme Court of the nation, the justices refused to recognize the constitutional revolution inherent in the Fourteenth Amendment.

Constitutions and the laws under them, if they are to govern a people, have to be sanctioned by the majority. Yet the United States as a whole was deeply divided over the authenticity of the Enforcement Acts and the meaning of the Reconstruction Amendments. Not even the Republican party was united in its resolve to nationalize the fundamental rights of citizenship. Radicals never held a majority in Congress. Democrats, North and South, were firmly convinced that the Fourteenth Amendment was never meant to execute a radical change in the nature of the Union and that the Enforcement Acts seriously exceeded constitutional authority. "The force acts," as a Dunning School historian astutely noted long ago, "were in fact out of joint with the times. They did not square with the public consciousness either North or South."[37]

Although the nation was divided over the Enforcement Acts and future prospects of its black citizens, it was united by laissez-faire constitutional principles. Like the white people of the South, many Northerners tended to believe that educated, property-owning, taxpaying citizens were the ones who should bear the responsibility of governing. Only the people who supported the government with their hard-earned dollars could be trusted to promote neutral public policy instead of passing special class legislation that would benefit one group at the expense of another. As the interminable "Negro problem" stretched on and on, Northern public opinion lined up behind the Southern demand for home rule and the restoration of legitimate constitutional government.

If Southern honor were to yield to Yankee values, the nation would have to maintain a united determination to impose permanent change on the recalcitrant South. A president and attorney general who would stand behind the effort to enforce federal rights, a Congress willing to back them up with stiff laws and the money to enforce them, a federal judiciary capable of recognizing changes in the system, and federal troops to keep the peace were all necessary if Reconstruction was to work over the long haul. It was not to be. "Even such atrocities as Ku Kluxing do not hold their attention, as long and as earnestly, as we should expect," Attorney General Amos Akerman had written of Northern Republicans in 1871. "The Northern mind being full of what is called progress runs away from the past."[38] The Southern mind was deeply rooted in its tradition. The former Confederates, although they had lost the war, stood their ground and eventually won exactly the peace settlement they wanted. A permanent establishment of fundamental rights for black citizens was left for a future generation to accomplish.

Notes

Chapter 1: Introduction

1. On Southern violence see, for example, John Hope Franklin, *The Militant South: 1800–1861* (Cambridge, Mass.: Belknap Press of Harvard University Press, 1956); Bertram Wyatt-Brown, *Southern Honor: Ethics and Behavior in the Old South* (New York: Oxford University Press, 1983); Edward Ayers, *Vengeance and Justice: Crime and Punishment in the Nineteenth Century South* (New York: Oxford University Press, 1984). On violence as a motif for Southern legal history see Paul Finkelman, "Exploring Southern Legal History," *North Carolina Law Review* 64 (1985): 77–116.

2. On the South Carolina Klan trials see Kermit L. Hall, "Political Power and Constitutional Legitimacy: The South Carolina Ku Klux Klan Trials, 1871–1872," *Emory Law Journal* 33 (Fall 1984): 921–51; Kermit L. Hall and Lou Falkner Williams, "Constitutional Tradition Amid Social Change: Hugh Lennox Bond and the Ku Klux Klan in South Carolina," *Maryland Historian* 16 (Fall–Winter 1985): 43–58; Lou Falkner Williams, "The South Carolina Ku Klux Klan Trials and Enforcement of Federal Rights, 1871–1872," *Civil War History* 39 (March 1993): 47–66; Williams, "The Constitution and the Ku Klux Klan on Trial: Federal Enforcement and Local Resistance in South Carolina, 1871–1872," *Georgia Journal of Southern Legal History* 2 (Spring–Summer 1993): 41–70; Robert J. Kaczorowski, *The Politics of Judicial Interpretation: The Federal Courts, the Department of Justice, and Civil Rights, 1866–1876* (New York: Oceana Press, 1985); Everette Swinney, "Suppressing the Ku Klux Klan: The Enforcement of the Reconstruction Amendments, 1870–1874" (Ph.D. dissertation: University of Texas, 1966).

3. On the South Carolina Klan see Francis B. Simkins, "The Ku Klux Klan in South Carolina," *Journal of Negro History* 12 (October 1927): 606–47; Herbert Shapiro, "The Ku Klux Klan During Reconstruction: The South Carolina Episode," *Journal of Negro History* 49 (January 1964): 34–55; J. C. A. Stagg, "The Problem of Klan Violence: The South Carolina Upcountry, 1868–1871," *Journal of American Studies* 8 (December 1974): 303–20; and Allen W. Trelease, *White*

Terror: The Ku Klux Klan Conspiracy and Southern Reconstruction (New York: Harper & Row, 1971).

4. The Ku Klux Klan reports for South Carolina contain a verbatim record of the first group of Klan trials in November 1871–January 1872; see United States Congress, *Report of the Joint Select Committee to Inquire into the Condition of Affairs in the Late Insurrectionary States*, 13 vols. (Washington, D.C.: U.S. Government Printing Office, 1872) (hereafter cited as *KKK Reports*), 5:1615–1990. The complete trial record is also reprinted in United States Circuit Court, *Proceedings in the Ku Klux Trials at Columbia, S.C. in the United States Circuit Court, November Term, 1871* (1872; reprint, New York: Negro Universities Press, 1969) (cited hereafter as *Proceedings*). The Minute Book of the U.S. Circuit Court of the District of South Carolina, January 1869–March 1872 (Accession 52A155, No. 293), the Sessions Index (Accession 52A155, No. 212), and 174 Case Files (Accession 52A155, Box 01) have also survived. These materials are at the National Archives Regional Branch in East Point, Georgia.

5. Quoted in Leon F. Litwack, "The Ordeal of Black Freedom," in *The Southern Enigma: Essays on Race, Class, and Folk Culture*, ed. Walter J. Fraser, Jr., and Winfred B. Moore, Jr. (Westport, Conn.: Greenwood Press, 1983), p. 7.

6. George M. Fredrickson argued that paternalism was never strong in South Carolina; racism was always the stronger force in the state. See "Masters and Mudsills: The Role of Race in the Planter Ideology of South Carolina," *South Atlantic Urban Studies* 2 (1978): 34–38.

7. Litwack, "Ordeal of Black Freedom," p. 9; James L. Roark, *Masters Without Slaves: Southern Planters in the Civil War and Reconstruction* (New York: Norton, 1977), pp. 84–85, 94–95, 106–7; Joel Williamson, *After Slavery: The Negro in South Carolina During Reconstruction, 1861–1877* (Chapel Hill: University of North Carolina Press, 1965), pp. 32–35; David H. Donald, "A Generation of Defeat," in *From the Old South to the New: Essays on the Transitional South*, ed. Walter J. Fraser, Jr., and Winfred B. Moore, Jr. (Westport, Conn.: Greenwood Press, 1981), pp. 7–11.

8. *Acts of the General Assembly of South Carolina Passed at the Sessions of 1864–65* (Columbia: Julian A. Selby, 1866), 271–304.

9. Ibid. The job restrictions not only limited the former slaves' access to meaningful work but also threatened the black middle class, which had dominated many trades before the War. On this point see Thomas Holt, *Black over White: Negro Political Leadership in South Carolina During Reconstruction* (Urbana: University of Illinois Press, 1977), pp. 20–21. See also Williamson, *After Slavery*, pp. 72–73; Eric Foner, *Reconstruction: America's Unfinished Revolution, 1863–1877* (New York: Harper & Row, 1988), p. 200; Francis B. Simkins and Robert H. Woody, *South Carolina During Reconstruction* (Chapel Hill: University of North Carolina Press, 1932), pp. 48–50.

10. T. Fraser Matthews to B. F. Perry, 21 August 1865, Benjamin F. Perry Papers, Alabama State Department of Archives and History, Montgomery, Alabama (hereafter cited as ASDAH). See also Steven A. Channing, *Crisis of Fear: Secession in South Carolina* (New York: Simon and Schuster, 1979), pp. 25–26, 35–36, 58–59.

11. Report of William Stone, 31 July 1868, Bureau of Refugees, Freedmen, and Abandoned Lands (hereafter cited as BRFAL), Record Group (hereafter cited as RG) 105, M869, roll 36, National Archives (hereafter cited as NA).

12. Williamson, *After Slavery*, pp. 34–41.

13. Ibid., pp. 88–91; Edward Magdol, *A Right to the Land: Essays on the Freedmen's Community* (Westport, Conn.: Greenwood Press, 1976), pp. 139–45; Willie Lee Rose, *Rehearsal for Reconstruction: The Port Royal Experiment* (New York: Oxford University Press, 1964). For historiographical information on educating the freedpeople see Robert C. Morris, "Educational Reconstruction," in *The Facts of Reconstruction*, ed. Eric Anderson and Robert W. Moss (Baton Rouge: Louisiana State University Press, 1991), pp. 141–66.

14. *Proceedings of the Colored People's Convention of the State of South Carolina* (Charleston: South Carolina Leader, 1865), p. 25.

15. A. C. Garlington to A. Baxter Springs, 17 February 1866, Springs Family Papers, G.I.C. to W. P. Miles, 18 April 1867, William Porcher Miles Papers, both in Southern Historical Collection, University of North Carolina, Chapel Hill (hereafter cited as SHC); J. M. Anderson to Gov. Perry, n.d., T. J. Moore to Gov. Perry, 27 September 1865, both in Perry Papers, ASDAH.

16. H. H. Alvord to Gen. Ely, 8 September 1865, BRFAL, RG 105, M869, Roll 34; George Pingree, Annual Report, 24 September 1867, BRFAL, RG 105, M869, Roll 35; F. W. Liedtke to Major E. L. Deane, 27 December, 1867, BRFAL, RG 105, M869, Roll 18, NA.

17. William Stone to Erasmus W. Everson, 18 August 1869, Everson Collection, South Carolina Historical Society (cited hereafter as SCHS), Charleston, S.C.

18. Wade Hampton to James Conner, 24 March 1867, Conner Family Papers, SCHS.

19. Wade Hampton to D. W. Ray, William H. Talley, J. P. Thomas, et al., *Charleston Mercury*, 29 August 1867 (transcription), Hampton Family Papers, South Caroliniana Library (hereafter cited SCL), University of South Carolina, Columbia, S.C.

20. Simkins and Woody, *South Carolina During Reconstruction*, pp. 86–87.

21. William Henry Trescot to Henry Wilson, 8 September 1867, in "Letter of William Henry Trescot on Reconstruction in South Carolina, 1867," *American Historical Review* 15 (1910): 580. Trescot advocated political participation by as many whites as were qualified to vote.

22. Holt, *Black over White*, pp. 35–39. Seventy of the 124 delegates were black.

23. Benjamin F. Perry, Speech at Anderson Court House, March 1868, pp. 10–11, Benjamin F. Perry Papers, SCL.

24. James B. Campbell to Frederick A. Ford, 3 August 1868, in *Two Letters from the Hon. James B. Campbell on Public Affairs and Our Duties to the Colored Race Published by the Democratic Central Executive Committee of South Carolina* (Charleston: Walker, Evans & Cogswell, 1868), p. 6; W. H. Trescot to R. K. Scott, 24 October 1868, Governor Robert K. Scott Papers, Letters Received, South Carolina Department of Archives and History, Columbia, S.C. (hereafter cited as SCDA).

25. On laissez-faire constitutional principles see Michael Les Benedict, "The Problem of Constitutionalism and Constitutional Liberty in the Reconstruction South," in *An Uncertain Tradition: Constitutionalism and the History of the South*, ed. Kermit L. Hall and James W. Ely, Jr. (Athens: University of Georgia Press, 1989), pp. 225–49; Benedict, "Laissez-Faire and Liberty: A Re-evaluation of the Meaning of Laissez-Faire Constitutionalism," *Law and History Review* 3 (1985): 293–331.

26. Benjamin F. Perry, Speech at Anderson Court House," March 1868, p. 11, Perry Papers, SCL.

27. See, for example, Richard Lathers, *South Carolina, Her Wrongs and the Remedy: Remarks of Col. Richard Lathers, Delivered at the Opening of the Taxpayers' Convention in Columbia, S.C., Tuesday, February 17, 1874*," pamphlet, SCL.

28. W. H. Trescot to R. K. Scott, 24 October 1868, Governor Scott Papers, Letters Received, SCDA.

29. Alfred Huger to B. F. Perry, 11 July 1867, Perry Papers, ASDAH. The state legislature was not strictly a "Negro legislature" as Huger contended. The senate had a white majority counting Democrats and white Republicans together. But Huger was correct that blacks were in the majority if both houses were counted together. Of the 156 state legislators, 85 were black Republicans, 10 in the senate and 75 in the house (Holt, *Black over White*, p. 97).

30. Richard N. Current, *Those Terrible Carpetbaggers* (New York: Oxford University Press, 1988), pp. 40–45, 214–35. See also Simkins and Woody, *South Carolina During Reconstruction*, pp. 369–70, 154–57; Williamson, *After Slavery*, pp. 382–85.

31. Current, *Those Terrible Carpetbaggers*, pp. 91–98.

32. Quote from S. Sumter to John, 29 March 1868, Waties-Parker Family Papers, SCL.

33. For a Dunning School interpretation of Reconstruction in South Carolina critical of the Republican legislature see John S. Reynolds, *Reconstruction in South Carolina, 1865–1877* (1905; reprint, New York: Negro Universities Press, 1969).

34. Holt, *Black over White*, pp. 96–121.

35. Williamson, *After Slavery*, pp. 371–80; William Stone to Erasmus W. Everson, 18 August 1869, Everson Collection, SCHS.

36. Williamson, *After Slavery*, pp. 148–51; Lacy K. Ford, *Origins of Southern Radicalism: The South Carolina Upcountry, 1800–1860* (New York: Oxford University Press, 1988), pp. 308–10; J. Mills Thornton III, "Fiscal Policy and the Failure of Radical Reconstruction in the Lower South," in *Region, Race, and Reconstruction: Essays in Honor of C. Vann Woodward*, ed. J. Morgan Kousser and James M. McPherson (New York: Oxford University Press, 1982), pp. 349–94. Governor Scott quoted in "The South Carolina Problem: The Epoch of Transition," *Scribner's Monthly*, June 1874, pp. 138–39.

37. Williamson, *After Slavery*, pp. 148–51; Ford, *Origins of Southern Radicalism*, pp. 308–10. For the story of South Carolina's efforts to make land available to the freedmen see Carol K. Rothrock Bleser, *The Promised Land: The History of the South Carolina Land Commission* (Columbia: University of South Carolina Press, 1969). On the yeomen farmers and the tax issue, see, for example, Edward and Elizabeth Lipscomb to Smith and Sally Lipscomb, 30 June 1869 and 11 April 1871, Edward Lipscomb Papers, SHC.

38. Benedict, "Problem of Constitutionalism," pp. 234–40; Benedict, "Laissez-Faire and Liberty," pp. 305–6. See also Kenneth S. Greenberg, *Masters and Statesmen: The Political Culture of American Slavery* (Baltimore: Johns Hopkins University Press, 1985), pp. 4–5.

39. E. P. Alexander to B. F. Perry, 21 August 1867, Perry Papers, ASDAH.

40. Benjamin F. Perry, "Second Letter from Ex-Gov. Perry to Governor Scott," 28 March 1871, Perry Papers, SCL; "Proceedings of the Tax-Payers' Convention of South Carolina, Held at Columbia, Beginning May 9, and Ending May 12, 1871," in *KKK Reports*, 3:485.

41. Testimony of James Chesnut, *KKK Reports*, 3:449.

42. "Proceedings of the Tax-Payers' Convention," ibid., p. 476.

43. Lathers, *South Carolina, Her Wrongs and the Remedy*. The reference to domination by "their own slaves" underscores the inability of many white South Carolinians to accept black freedom.

44. Alfred Huger to Gov. Perry, 21 July 1867, Perry Papers, ASDAH.

45. David Schenck Journal, Vol. 6, 11 July 1872, David Schenck Collection, SHC. Schenck was a North Carolinian.

46. R. H. Woody, "The South Carolina Election of 1870," *North Carolina Historical Review* 8 (April 1931): 168–86; Trelease, *White Terror*, pp. 350–51.

47. Williamson, *After Slavery*, pp. 352–55; Woody, "Election of 1870," pp. 174–76; Alrutheus Ambush Taylor, *The Negro in South Carolina During the Reconstruction* (1924; reprint, New York: AMS, 1971), pp. 193–97.

48. Woody, "Election of 1870," pp. 172–76.

49. A. H. Valentine to R. K. Scott, 20 September 1870, Governor Scott Papers, Letters Received, SCDA. See also affidavits of 1870 Election, Spartanburg

County, Elections File, 1870, Green Files, SCDA, especially the testimony of Clem Bowden, William Madison, and Tom Fisher. Joel Williamson has denied that the Ku Klux Klan was inherently political because Klan violence did not begin until after the election of 1870. Evidence in the Governor's Papers, affidavits in the Green Files, and the Ku Klux Klan reports all indicate that Klan violence started before the election.

50. Affidavits of Election, 1870, Green Files, SCDA, testimony of Tench Blackwell; A. B. Springs to John Springs, 22 October 1870, Springs Family Papers, SHC; Woody, "Election of 1870," pp. 183–84; *KKK Reports*, 3:123–24, 82; Trelease, *White Terror*, p. 351.

51. Williamson, *After Slavery*, pp. 352–56.

52. *KKK Reports*, vols. 3, 4, and 5, passim; see also Trelease, *White Terror*, passim; and Simkins, "Ku Klux Klan in South Carolina," passim.

53. Shapiro, "Klan During Reconstruction," pp. 35–39.

54. J. P. Kinard to R. K. Scott, 19 April 1870, A. P. Turner to Scott, 23 December 1869, H. K. Robert to Scott, 14 January 1870, James M. Brisco to Scott, 8 June 1869, Jemy Hollinshead to Scott, 22 July 1869, all in Governor Scott Papers, SCDA.

55. George W. Williams to R. K. Scott, 14 April 1869, ibid.; Shapiro, "Klan During Reconstruction," p. 39.

Chapter 2: Klan Crime and the South Carolina Whites

1. Julian J. Petty, *The Growth and Distribution of Population in South Carolina* (Columbia: State Planning Board, 1943), Appendix F. Figures are for 1870.

2. Lacy K. Ford, "Labor and Ideology in the South Carolina Up-Country: The Transition to Free-Labor Agriculture," in *The Southern Enigma: Essays on Race, Class, and Folk Culture*, ed. Walter J. Fraser, Jr., and Winfred B. Moore, Jr. (Westport, Conn.: Greenwood Press, 1983), pp. 25–41; Ford, "Yeoman Farmers in the South Carolina Upcountry: Changing Production Patterns in the Late Antebellum Era," *Agricultural History* 60 (Fall 1986): 17–37; Ford, "Rednecks and Merchants: Economic Development and Social Tensions in the South Carolina Upcountry, 1865–1900," *Journal of American History* 71 (September 1984): 298–303; Ford, *Origins of Southern Radicalism*, pp. 71–75, 245–55. On "safety-first" agriculture see Gavin Wright, *The Political Economy of the Cotton South: Households, Markets, and Wealth in the Nineteenth Century* (New York: Norton, 1978), pp. 55–74.

3. Ford, "Labor and Ideology," pp. 25–41; Richard Sutch and Roger Ransom, "Sharecropping: Market Response or Mechanism of Race Control?" in *What was Freedom's Price?*, ed. David G. Sansing (Jackson: University Press of Mississippi, 1978), p. 61; A. B. Springs to E. B. Springs, 19 September, 1870, Springs

Family Papers, SHC; Report of Major Pingree, 31 December 1867, BRFAL, RG 105, M869, roll 35, NA.

4. John William De Forest, *A Union Officer in the Reconstruction*, ed. James H. Croushore and David M. Potter (New Haven: Yale University Press, 1948), pp. 126–27; Richard H. Abbott, *The Republican Party and the South, 1855–1877: The First Southern Strategy* (Chapel Hill: University of North Carolina Press, 1986), p. 111; A. B. Springs to John Springs, 22 October 1870, Springs Family Papers, SHC. On the Union League movement in Alabama and Mississippi see Michael W. Fitzgerald, *The Union League Movement in the Deep South: Politics and Agricultural Change During Reconstruction* (Baton Rouge: Louisiana State University Press, 1989).

5. J. J. Pringle Smith to W. P. Miles, 2 April 1872, Miles Papers, SHC; W. R. Robertson to A. B. Springs, 23 August 1870, Springs Family Papers, SHC; *Yorkville Enquirer*, 24 September 1868.

6. J. A. Jackson to John B. Hubbard, 3 July 1870, John Burke to John B. Hubbard, 10 October 1870, both in General Assembly of South Carolina at the Regular Session, 1877–78, *Report of the Joint Investigating Committee on Public Frauds: Reports and Resolutions of the State of South Carolina, 1877–78* (1878).

7. Otis A. Singletary, *Negro Militia and Reconstruction* (1957; reprint, New York: McGraw-Hill, 1963), pp. 20–24; Reynolds, *Reconstruction in South Carolina*, pp. 114–15; Williamson, *After Slavery*, pp. 260–61; Robert K. Scott, *Annual Message to Senate and House*, January 1871, Legislative System, Green Files, SCDA.

8. Joseph Crews to Capt. Hubbard, 3 July 1870, in General Assembly, *Report of the Joint Investigating Committee*, p. 1687.

9. *Yorkville Enquirer*, 15, 22 September, 6 October 1870. For a quieter voice of restraint see [Julius J. Fleming], *The Juhl Letters to the Charleston Courier: A View of the South, 1865–1871*, ed. John Hammond Moore (Athens: University of Georgia Press, 1974), pp. 371–72. For an excellent discussion of Second Amendment issues for African Americans see Robert J. Cottrol and Raymond T. Diamond, "The Second Amendment: Toward an Afro-Americanist Reconsideration," *Georgetown Law Journal* 80 (December 1991): 308–61.

10. On black troops and the white mind, see Lawrence J. Friedman, *The White Savage: Racial Fantasies in the Postbellum South* (Englewood Cliffs, N.J.: Prentice-Hall, 1970), pp. 11–17. On the South and the military tradition, see Franklin, *Militant South*.

11. Leon F. Litwack, *Been in the Storm So Long* (New York: Random House Vintage Books, 1980), p. 268; W. F. de Saussure to B. F. Perry, 31 July 1865, Edward Frost to Perry, 30 August 1865, W. T. Burnett to Perry, 4 October 1865, all in Perry Papers, ASDAH; *Charleston Mercury*, 26 January 1865, quoted in Friedman, *White Savage*, p. 15.

12. It is necessary to keep in mind that the sources on the black militia were generally written by whites who were locked into the notion that any behavior on the part of blacks which was disallowed during slavery was intolerably insolent. Leland, a Ph.D. and president of a girls' school in Laurens, was arrested and jailed as a suspected Klansman in 1871; see John A. Leland, *A Voice from South Carolina* (1879; reprint, Freeport, N.Y.: Books for Libraries Press, 1971). J. A. Leland to R. K. Scott, 4 November 1870, Governor Scott Papers, SCDA; Mrs. J. Ward Motte to Robert Motte, 2 August 1870, Lalla Pelot Papers, Perkins Library, Duke University, Durham, N.C. (hereafter cited as Duke); Peggy Lamson, *The Glorious Failure: Black Congressman Robert Brown Elliott and the Reconstruction in South Carolina* (New York: Norton, 1973), pp. 90–91; Williamson, *After Slavery*, p. 261; *KKK Reports*, 5:1425.

13. *KKK Reports*, 3:79–80, testimony of David T. Corbin; compare Reynolds, *Reconstruction in South Carolina*, p. 184. Klansmen broke into the jail where the black suspects were held, took them out, and brutally murdered them. See Trelease, *White Terror*, pp. 356–58.

14. *KKK Reports*, 3:241, 248; Mrs. J. Ward Motte to Robert Motte, 2 August 1870, Pelot Papers, Duke; Taylor, *Negro in South Carolina*, pp. 190–91; Henry W. Thompson, *Ousting the Carpetbagger from South Carolina* (Columbia, S.C.: R. L. Bryan, 1926), p. 50.

15. General Assembly, *Report of the Joint Investigating Committee*, pp. 1679, 1684. This report is the best source of information on the black militia, but one must remember that it was published by the Redeemer government to bring as much reproach as possible on the Republicans. Still, it contains unimpeachable evidence in the form of letters and financial accounts from the records of the previous period. Used with care, the testimony of the various witnesses who participated demonstrates that a large percentage of the militia expenses was a huge fraud on the state. On this point see also Lamson, *Glorious Failure*, pp. 97–98. For the community standing of black militia leaders see Magdol, *Right to the Land*, pp. 109–36.

16. General Assembly, *Report of the Joint Investigating Committee*, pp. 1689–93, 1709–13.

17. James Chesnut referred to sixteen thousand new Winchesters in his testimony before the congressional investigating committee. This number is not corroborated in the report of the committee on public frauds. See *KKK Reports*, 3:463. Even if Chesnut was correct, there were still not enough guns to distribute among all the militia.

18. B. G. Yocum to John B. Hubbard, 2 September 1870, in General Assembly, *Report of the Joint Investigating Committee*, p. 1686; *KKK Reports*, 3:239; *Yorkville Enquirer*, 6 October 1870; [Fleming], *Juhl Letters*, p. 356.

19. *Proceedings*, pp. 216–21; *KKK Reports* 3:1763–64.

20. *South Carolina Statutes at Large*, 8:538.

21. Forrest G. Wood, *Black Scare: The Racist Response to Emancipation and Reconstruction* (Berkeley: University of California Press, 1970), pp. 140–41; Joel Williamson, *The Crucible of Race: Black-White Relations in the American South Since Emancipation* (New York: Oxford University Press, 1984), pp. 17–19; Williamson, *After Slavery*, pp. 248–49; H. M. Henry, "The Police Control of the Slave in South Carolina" (Ph.D. dissertation, Vanderbilt University, 1914), pp. 28–52.

22. *Yorkville Enquirer*, 23 March 1871. For evidence that blacks also considered the antebellum patrol system and the Klan "bout de same," see Gladys-Marie Fry, *Nightriders in Black Folk History* (Knoxville: University of Tennessee Press, 1975), pp. 154–56.

23. Trelease, *White Terror*, pp. 349–80; *KKK Reports*, 5:passim.

24. The murders reported were in Laurens, York, Spartanburg, and Union counties (*KKK Reports*, 3:ii–xxxv, 4:919–22). The *KKK Reports* documented 213 whippings in Spartanburg County. Allen Trelease estimated approximately 600 total whippings for York County. (*White Terror*, p. 365).

25. Trelease emphasized political motivation as the impetus for Klan atrocities (*White Terror*, p. xvii). Joel Williamson found the white fear of the black militia more important (*After Slavery*, p. 261). J. C. A. Stagg emphasized problems of class, specifically disputes over land tenure and labor contracts, as the basis for Klan activity ("Problem of Klan Violence," pp. 303–20). The Dunning School interpretation of the Klan in South Carolina is in Reynolds, *Reconstruction in South Carolina*. An early revisionist account is Simkins, "The Ku Klux Klan in South Carolina," pp. 606–47. For an analysis of the Georgia Klan as the repositor of Southern values see Charles L. Flynn, Jr., "The Ancient Pedigree of Violent Repression: Georgia's Klan as a Folk Movement," in *The Southern Enigma: Essays in Race, Class, and Folk Culture*, ed. Walter J. Fraser, Jr., and Winfred B. Moore, Jr. (Westport, Conn: Greenwood Press, 1983), pp. 189–90.

26. *KKK Reports*, vols. 3, 4, and 5:passim.

27. Ibid., 3:41–42, 274–75.

28. Ibid., pp. 365–67.

29. Ibid., pp. 3:27–28, 4:580, 5:1705.

30. Ibid., 3:189.

31. Ibid., 5:1939–74.

32. The situation in South Carolina was not unlike the legal pluralism anthropologist Clifford Geertz described in Third World countries, where traditional local folkways are suddenly confronted with imported, modern (usually Western) concepts of law and justice. See Geertz, "Local Knowledge: Fact and Law in Comparative Perspective," in *Local Knowledge: Further Essays in Interpretive Anthropology* (New York: Basic Books, 1983), pp. 219–20. On the conflict

between established custom and law see Stanley Diamond, "The Rule of Law Versus the Order of Custom," in *The Rule of Law*, ed. Robert Paul Wolff (New York: Simon and Schuster, 1971), pp. 115–43.

33. Wyatt-Brown, *Southern Honor*, passim; Ayers, *Vengeance and Justice*, pp. 26–27.

34. Wyatt-Brown, *Southern Honor*, pp. 362–401.

35. See, however, Kathleen M. Blee, *Women of the Klan: Racism and Gender in the 1920s* (Berkeley: University of California Press, 1991), pp. 11–16.

36. Wyatt-Brown, *Southern Honor*, pp. 292–300; cf. Winthrop D. Jordan, *White over Black: American Attitudes Toward the Negro, 1550–1812* (Chapel Hill: University of North Carolina Press, 1968), pp. 148–49.

37. Jordan, *White over Black*, pp. 136–54; Wyatt-Brown, *Southern Honor*, p. 388.

38. John F. Lucas to Maude Stewart, 19 April 1916, Ku Klux Klan General Collection, SCHS. I am indebted to Stephen Hoffius of the *South Carolina Historical Magazine* for calling this letter to my attention.

39. *KKK Reports*, 3:212, 5:1407; David Schenck Journal, 18 December 1869, SHC. For an excellent assessment of white male reaction to interracial sex between white women and black men see Trudier Harris, *Exorcising Blackness: Historical and Literary Lynching and Burning Rituals* (Bloomington: Indiana University Press, 1984), pp. ix-xiii, 1–23.

40. *KKK Reports*, 5:1864–65.

41. Ibid., 3:524–25.

42. Ibid., pp. 576–77.

43. Ibid., 5:1860–62, 1744–46.

44. Ibid., pp. 1860–61.

45. Ibid., 3:586.

46. Wyatt-Brown, *Southern Honor*, p. 53; Susan Griffin, *Rape: The Power of Consciousness* (San Francisco: Harper & Row, 1979), pp. 17–19; Nell Irvin Painter, "'Social Equality,' Miscegenation, Labor, and Power," in *The Evolution of Southern Culture*, ed. Numan V. Bartley (Athens: University of Georgia Press, 1988), pp. 58–63; Jacqueline Dowd Hall, "The Mind That Burns in Each Body: Women, Rape, and Racial Violence," *Southern Exposure* 12 (November 1984): 61–65; Harris, *Exorcising Blackness*, pp. x–xi, 2–3; Elizabeth Fox-Genovese, *Within the Plantation Household: Black and White Women in the Old South* (Chapel Hill: University of North Carolina Press, 1988), pp. 294–95.

47. On violence as a tradition in the South, see, for example, W. J. Cash, *The Mind of the South* (New York: Knopf, 1941); Sheldon Hackney, "Southern Violence," *American Historical Review* 74 (February 1969): 906–25; Richard Maxwell Brown, *Strain of Violence: Historical Studies of Violence and Vigilantism* (New York: Oxford University Press, 1975); Ayers, *Vengeance and Justice*; and Wyatt-Brown, *Southern Honor*.

48. Leland, *Voice from South Carolina*, pp. 55–56.

49. Williamson, *After Slavery*, pp. 330–32; Report of William Stone, 1 October 1868, BRFAL, RG 105, M869, Roll 36, NA; Hubbard to Scott, 14 February 1871, Governor Scott Papers, SCDA; William Stone to Major H. Neide, 19 September 1868, BRFAL, RG 105, M869, Roll 18, NA; Testimony of David T. Corbin, *KKK Reports*, 5:69–70.

50. Report of William Stone, March 1867, BRFAL, RG 105, M869, Roll 35; Report of J. B. Dennis, December 1867, BRFAL, RG 105, M869, Roll 18, NA; *KKK Reports*, 5:69.

51. H. E. Hayne to Scott, 9 October 1868, Gov. Scott Papers, SCDA; Edward Lipscomb to Smith and Sally Lipscomb, 30 June 1869, Lipscomb Family Papers, SHC.

52. *KKK Reports*, 5:1487, 1552–53.

53. Report of Major Merrill, ibid. pp.1599–1606; Presentment of York County Grand Jury, ibid., pp.1611–12.

54. Report of Major Merrill, ibid., pp.1601–2.

Chapter 3: Federal Intervention and Southern Resistance

1. Robert K. Scott to U. S. Grant, [November 1871], Robert K. Scott Papers, Ohio Historical Society, Columbus, Ohio (cited hereafter as OHS). For an excellent narrative of events in South Carolina see Trelease, *White Terror*, pp. 362–80.

2. *Yorkville Enquirer*, 19 January 1871; Robert K. Scott to the Senate and House of Representatives, 16 January 1871, Governor Scott Messages, Legislative System, Green Files, SCDA.

3. *U.S. Statutes at Large*, 16:140–46. See also Harold M. Hyman, *A More Perfect Union: The Impact of the Civil War and Reconstruction on the Constitution* (New York: Knopf, 1973), p. 526; Herman Belz, *Emancipation and Equal Rights: Politics and Constitutionalism in the Civil War Era* (New York: Norton, 1978), pp. 126–27; Everette Swinney, *Suppressing the Ku Klux Klan: The Enforcement of the Reconstruction Amendments, 1870–1877* (New York: Garland, 1987), pp. 57–58; William Watson Davis, "The Federal Enforcement Acts," in *Studies in Southern History and Politics Inscribed to William Archibald Dunning* (New York: Columbia University Press, 1914), pp. 207–12. The second Enforcement Act of February 1871 provided national supervision for congressional elections. It was framed primarily to curb election fraud in the North and was not used in the Ku Klux Klan trials in the South. See *U.S. Statutes at Large*, 16:433–40.

4. Report of Major Merrill, *KKK Reports*, 5:1599–1606.

5. Arthur Zilversmit, "Grant and the Freedmen," in *New Perspectives on Race and Slavery in America: Essays in Honor of Kenneth M. Stampp*, ed. Robert H. Abzug and Stephen E. Maizlish (Lexington: University Press of Kentucky, 1986), p. 133; Trelease, *White Terror*, pp. 383–88; U. S. Grant to the Senate and House

of Representatives, 23 March 1871, in James D. Richardson, ed., *A Compilation of the Messages and Papers of the Presidents* (New York: Bureau of National Literature, 1897), 9:4081–82. *U.S. Statutes at Large,* 17:13–15.

6. *U.S. Statutes at Large,* 17:13–15.

7. The authorization to suspend habeas corpus expired at the end of the next regular session of Congress in 1872 and was never extended (*U.S. Statutes at Large,* 17:13–15). Historians have debated whether Congress believed it had constitutional authority to protect blacks from private aggression or felt compelled to remain within the state-action concept of federal power under the Fourteenth Amendment. For the former argument see Laurent B. Frantz, "Congressional Power to Enforce the Fourteenth Amendment Against Private Acts," *Yale Law Journal* 73 (July 1964): 1354–57; for the latter see Alfred Avins, "The Ku Klux Klan Act of 1871: Some Reflected Light on State Action and the Fourteenth Amendment," *St. Louis University Law Journal* 11 (Spring 1967): 377–79.

8. Swinney, *Suppressing the Ku Klux Klan,* pp. 166–70; Belz, *Emancipation and Equal Rights,* p. 129; Davis, "Federal Enforcement Acts," p. 212.

9. On the work of the committee see Trelease, *White Terror,* pp. 392–95. The report of the subcommittee for South Carolina filled three volumes. See *KKK Reports,* vols. 3–5. Volume 5 of the *KKK Reports* contains a verbatim report of the U.S. Circuit Court session in November and December 1871, when the first group of Klan trials for South Carolina was held.

10. Akerman replaced Ebenezer Rockwood Hoar, Grant's first attorney general, who had lost the support of the Senate by writing opinions unfavorable to the Radicals and failing to consult the senators on his candidates for district attorneys and judges. Needing Southern support for his Santo Domingo Treaty, Grant asked Hoar to resign to enable him to appoint a Southerner to a cabinet position. See Homer Cummings and Carl McFarland, *Federal Justice: Chapters in the History of Justice and the Federal Executive* (New York: Macmillan, 1937), pp. 225–29.

11. Akerman to James Jackson, 20 November 1871, Amos T. Akerman Papers, Alderman Library, University of Virginia, Charlottesville, Virginia (hereafter cited as UVA). An excellent assessment of Akerman's career is William S. McFeely, "Amos T. Akerman: The Lawyer and Racial Justice," in *Region, Race, and Reconstruction: Essays in Honor of C. Vann Woodward,* ed. J. Morgan Kousser and James M. McPherson (New York: Oxford University Press, 1982), pp. 395–415. See also William S. McFeely, *Grant: A Biography* (New York: Norton, 1981), pp. 367–74.

12. Report of Major Merrill, *KKK Reports,* 5:1602; Akerman to Gen. Alfred H. Terry, 18 November 1871, and Akerman to B. D. Silliman, 9 November 1871, Akerman Papers, UVA; *New York Times,* 31 October 1871; Trelease, *White Terror,* pp. 402–3.

13. Lewis Merrill to R. K. Scott, 17 July 1871, Scott Papers, OHS; Report of Major Merrill, *KKK Reports*, 5:1599–1606.

14. Akerman to E. P. Jacobson, 18 August 1871, Akerman to B. D. Silliman, 9 November 1871, Akerman to Gen. A. H. Terry, 18 November 1871, all in Akerman Papers, UVA.

15. The counties were Spartanburg, York, Marion, Chester, Laurens, Newberry, Fairfield, Lancaster, and Chesterfield (Richardson, *Messages and Papers*, 9:4089–92). Including Marion County was a mistake. Grant issued another proclamation on 3 November substituting Union County for Marion (ibid., pp. 4092–93). On Grant's sensitivity to the charge of being a military dictator see Zilversmit, "Grant and the Freedmen," p. 134, and McFeely, *Grant*, p. 370.

16. Report of Major Merrill, *KKK Reports*, 5:1602–3; Trelease, *White Terror*, pp. 403–6.

17. Report of Major Merrill, *KKK Reports*, 5:1602–3; Mary Davis Brown Diary, 17 October 1871, SCL; Trelease, *White Terror*, pp. 403–6. See also *Statement of Dr. Bratton's Case, Being Explanatory of the Ku-Klux Prosecutions in the Southern States* (London, Ontario: Free Press, 1872).

18. Major Merrill's Report, *KKK Reports*, 5:1602–4. Federal district attorney D. T. Corbin reported that approximately three hundred Klansmen had made confessions, and another three hundred blacks had given statements to federal officials detailing the atrocities committed against them by the Klan. These crimes, Corbin stated, "exhibit a catalogue of crimes probably never surpassed, if equalled, in the history of any country" (Corbin to A. T. Akerman, 13 November 1871, Department of Justice, Source Chronological Files for South Carolina, Record Group 60, M947, NA; hereafter cited as SCF, S.C.).

19. Brown Diary, 15, 16, 17 October, 10 November 1871, SCL.

20. Iredell Jones to My Dear Wife, 22, 30 October, 15 November 1871, Iredell Jones Papers, Duke. Jones's self-proclaimed innocence seems doubtful. The Iredell Jones Papers at the South Caroliniana Library contain documents, signed by Jones, authorizing the organization of a Klan in Rock Hill. See also "General Orders" for Klan business in Jones Papers, SCL.

21. Iredell Jones to My Dear Wife, 24 October 1871, Jones Papers, Duke; Leland, *Voice from South Carolina*, pp. 98–132; *Yorkville Enquirer*, 26 October, 2, 9 November 1871.

22. Report of Major Merrill, *KKK Reports*, 5:1602; Amos T. Akerman, Annual Report, *New York Times*, 16 January 1872; D. T. Corbin to A. T. Akerman, 13 November 1871, SCF, S.C.; R. K. Scott, Annual Message, 28 November 1871, Legislative System, Green Files, SCDA; Trelease, *White Terror*, pp. 404–6.

23. *U.S. Statutes at Large*, 16:44–45.

24. Any combination of two judges could sit together or any of the judges could hold court alone (ibid.; Kermit L. Hall, "The Civil War Era as a Crucible

for Nationalizing the Federal Courts," *Prologue: Journal of the National Archives* 7 [Spring 1975]: 183–86).

25. *Dictionary of American Biography*, 1964 ed., s.v. "Hugh Lennox Bond"; James G. Randall and David Donald, *The Civil War and Reconstruction*, 2d ed. (Lexington, Mass.: D. C. Heath, 1969), pp. 195–96. On Bond's political career and commitment to a Radical Republican ideology of "equal access to law" see Richard P. Fuke, "Hugh Lennox Bond and Radical Ideology," *Journal of Southern History* 45 (November 1978): 569–86.

26. W. A. Low, "The Freedmen's Bureau and Civil Rights in Maryland," *Journal of Negro History* 37 (July 1952): 232, 241–42.

27. [Hugh L. Bond] to Kate [Bond], 1 January 1865 and n.d., Bond-McCullogh Papers, Maryland Historical Society, Baltimore, Maryland (cited hereafter as MHS).

28. Jean H. Baker, *The Politics of Continuity: Maryland Politics from 1858 to 1870* (Baltimore: Johns Hopkins University Press, 1973) pp. 181–88.

29. U.S. Congress, Senate, *Journal of the Executive Proceedings*, vol. 17 (Washington, D.C.: U.S. Government Printing Office, 1901), pp. 536–37.

30. Hugh Bond to Anna Bond, 14 June 1871 and n.d., Hugh Lennox Bond Papers, MHS.

31. 4 Wallace 333; U. R. Brooks, *South Carolina Bench and Bar* (Columbia, S.C.: State Company, 1908), pp. 336–45; *City of Charleston Year Book—1895* (Charleston, S.C.: N.p., 1895), pp. 376–85.

32. U.S. Circuit Court, District of South Carolina, Minute Book, January 1869–March 1872, Federal Records Center, East Point, Georgia, pp. 457–94 (hereafter cited as Minute Book).

33. Hugh Bond to Anna Bond, n.d. [November 1871], 26 November 1871, and n.d. [1871], Bond Papers, MHS; Hampton to A. Burt, 22 October 1871, Wade Hampton Papers, Duke.

34. Hampton to A. Burt, 22 October 1871, Hampton Papers, Duke.

35. J. M. Wallace to Ben, 21 February 1870, Wallace, Rice, Duncan Family Papers, SCL.

36. *Charleston Daily Courier*, 25 November 1871.

37. Bernard C. Steiner, *Life of Reverdy Johnson* (1914; reprint, New York: Russell & Russell, 1970), pp. 118–35; James Brooks and Reverdy Johnson, *A Correspondence Between the Hon. James Brooks of New York and the Hon. Reverdy Johnson of Baltimore on the State of the Country* (Baltimore: Sun Book and Job Office, 1872), pp. 7–15; Reverdy Johnson, *Speeches of Hon. Reverdy Johnson on the Military Reconstruction Bill* (Washington, D.C.: Congressional Globe Office, 1867), pp. 3–5, 8–9; Reverdy Johnson, "Speech on Grant and the Ku Klux Bill," *Charleston Daily Courier*, 6 November 1871; "Reverdy Johnson," Dielman-Hayward Files, MHS.

38. Steiner, *Reverdy Johnson*, p. 37; Hugh Bond to Anna Bond, 26, 28 November 1871, Bond Papers, MHS; "In Memoriam: Reverdy Johnson," in *Proceedings of the Bench and Bar of the Supreme Court of the United States* (Washington, D.C.: Joseph L. Pearson, 1876).

39. *Biographical Encyclopedia of Ohio of the Nineteenth Century* (Cincinnati: Galaxy Publishing Co., 1876), pp. 433–34; Henry Stanbery, "Speech at the Great Democratic Banquet in the City of Washington, 8 January, 1868," in *An Appeal to the Senate to Modify Its Policy, and Save from Africanization and Military Despotism the States of the South* (Washington, D.C.: Democratic Executive Committee, 1868).

40. *Biographical Directory of South Carolina Senate*, 2 vols. (Columbia: University of South Carolina Press, 1986), 1:327–30.

41. Akerman to D. T. Corbin, 23 November 1871, Department of Justice, Letters Sent by the Department of Justice, Instructions to United States Attorneys and Marshals, Book C, RG 60, NA (hereafter cited as Instruction Book); Akerman to D. T Corbin, 6 December 1871, Akerman Papers, UVA.

42. For biographical information on Chamberlain see Chapter 1.

43. The *New York Times, New York Herald Tribune*, and *Chicago Tribune* all carried the trial story throughout this court session. Quotations from *Charleston Daily Courier*, 27, 29 November 1871, 6 January 1872.

44. Minute Book, pp. 510–12; *KKK Reports*, 5:1615–17; *Charleston Daily Courier*, 29 November 1871.

45. Minute Book, pp. 510–12; *KKK Reports*, 5:1615–17; Hugh Bond to Anna Bond, 26 November 1871; *Charleston Daily Courier*, 29 November 1871.

46. Corbin cited a case, *Clair v. the State*, in which the Supreme Court ordered a new trial on the grounds that the jury was chosen incorrectly (*KKK Reports*, 5:1616; Minute Book, pp. 512–13).

47. *KKK Reports*, 5:1617–19; Minute Book, pp. 513–15; Hall, "Political Power," p. 938.

48. Hall, "Political Power," p. 938; Minute Book, pp. 515–16.

49. *Charleston Daily Courier*, 19 December 1871; Hugh Bond to Anna Bond, 14 April 1872, Bond Papers, MHS. On the attitude of white Southerners toward blacks in the courts, see, for example, Eli H. Baxter to A. B. Springs, 14 May 1867, Springs Family Papers, and Edward Lipscomb to Smith and Sally Lipscomb, 30 June 1869, Lipscomb Family Papers, both in SHC.

Chapter 4: The Constitution and the Klan on Trial

1. Thirteenth Amendment arguments were not included in the prosecution's efforts or in the remarks of the judges.

2. The first group of Klan trials in November 1871–January 1872 was reported verbatim in *KKK Reports*, 5:1615–1990. The trial record is also in *Proceedings*.

The following criminal court records have also survived: Minute Book; U.S. Circuit Court, District of South Carolina, Sessions Index, 1866–1912 (Accession 52A155 No. 212), and 174 Case Files, U.S. Circuit Court Criminal Cases, 1874–1911 (Accession 52A155 Box No. 01). These materials are at the National Archives Regional Branch in East Point, Georgia.

3. *Proceedings*, p. 420.

4. Akerman to Corbin, 10 November 1871, Instruction Book C; Corbin to Akerman, 13, 17 November 1871, SCF, S.C.

5. 25 Federal Cases 701 (1871). Six other men were indicted along with Crosby. The indictment is printed in *Proceedings*, pp. 825–32.

6. Corbin to A. T. Akerman, 3 December 1871, SCF, S.C.; *KKK Reports* 3:1637.

7. Corbin to A. T. Akerman, 17 November 1871, SCF, S.C.

8. Ibid.; Corbin to Akerman, 13 November 1871, SCF, S.C. Other federal prosecuting attorneys in the South shared Corbin's nationalistic view of the Fourteenth Amendment. See Kaczorowski, *Politics of Judicial Interpretation*, passim.

9. *U.S. Statutes at Large*, 16:141.

10. Criminal Case Records, S.C., roll number 105 and 131; *KKK Reports*, 5:1577–78.

11. Corbin to A. T. Akerman, 13 November 1871, SCF, S.C. For an argument that Congress intended the Fourteenth Amendment to secure the right to bear arms to the former slaves, see Cottrol and Diamond, "Second Amendment," pp. 343–46.

12. Corbin to A. T. Akerman, 13 November 1871, SCF, S.C.; Akerman to John A. Minnis, 16 August 1871, Instruction Book B–1, Akerman to D. T. Corbin, 16 November 1871, Instruction Book C.

13. Federal prosecutors managed to convict in North Carolina, but the trials did not become the showcase for constitutional experimentation that the South Carolina trials would prove to be. The North Carolina indictments contained three counts. The federal grand jury in North Carolina indicted the KKK members for conspiring "by intimidation and force" to violate the first section of the Enforcement Act of 31 May 1871. Other counts charged the defendants with beating a specific black citizen to prevent his voting in future elections and because he had voted in previous elections (U.S. Circuit Court, Eastern District of North Carolina, Minute Docket of Criminal Proceedings, 1867–78, p. 230; U.S. Circuit Court, Eastern District of North Carolina, Criminal Case Files, 1866–92, Case number 106, *U.S. v. Randolph Shotwell*, NA, East Point, Georgia). Another indictment that was not used in a trial contained considerable experimentation on constitutional issues. See Case File number 106.

14. Criminal Case Files, S.C., roll number 172, NA, East Point, Georgia. Indictment is reprinted in *Proceedings*, pp. 825–32. For Corbin's argument on the

eleventh count see *Proceedings*, p. 121; see also Corbin to Akerman, 13 November 1871, SCF, S.C.; Hall, "Political Power," 929–30.

15. *KKK Reports*, 3:1645; *Proceedings*, pp. 831–32.

16. *Proceedings*, pp. 65, 826–31; *U.S. Statutes at Large*, 16:141; Corbin to Akerman, 13 November 1871, SCF, S.C.

17. *Proceedings*, p. 831.

18. Corbin to Akerman, 3 December 1871, SCF, S.C.

19. *Proceedings*, pp. 16–33, 68–78.

20. See *Barron v. Baltimore*, 7 Peters 243 (1833).

21. *Proceedings*, pp. 30–31.

22. Ibid. and pp. 79–83. Stanbery's argument was absurd because the primary thrust of many of the Klan raids had been to convince Republicans, both black and white, that they must no longer vote the Radical ticket.

23. *Proceedings*, pp. 24–27.

24. Johnson stated that the Thirteenth Amendment gave the former slaves "every right . . . belonging to a freeman," but he failed to address the problem of what rights accompany freedom (*Proceedings*, p. 71). On this point see also Kaczorowski, *Politics of Judicial Interpretation*, pp. 124–25.

25. *Proceedings*, pp. 73–77.

26. Ibid., pp. 79–83. The defense attorneys insisted throughout the trials that the government was attempting to try the defendants for ordinary crimes. The common law crimes were included in the indictments, under the provisions of the Enforcement Act of 1870, as a measure of punishment for the Klan conspiracy against the political rights of the victims.

27. Ibid., pp. 83–88.

28. Ibid., pp. 54–56.

29. Ibid., pp. 56–57.

30. Ibid., pp. 34–58.

31. Ibid., pp. 58–67. Although the trial record is printed in both the *KKK Reports*, vol. 5, and the *Proceedings*, Corbin's arguments on the motion to quash are not included in the *KKK Reports*.

32. *Proceedings*, pp. 61–66.

33. Ibid.

34. Ibid., pp. 63–67.

35. See *Proceedings*, pp. 794–96.

36. For an analysis of Judge Bond's constitutional scruples on civil rights enforcement see Hall and Williams, "Constitutional Tradition," pp. 43–58. For a conflicting opinion see Kaczorowski, *Politics of Judicial Interpretation*, pp. 127–29.

37. *Proceedings*, p. 90.

38. Ibid.

39. Ibid., p. 91. Bond's decision in another important Reconstruction case sheds more light on his understanding of the state-action concept. In *U.S. v. Petersburg Judges of Elections*, 27 Federal Cases 506 (1874), he noted that no way had been devised to punish states for obstructing voters. Therefore, the national government was forced to rely on punishing individuals guilty of crimes against civil rights.

40. Bond indicated, however, that *someone* should take responsibility for hanging the Klansmen who had perpetrated the crime (Hugh Bond to Anna Bond, n.d., Bond Papers, MHS).

41. *Proceedings*, pp. 91–92.

42. See Michael Les Benedict, "Preserving the Constitution: The Conservative Basis of Radical Reconstruction," *Journal of American History* 61 (June 1974): 76–77.

43. Ibid. For an excellent discussion of the Supreme Court's adherence to traditional dual federalism see Michael Les Benedict, "Preserving Federalism: Reconstruction and the Waite Court," *Supreme Court Review* (Chicago: University of Chicago Press, 1979), pp. 39–79.

44. *Proceedings*, p. 92.

45. *Proceedings*, pp. 95–111; Hall, "Political Power," pp. 938–40.

46. For the facts of the *Avery* case see the discussion of *U.S. v. Robert Hayes Mitchell* below. *Proceedings*, pp. 109–12, 140–42; *U.S. v. James W. Avery*, 13 Wall 251 (1871).

47. 26 Federal Cases 1283 (1871). The verbatim trial report is in *Proceedings*, pp. 146–459.

48. *Proceedings*, pp. 139–43; Minute Book, pp. 525–27, 530–31. The more influential leaders of the Klan in York County, including James W. Avery, J. Rufus Bratton, John Bratton, and the two sons of "Squire" Samuel Brown were included in the indictment with the murder count. Most of those indicted for murder had fled and were thus unavailable for trial.

49. *Proceedings*, pp. 146–54. Historians are divided on the meaning of the Second Amendment. For an argument that the amendment was intended to guarantee a sound militia see Lawrence D. Cress, "An Armed Community: The Origins and Meaning of the Right to Bear Arms," *Journal of American History* 71 (1984): 22–42. For the argument that the amendment guarantees an individual the right to bear arms see Robert E. Shalhope, "The Ideological Origins of the Second Amendment," *Journal of American History* 69 (December 1982): 599–614, and Stephen P. Halbrook, *That Every Man Be Armed: The Evolution of a Constitutional Right* (Albuquerque: University of New Mexico Press, 1985). For a combination of the two arguments see David T. Hardy, "The Second Amendment and the Historiography of the Bill of Rights," *Journal of Law and Politics* 4(1987): 1–62. See also Cottrol and Diamond, "Second Amendment," pp. 343–46.

50. *Proceedings*, pp. 146–544; 13 Wall 251 (1871).

51. *KKK Reports*, 3:1657, 1670. Corbin resurrected the Second Amendment charge in the April 1872 session of the circuit court. See below, Chapter 5.

52. *Proceedings*, pp. 449–51.

53. It is unclear from the record whether Jim Williams, alias Rainey, was related to Amzi Rainey, the victim of the Klan attack in *U.S. v. Allen Crosby*. Amzi Rainey was not murdered.

54. See, for example, *Proceedings*, pp. 339, 343, 346–47, 371, 351, 359–61, Corbin on p. 325.

55. Ibid., pp. 247, 249, 389–92; on Mitchell's role in the outrage see pp. 457–59. For an analysis of the party that followed the murder, see Lacy K. Ford, Jr., "One Southern Profile: Modernization and the Development of White Terror in York County, 1856–1876" (Master's thesis, University of South Carolina, 1976), pp. i–iii.

56. Constitution and by-laws in *Proceedings*, pp. 175–76.

57. *Proceedings*, pp. 432–33.

58. Ibid., pp. 178, 203, 283–84.

59. Ibid., pp. 244–49, 257–67, 277–78.

60. Ibid., pp. 231, 290–91. Arson was very common in upcountry South Carolina. The evidence is so convoluted it is difficult to ascertain exactly when the fires started and who burned what. Basically, however, the freedmen attacked property of whites (barns, gin houses) to retaliate for outrages committed against blacks. Many fires followed the various Ku Klux Klan outrages. The *Yorkville Enquirer* on one occasion (16 February 1871) actually admitted that Klan outrages had preceded black arson. White arson focused on any means the blacks had of getting ahead; black schools and churches were a favorite target. On arson as a weapon of retaliation of the powerless see Albert C. Smith, "Southern Violence Reconsidered: Arson as Protest in Black-Belt Georgia, 1865–1910," *Journal of Southern History* 51 (November 1985): 527–64. On the difference between black and white arson see Magdol, *Right to the Land*, pp. 129–30.

61. *Proceedings*, pp. 302, 306, 311–12, 342–43, 346–47, 405, 413.

62. Ibid., pp. 399–401, 412–15.

63. Ibid., pp. 413–15. The government was trying desperately to get Dr. Bratton, who had escaped to London, Ontario. U.S. government agents kidnapped Bratton when Canadian officials refused to extradite him. The Canadian government sharply protested the action, however, and the United States returned the suspect (Louis F. Post, "A 'Carpetbagger' in South Carolina," *Journal of Negro History* 10 [January 1925]: 40–79). After a five-year exile Bratton was pardoned by Rutherford B. Hayes and allowed to return to South Carolina.

64. *Proceedings*, pp. 399–400, 405–6, 414–15.

65. Ibid., pp. 405–6.

66. Ibid., pp. 151, 425–26.

67. For a list of jurors by race and place of residence see Minute Book, p. 532.

68. *Proceedings*, pp. 427–29.

69. Ibid., pp. 430–31.

70. Ibid., pp. 432–43.

71. Ibid., pp. 444–45.

72. Ibid., pp. 448–49.

73. Ibid., p. 451.

74. Ibid.

75. When he was sentenced, Mitchell declared that he would have pleaded guilty, but his attorney would not let him.

Chapter 5: The Ku Klux Klan in Court

1. *Proceedings*, passim.

2. For the trial see ibid., pp. 460–606; explanation of indictment on pp. 586–87. See also Hugh Bond to Anna Bond, 18 December 1871, Bond Papers, MHS. This is a different Mitchell from the person tried in *U.S. v. Robert Hayes Mitchell*.

3. *Proceedings*, pp. 473–74, 480, 496, 510, 516.

4. Ibid., pp. 501–11.

5. See, for example, *Charleston Daily Courier*, 2, 11, 29 November, 14, 15, 21, 22 December 1871.

6. *Proceedings*, pp. 481, 487, 489, 498, 507–8. National newspapers followed the Klan trials carefully; both the *New York Times* and *Chicago Tribune*, for example, featured daily coverage of the South Carolina trials through December 1871.

7. *Proceedings*, pp. 593–94.

8. Ibid., pp. 585–87.

9. *New York World*, 26 December 1871, as quoted in *Charleston Daily Courier*, 4 January 1872; see also *Charleston Daily Courier*, 22 December 1871.

10. *Proceedings*, pp. 477, 480, 490–92, 520.

11. Ibid., pp. 563, 580.

12. Ibid., pp. 518, 522–24, 530–56, 580. On cross-examination the witnesses lacked such accurate recall about other Klan atrocities.

13. Ibid., pp. 480, 491–92, 572, 575–76, 600.

14. Ibid., pp. 480, 572; Ben Pitman to A. T. Akerman, 29 December 1871, SCF, S.C.

15. *Proceedings*, pp. 593–94.

16. For the trial record see ibid., pp. 607–53.

17. The indictment is reprinted in *KKK Reports*, 5:1919–20; *Proceedings*, pp. 608, 628.

18. *Proceedings*, pp. 615–16, 623, 638.

19. Ibid., pp. 610, 619, 623, 635.

20. Ibid., p. 645.

21. Leonard Levy, *Origins of the Fifth Amendment: The Right Against Self-Incrimination* (New York: Oxford University Press, 1968), pp. 375–76, 405–7; David M. Gold, "The Defendant Takes the Stand," in *The Shaping of Nineteenth-Century Law: John Appleton and Responsible Individualism* (New York: Greenwood Press, 1990), pp. 60–66. The *Charleston Daily Courier*, 23 April 1872, complained that Judge Bond refused to allow defendants to testify. The convicted Klansmen were allowed to make "mitigating" statements to the judges before sentencing.

22. *Proceedings*, pp. 526–29.

23. Ibid., pp. 641–43. A witness for the prosecution also referred to the raid on Millar's place; see p. 625.

24. Ibid., pp. 643–44. For an interview with another Klansman who had received a whipping at the hands of the Klan and decided to join "so that I could live in peace," see *New York Times*, 11 November 1871.

25. *Proceedings*, pp. 611–13.

26. Ibid., pp. 628–31, 635–38.

27. Ibid., pp. 644–46, 649–51.

28. The trial is in ibid., pp. 654–763. Although the last name is identical to that in *U.S. v. James W. Avery*, the Klan case previously certified to the Supreme Court on a division of opinion, this is a different defendant.

29. *Proceedings*, pp. 654–72.

30. Ibid., pp. 672–86.

31. Ibid., pp. 689–91.

32. Ibid., pp. 692–93.

33. Ibid., pp. 695–99. See also U.S. Circuit Court, District of South Carolina, Criminal Case Files, number 156.

34. *Proceedings*, pp. 692–99; affidavit on p. 695. See also testimony of Rev. Cooper, p. 710. The black women testified that they had been in and out of the bedroom during the night to attend Avery's baby, who was sick. Their testimony differed, however, on the nature of the infant's distress; cf. pp. 717 and 726.

35. Ibid., p. 748. Mrs. Mary Avery, Robert E. Cooper, and the servants, Louisa Chambers and Kitty Avery, were all charged with conspiracy to prevent Postle from testifying in the case and to obstruct justice. The indictment is in the Criminal Case Files, number 156.

36. *Proceedings*, pp. 729–31, 688, 690–91.

37. Ibid., pp. 748–63. See also Minute Book, pp. 558–59, 573.

38. The proceedings against McMaster are included verbatim in the appendixes to *Proceedings*, pp. 799–812. The decision of the court, however, is missing.

39. *Charleston Daily Courier*, 8 January 1872. The Minute Book lists the trial, p. 566, but does not indicate a verdict. McMasters ran for Congress on the "Straight-out" Democratic ticket in 1884. See McMasters's scrapbook in F. W. McMasters Papers, SCL.

40. Williams replaced Akerman, who resigned in December 1871.

41. F. W. McMaster to G. H. Williams, 11 June 1873, Affidavit of J. P. Castor and J. J. Steele, n.d., Corbin to G. H. Williams, 26 April 1873, all in SCF, S.C. For disposal of the case and all the other Klan cases, see U.S. Circuit Court, District of South Carolina, Sessions Index.

42. Hugh Bond to Anna Bond, 26 November, 18 December 1871, Bond Papers, MHS; grand jury charge in *Proceedings*, p. 12; jury charge in *U.S. v. R. H. Mitchell*, ibid., pp. 449–51.

43. Guilty pleas in *Proceedings*, pp. 110–11, 764–87; Returns for the Annual Report of the Attorney General, District of South Carolina, 6 January 1872, SCF, S.C.; Akerman to Corbin, 15 December 1871, 1 January 1872, both in Akerman Papers, UVA.

44. 13 Wall 251 (1871). See Chapter 4 above.

45. Certificate of Division is in Supreme Court Appellate Case Files, case number 6161, NA.

46. See, for example, Benedict, "Preserving the Constitution," pp. 65–90; Donald G. Nieman, *Promises to Keep: African-Americans and the Constitutional Order, 1776 to the Present* (New York: Oxford University Press, 1991), pp. 82–83, 89–93.

47. Akerman to D. T. Corbin, 15 December 1871, Akerman to Lewis Merrill, 8 January 1872, both in Akerman Papers, UVA; *New York Times*, 14 December 1871; McFeely, "Amos T. Akerman," p. 409.

48. Benjamin B. Kendrick, ed., *Journal of the Joint Committee of Fifteen on Reconstruction* (1914; reprint, New York: Negro Universities Press, 1969), pp. 191–92; *U.S. v. Benjamin B. Rosenberg*, 7 Wall 580 (1869).

49. *U.S. v. James W. Avery*, 13 Wall 251 (1872). See also Charles Fairman, *Reconstruction and Reunion, 1864–88*, 2 vols. (New York: Macmillan, 1987), 2:211–13. The Supreme Court may well have followed precedent without Williams's recommendation.

50. *Proceedings*, pp. 794–95.

51. Ibid., pp. 797–98.

52. *U.S. Statutes at Large*, 14:385; *U.S. Statutes at Large*, 15:44.

53. Fairman, *Reconstruction and Reunion*, 1:581–83, 2:213–14.

54. Ibid., 2:214–15. The Supreme Court accepted this argument when Stanbery made it again in *U.S. v. Reese*, 92 U.S. 214 (1876).

55. Fairman, *Reconstruction and Reunion*, 2:216–17.

56. Hugh Bond to Anna Bond, 14 April 1872, Bond Papers, MHS.

57. Fairman, *Reconstruction and Reunion*, 2:217–20.

58. Corbin to A. T. Akerman, 3 November 1871, Corbin to G. H. Williams, 20 February 1871, Corbin to G. H. Williams, 22 November 1872, all in SCF, S.C.

59. Lewis Merrill to G. H. Williams, 30 September 1872, Corbin to G. H. Williams, 22 November 1872, both in SCF, S.C.

60. W. H. Brown to R. M. Wallace, 13 April 1872, Corbin to G. H. Williams, 1 June 1872, ibid.

61. Corbin to A. T. Akerman, 3 December 1871. Both Avery and Bratton were indicted in the case, which was certified to the Supreme Court on a division of opinion, *U.S. v. James W. Avery, et al.*, 13 Wall 251 (1872). On the government's efforts to trace Avery and Bratton see Lewis Merrill to A. T. Akerman, 8 December 1871, and Lewis Merrill to Adjutant General, 11 July 1872, SCF, S.C.

62. For information on the Canadian perception of Bratton's case see *Statement of Dr. Bratton's Case*, pp. 3–18.

63. Post, "A 'Carpetbagger' in South Carolina," pp. 60–61; Fred Landon, "The Kidnapping of Dr. Rufus Bratton," *Journal of Negro History* 10 (July 1925): 330–33; *Statement of Dr. Bratton's Case*, pp. 3, 18. Bratton remained in Canada for several years as a practicing physician. His wife and friends in South Carolina continued during his absence to work for his freedom. He was eventually pardoned by President Rutherford Hayes, whereupon he returned to South Carolina (J. R. Bratton to Dear Brother, 20 April 1875, Mrs. J. R. Bratton to D. T. Corbin, 25 August 1873, both in Bratton Family Papers, SCL).

64. *Charleston Daily Courier*, 6, 8, 9 January 1872.

65. Ibid., 4, 6, 12 April 1872; G.I.C. to William Porcher Miles, 4 April 1872, Miles Papers, SHC.

66. Hugh Bond to Anna Bond, 11, 14 April 1872, Bond Papers, MHS; *Charleston Daily Courier*, 11, 12, 13 April 1872. See also Criminal Docket, United States Circuit Court for South Carolina, April Term 1872, in SCF, S.C.

67. Although there is no verbatim report of the Klan trials after the November 1871 term, the *Charleston Courier* (despite its partisan editorial comment) provided extensive coverage. Corbin had persuaded Attorney General Williams to hire a stenographer, but the man chosen was "incapacitated since here from drink," and Corbin had to fire him. See Corbin to J. Falls, 18 April 1872, SCF, S.C.

68. *Proceedings*, pp. 505–7.

69. *Charleston Daily Courier*, 20, 26 April 1872; U.S. Circuit Court, District of South Carolina, Criminal Case Files, number 30; *U.S. v. Elijah Ross Sapaugh*, Supreme Court Appellate Case Files, number 6482, NA. See also Criminal Case Docket, District of South Carolina, April Term 1872, SCF, S.C.; *Charleston Daily Courier*, 16, 17, 18, 19, 27 April 1872.

70. *Charleston Daily Courier*, 20 April 1872.

71. Ibid.

72. Ibid.; Criminal Docket, United States Circuit Court for South Carolina, April Term 1872, SCF, S.C.

73. *Charleston Daily Courier*, 6 January, 16, 17, 18, 19, 27 April 1872; Criminal Case Docket, District of South Carolina, April Term 1872, and Corbin to George Williams, 15 December 1872, SCF, S.C.

74. Corbin to George Williams, 22 July, 22 November 1872, Merrill to Adjutant General, 11 July 1872, all in SCF, S.C.

75. Hugh Bond to Anna Bond, 18 April 1872, 18 December 1871, Bond Papers, MHS.

76. Corbin to George Williams, 15 December 1872, SCF, S.C.

77. Motion in Arrest of Judgment in U.S. Circuit Court, District of South Carolina, Criminal Case Files, number 30.

78. Williams to Corbin, 26 September, 29 October 1874, Instruction Book E; Corbin to Williams, 16 December 1874, SCF, S.C.

Chapter 6: Sentencing and the End of Reconstruction

1. Hugh Bond to Anna Bond, 14 June 1871, Bond Papers, MHS.

2. "Objections to the New Constitution of South Carolina," in Walter L. Fleming, ed., *Documentary History of Reconstruction*, 2 vols. (Cleveland: Arthur H. Clark, 1906–7) 1:456.

3. On this point see John P. Frank and Robert J. Munro, "The Original Understanding of 'Equal Protection of the Laws,'" *Columbia Law Review* 50 (February 1950): 131–69; Harold M. Hyman and William M. Wiecek, *Equal Justice Under Law: Constitutional Development, 1835–1875* (New York: Harper Torchbooks, 1982), pp. 335–515.

4. B. H. Bristow to D. H. Starbuck, 2 October 1871, Instruction Book B; *Charleston Daily Courier*, 24 October 1871, quoting *New York Sun*, n.d.

5. *New York Times*, 30 October 1871, quoting *Columbia* (S.C.) *Phoenix*, 26 October 1871.

6. Confessions and sentences are in *Proceedings*, pp. 764–91; quotations on pp. 772, 773, 775, 799.

7. Ibid., pp. 791, 771, 785, 788.

8. Ibid., pp. 789–91.

9. *U.S. Statutes at Large*, 16:141.

10. See *Proceedings*, pp. 764–91; Minute Book, pp. 84–85, 87–88.

11. Sentences for those who confessed are in *Proceedings*, pp. 764–87.

12. Ibid., pp. 786–87.

13. Ibid., pp. 767–68; *New York Tribune*, 23 November 1871. A clipping from the *Paris* (Texas) *News*, 6 September 1933, titled "Backward Glances," impli-

cated Brown as a behind-the-scenes Klan leader. Worth Duncan related that Brown asked him to deliver a Winchester cartridge to J. Banks Lyle, who was allegedly the highest Klan official in South Carolina. Within a few days the Battle of Turkey Creek Bridge was fought between the Klan and some black militia. Lyle left South Carolina to avoid prosecution and lived for many years in Texas, where he ran a school. He had run a classical school in South Carolina before the Civil War (Clipping in J. Banks Lyle Papers, SCL).

14. *Proceedings*, pp. 767–68.

15. Ibid., p. 768.

16. Randolph Abbott Shotwell, *The Papers of Randolph Abbott Shotwell*, ed. J. G. de Roulhac Hamilton, 3 vols. (Raleigh: North Carolina Historical Commission, 1936), 3:326–29.

17. Ibid.; *Proceedings*, pp. 767–68.

18. Shotwell, *Papers*, pp. 248–49, 326–32, 349–50, 384. Shotwell reported that Brown's congressman, A. S. Wallace, had suggested that Brown should be released only on the condition that he reveal the whereabouts of his two sons in exile and arrange for them to exchange places with him.

19. *Proceedings*, pp. 789–90.

20. Ibid., pp. 789–91. For a discussion of the role of dehumanization of the victim in fostering violence see Herbert C. Kelman, "Violence Without Moral Restraint," in *Varieties of Psycho History*, ed. George M. Kren and Leon H. Rapporport (New York: Springer, 1976), pp. 282–314.

21. Hugh Bond to Anna Bond, 9 February 1871, Bond Papers, MHS; *Proceedings*, pp. 774, 782, and passim; Baker, *Politics of Continuity*, pp. 183–84.

22. *Proceedings*, pp. 457–59.

23. Ibid., pp. 603–6.

24. Ibid., pp. 651–53.

25. D. T. Corbin to G. H. Williams, 26 April 1873, SCF, S.C.

26. Minute Book, pp. 53–54, 80, 84–85, 87–89. Robert Hayes Mitchell testified that Riggins was a Klan chief. See *Proceedings*, p. 457.

27. Returns for the Annual Report of the Attorney General, 1871–72, SCF, S.C.; Williams to D. T. Corbin, 7 December 1872, Instruction Book C, pp. 535–36.

28. Lewis Merrill to George Williams, 30 September 1872, SCF, S. C.

29. Williams to A. J. Evans, 16 April 1873, Instruction Book C, p. 696. President Grant began around the same time to pardon those Klansmen who were already serving sentences. See Kaczorowski, *Politics of Judicial Interpretation*, pp. 111–12.

30. Williams to Virgil S. Lusk, 21 June 1873, quoted in Kaczorowski, *Politics of Judicial Interpretation*, p. 111; Williams to V. S. Lusk, 25 April 1874, Instruction Book D, p. 511.

31. Williams to A. J. Evans, 16 April 1873, Instruction Book C. On the effort to economize see, for example, Williams to R. M. Wallace, 27 August 1872, and Williams to D. T. Corbin, 29 August 1872, ibid., pp. 438–39, 440–41.

32. Williams allegedly used government funds to purchase a handsome carriage, complete with horses and liveried servants. See Sidney Teiser, "Life of George H. Williams: Almost Chief-Justice," *Oregon Historical Quarterly* 47 (December 1946): 421–29, Everette Swinney, "Enforcing the Fifteenth Amendment, 1870–1877," *Journal of Southern History* 28 (May 1962): 206–7.

33. See, for example, Williams to Corbin, 9 November 1872, Instruction Book C, p. 575, and Williams to Corbin, 23 April 1872, Instruction Book D, p. 2; W. D. Parker, J. B. Kershaw, and R. M. Sims to George H. Williams, 30 July 1873, SCF, S.C. General J. B. Kershaw, a leading South Carolina Democrat who visited Grant and persuaded him to adopt a policy of forgiveness, was reportedly the Grand Cyclops of the Ku Klux Klan in South Carolina in 1874. See J. C. Winnsmith to U. S. Grant, 5 October 1874, SCF, S.C; Kaczorowski, *Politics of Judicial Interpretation*, pp. 110–13; William Gillette, *Retreat from Reconstruction, 1869–1879* (Baton Rouge: Louisiana State University Press, 1979), pp. 36–37.

34. Lawanda Cox, "Reflections on the Limits of the Possible," in *Lincoln and Black Freedom: A Study in Presidential Leadership* (Urbana: University of Illinois Press, 1985), pp. 156–69.

35. R. M. Wallace to George H. Williams, 3 September 1874, L. C. Carpenter to U. S. Grant, 26 August, 4 September 1874, J. C. Winnsmith to U. S. Grant, 5 October 1874, Gov. T. J. Moses, Jr., to George H. Williams, 26 September 1874, all in SCF, S.C.

36. Williams to D. T. Corbin, 3 September 1874, Instruction Book C, pp. 13–14; Gillette, *Retreat from Reconstruction*, pp. 36–37.

37. Williams to G. Wiley Wells, 19 December 1874, Instruction Book E, p. 201.

38. Gillette, *Retreat from Reconstruction*, pp. 54–55, 370–71; Cox, "Reflections on the Possible," pp. 166–69.

39. Michael Perman, *The Road to Redemption: Southern Politics, 1869–1879* (Chapel Hill: University of North Carolina Press, 1984), pp. 169–70; Perman, "Counter Reconstruction: The Role of Violence in Southern Redemption," in *The Facts of Reconstruction: Essays in Honor of John Hope Franklin*, ed. Eric Anderson and Alfred A. Moss, Jr. (Baton Rouge: Louisiana State University Press, 1991), pp. 132–33.

40. George Brown Tindall, *South Carolina Negroes, 1877–1900* (Columbia: University of South Carolina Press, 1952), pp. 19–22; William J. Cooper, Jr., *The Conservative Regime: South Carolina, 1877–1890* (Baltimore: Johns Hopkins University Press, 1968), p. 28; George C. Rable, *But There Was No Peace: The Role of Violence in the Politics of Reconstruction* (Athens: University of Georgia Press, 1984), pp. 163–77.

41. Hampton M. Jarrell, *Wade Hampton and the Negro: The Road Not Taken* (Columbia: University of South Carolina Press, 1950), pp. 158–73; Alfred B. Williams, *Hampton and His Redshirts: South Carolina's Deliverance in 1876* (Charleston: Walker, Evans & Cogswell, 1935), pp. 161–63.

42. See, for example, Reynolds, *Reconstruction in South Carolina*, pp. 344–47.

43. Benjamin R. Tillman, *The Struggles of '76: Address Delivered at the Red Shirt Reunion, Anderson, S.C., August 25th, 1909*, pp. 14, 28, pamphlet, SCL. Tillman claimed he had personally taken part in four race riots during the election of 1876. See also D. T. Corbin to Alphonso Taft, 9 October 1876, R. W. Wallace to A. Taft, 18 October 1876, D. H. Chamberlain to U. S. Grant, 11 October 1876, all in SCF, S.C., Reynolds, *Reconstruction in South Carolina*, pp. 344–47, 375–81; Williamson, *After Slavery*, pp. 268–72.

44. F. to J. H. Aycock, 21–22 September 1876, J. H. Aycock Papers, SCL. See also Tillman, *Struggles of '76*, pp. 56–67; Senate Miscellaneous Documents, 44th Cong., 2d sess., No. 48. For an excellent narrative account of the Ellenton riots see Rable, *But There Was No Peace*, pp. 173–77.

45. Perman, "Counter Reconstruction," p. 132; Tindall, *South Carolina Negroes*, p. 14; Williams, *Hampton and His Redshirts*, p. 365.

46. George Brown Tindall, *The Disruption of the Solid South* (New York: Norton, 1972), pp. 9–10; Vincent P. De Santis, *Republicans Face the Southern Question: The New Departure Years, 1877–1897* (Baltimore: Johns Hopkins Press, 1959), pp. 66–103; Robert M. Goldman, *"A Free Ballot and a Fair Count": The Department of Justice and the Enforcement of Voting Rights in the South, 1877–1893* (New York: Garland, 1990), p. 98. The classic, though much disputed, account of the Compromise of 1877 is C. Vann Woodward, *Reunion and Reaction: The Compromise of 1877 and the End of Reconstruction* (Boston: Little, Brown, 1951).

Chapter 7: Enforcement in the Supreme Court

1. *U.S. v. Hall*, 26 Federal Cases, 79–82 (1871). See also Kaczorowski, *Politics of Judicial Interpretation;* pp. 14–17.

2. 13 Wall 251 (1872); Supreme Court Appellate Case Files, file number 6482, NA. For discussion of these cases see Chapter 5 above.

3. 16 Wallace 36 (1873); Kaczorowski, *Politics of Judicial Interpretation*, p. 143.

4. Charles Fairman, *Mr. Justice Miller and the Supreme Court, 1862–1890* (Cambridge, Mass.: Harvard University Press, 1939), pp. 179–81.

5. 16 Wall 36 (1873), pp. 67, 71–83.

6. Ibid., pp. 96, 112–13, 129. The dissenting opinions of Field and Joseph Bradley also pointed the direction for future use of the amendment in the area of substantive due process and liberty of contract.

7. See Kaczorowski, *Politics of Judicial Interpretation*, pp. 150–66.

8. Loren Miller, *The Petitioners: The Story of the Supreme Court of the United States and the Negro* (New York: Pantheon Books, 1966), pp. 108–9; C. Peter Magrath, *Morrison R. Waite: The Triumph of Character* (New York: Macmillan, 1963), p. 120; Nieman, *Promises to Keep*, p. 95; Kaczorowski, *Politics of Judicial Interpretation*, pp. 175–76.

9. *U.S. v. Cruikshank*, 92 U.S. 542 (1876), pp. 542–43.

10. Bradley to Woods, 3 January 1871, quoted in Magrath, *Morrison R. Waite*, p. 121.

11. 16 Wallace 36 (1873), p. 122; Leon Friedman, "Joseph P. Bradley," in *The Justices of the United States Supreme Court, 1789–1969: Their Lives and Major Opinions*, 4 vols., ed. Leon Friedman and Fred L. Israel, (New York: Chelsea House, 1969), 2:1196–97. See also John Anthony Scott, "Justice Bradley's Evolving Concept of the Fourteenth Amendment from the Slaughterhouse Cases to the Civil Rights Cases," *Rutgers Law Review* 25 (Summer 1971): 552–69.

12. *U.S. v. Cruikshank*, 25 Federal Cases 707 (1874).

13. 25 Federal Cases 707 (1874), pp. 712–13; Scott, "Bradley's Evolving Concept of the Fourteenth Amendment," pp. 558–59; Kaczorowski, *Politics of Judicial Interpretation*, pp. 179–83.

14. George H. Williams and S. F. Phillips, Brief for the United States, *U.S. v. Cruikshank*, in *Landmark Briefs and Arguments of the Supreme Court of the United States: Constitutional Law*, ed. Philip B. Kurland and Gerhard Casper (Arlington, Va: University Publications of America, 1975), 7:290–91; see also Kaczorowski, *Politics of Judicial Interpretation*, pp. 206–7.

15. 7 Peters 243 (1833).

16. David S. Bryon, Brief for Defendants, *U.S. v. Cruikshank*, in *Landmark Briefs*, ed. Kurland and Casper, 7:316–42.

17. *U.S. v. Cruikshank*, 92 U.S. 542 (1875), pp. 549–54.

18. 92 U.S. 542 (1875), pp. 553–54. For an excellent analysis of *Cruikshank* see Kaczorowski, *Politics of Judicial Interpretation*, pp. 214–17.

19. Miller, *Petitioners*, pp. 111–12.

20. 92 U.S. 542 (1876), p. 556; *U.S. v. Reese*, 92 U.S. 214 (1876).

21. For background information on *Reese* see William Gillette, "Anatomy of a Failure: Federal Enforcement of the Right to Vote in the Border States During Reconstruction," in *Radicalism, Racism, and Party Realignment: The Border States During Reconstruction*, ed. Richard O. Curry, (Baltimore: Johns Hopkins Press, 1969), pp. 265–304.

22. 92 U.S. 214 (1876), pp. 216–21.

23. Ibid., pp. 242–43.

24. Nieman, *Promises to Keep*, pp. 98–99; Kaczorowski, *Politics of Judicial Enforcement*, p. 213.

25. The law had become section 5519 of the Revised Statutes in 1873.

26. *U.S. v. Harris*, 106 U.S. 629 (1883), pp. 638–39; Miller, *Petitioners*, pp. 113–14.

27. 109 U.S. 3 (1883). Only one of the cases was from the South, a railroad accommodations case from Memphis, Tennessee. The other cases were from New York, Kansas, Missouri, and California.

28. Bertram Wyatt-Brown, "The Civil Rights Act of 1875," *Western Political Quarterly* 18 (December 1965): 763–75; Belz, *Emancipation and Equal Rights*, pp. 134–35; John Hope Franklin, "Enforcement of the Civil Rights Act of 1875," *Prologue: Journal of the National Archives* 6 (Winter 1974): 225–35.

29. 109 U.S. 3 (1883), pp. 10–12.

30. Ibid., pp. 23–25.

31. Ibid., p. 43.

32. Ibid., pp. 46, 51–54, 61.

33. Fairman, *Reconstruction and Reunion*, 2:486–87.

34. 110 U.S. 651 (1884), pp. 657–58.

35. For information on federal enforcement efforts after Redemption see Goldman, *"A Free Ballot and a Fair Count"*; Nieman, *Promises to Keep*, pp. 100–101.

36. Cooper, *Conservative Regime*, p. 94; J. Morgan Kousser, *The Shaping of Southern Politics: Suffrage Restriction and the Establishment of the One-Party South, 1880–1910* (New Haven: Yale University Press, 1974), pp. 45–50, 84–91.

37. Davis, "Federal Enforcement Acts," p. 228.

38. Akerman to Benjamin Conley, 28 December 1871, Akerman Papers, UVA.

Bibliography

United States Government Records

Bureau of Refugees, Freedmen, and Abandoned Lands. Record Group 105. M869. Records of the Assistant Commissioner for the State of South Carolina, 1865–70. National Archives, Washington, D.C.

Department of Justice. Record Group 60. Letters Sent by the Department of Justice, Instructions to United States Attorneys and Marshals, Books A–G, 1870–77. National Archives, Washington, D.C.

Department of Justice. Record Group 60. M947. Source Chronological Files for South Carolina, Letters Received by the Department of Justice from South Carolina, 1871–84. National Archives, Washington, D.C.

Richardson, James D., ed. *A Compilation of the Messages and Papers of the Presidents.* Vol. 9. New York: Bureau of National Literature, 1897.

U.S. Circuit Court. District of South Carolina. Criminal Case Files. National Archives, East Point, Georgia.

————. Minute Book, 1869–72. National Archives, East Point, Georgia.

————. Sessions Index. National Archives, East Point, Georgia.

U. S. Circuit Court. Eastern District of North Carolina. Criminal Case Files, 1866–92. National Archives, East Point, Georgia.

————. Minute Docket of Criminal Proceedings, 1867–78. National Archives, East Point, Georgia.

U. S. Circuit Court. *Proceedings in the Ku Klux Trials at Columbia, S.C. in the United States Circuit Court, November Term, 1871.* 1872. Reprint, New York: Negro Universities Press, 1969.

U. S. Congress. *Report of the Joint Select Committee to Inquire into the Condition of Affairs in the Late Insurrectionary States.* 13 vols. Washington, D.C.: U.S. Government Printing Office, 1872.

U. S. Congress. Senate. *Journal of the Executive Proceedings.* Vol. 17. Washington, D.C.: U.S. Government Printing Office, 1901.

U. S. Statutes at Large. Vols. 16 and 17. 1871–73.

South Carolina State Records

Chief Constable John B. Hubbard Papers. South Carolina Department of Archives and History, Columbia, South Carolina.

Elections File, 1870. Green Files. South Carolina Department of Archives and History, Columbia, South Carolina.

General Assembly of South Carolina at the Regular Session, 1877–78. *Report of the Joint Investigating Committee on Public Frauds. Reports and Resolutions of the State of South Carolina, 1877–78.* 1878.

Governor Robert K. Scott Papers. South Carolina Department of Archives and History, Columbia, South Carolina.

Legislative System. Green Files. South Carolina Department of Archives and History, Columbia, South Carolina.

Military Affairs. Green Files. South Carolina Department of Archives and History, Columbia, South Carolina.

Cases

Civil Rights Cases, 103 U.S. 3 (1883).

Ex Parte T. Jefferson Greer, Supreme Court Appellate Case Files, number 6200 (1872), National Archives; Washington, D.C.

Ex Parte Yarbrough, 110 U.S. 651 (1883).

Slaughter House Cases, 16 Wallace 36 (1873).

U.S. v. J. W. Avery, 13 Wall 251 (1872).

U.S. v. Crosby, 25 Federal Cases 701 (1871).

U.S. v. Cruikshank, 25 Federal Cases 707 (1874).

U.S. v. Cruikshank, 92 U.S. 542 (1876).

U.S. v. Hall, 26 Federal Cases 79 (1871).

U.S. v. Harris, 106 U.S. 629 (1883).

U.S. v. Mitchell, 26 Federal Cases 1283 (1871).

U.S. v. Reese, 92 U.S. 214 (1876).

U.S. v. Benjamin B. Rosenberg, 7 Wall 580 (1869).

U.S. v. Elijah Ross Sapaugh, Supreme Court Appellate Case Files, number 6482 (1873), National Archives, Washington, D.C.

Manuscripts

Amos T. Akerman Papers. Alderman Library, University of Virginia, Charlottesville, Virginia.

J. H. Aycock Papers. South Caroliniana Library, University of South Carolina, Columbia, South Carolina.

Hugh Lennox Bond Papers. Maryland Historical Society, Baltimore, Maryland.

Bond-McCullogh Papers. Maryland Historical Society, Baltimore, Maryland.

Bratton Family Papers. South Caroliniana Library, University of South Carolina, Columbia, South Carolina.

Mary Davis Brown Diary. South Caroliniana Library, University of South Carolina, Columbia, South Carolina.

Conner Family Papers. South Carolina Historical Society, Charleston, South Carolina.

Everson Collection. South Carolina Historical Society, Charleston, South Carolina.

Hampton Family Papers. South Caroliniana Library, University of South Carolina, Columbia, South Carolina.

Wade Hampton Papers. Perkins Library, Duke University, Durham, North Carolina.

Iredell Jones Papers. Perkins Library, Duke University, Durham, North Carolina.

Iredell Jones Papers. South Caroliniana Library, University of South Carolina, Columbia, South Carolina.

Lipscomb Family Papers. Southern Historical Collection, University of North Carolina, Chapel Hill, North Carolina.

J. Banks Lyle Papers. South Caroliniana Library, University of South Carolina, Columbia, South Carolina.

F. W. McMasters Papers. South Caroliniana Library, University of South Carolina, Columbia, South Carolina.

William Porcher Miles Papers. Southern Historical Collection, University of North Carolina, Chapel Hill, North Carolina.

Lalla Pelot Papers. Perkins Library, Duke University, Durham, North Carolina.

Benjamin F. Perry Papers. Alabama Department of Archives and History, Montgomery, Alabama.

Benjamin F. Perry Papers. South Caroliniana Library, University of South Carolina, Columbia, South Carolina.

David Schenck Collection. Southern Historical Collection, University of North Carolina, Chapel Hill, North Carolina.

Robert K. Scott Papers. Ohio Historical Society, Columbus, Ohio.

William Dunlop Simpson Papers. Perkins Library, Duke University, Durham, North Carolina.

Springs Family Papers. Southern Historical Collection, University of North Carolina, Chapel Hill, North Carolina.

Wallace, Rice, Duncan Family Papers. South Caroliniana Library, University of South Carolina, Columbia, South Carolina.

Waties-Parker Family Papers. South Caroliniana Library, University of South Carolina, Columbia, South Carolina.

Other Primary Sources

Brooks, James, and Johnson, Reverdy. *A Correspondence Between the Hon. James Brooks of New York and the Hon. Reverdy Johnson of Baltimore on the State of the Country*. Baltimore: Sun Book and Job Office, 1872.

Campbell, James B. *Two Letters from the Hon. James B. Campbell on Public Affairs and Our Duties to the Colored Race Published by the Democratic Central Executive Committee of South Carolina*. Charleston: Walker, Evans & Cogswell, 1868.

Chamberlain, D. H. *Arguments of D. H. Chamberlain During the Ku Klux Trials at Columbia, S.C.* Columbia: Republican Printing Co., 1872.

————. *Present Phases of Our So-Called Negro Problem*. Open Letter to the Right Honorable James Bryce, M.P., of England, 27 August 1904. South Caroliniana Library, University of South Carolina, Columbia, South Carolina.

————. "Reconstruction and the Negro." *North American Review* 78 (February 1879): 161–73.

Corbin, David T. *Argument of Hon. D. T. Corbin in the Trial of the Ku-Klux Before the United States Circuit Court*. Washington, D.C.: Chronicle Publishing, 1872.

De Forest, John William. *A Union Officer in the Reconstruction*. Edited by James H. Croushore and David M. Potter. New Haven: Yale University Press, 1948.

[Fleming, Julius J.]. *The Juhl Letters to the Charleston Courier: A View of the South, 1865–1871*. Edited by John Hammond Moore. Athens: University of Georgia Press, 1974.

Fleming, Walter L., ed. *Documentary History of Reconstruction*. 2 vols. Cleveland: Arthur H. Clark, 1906–7.

Green, James. *Personal Recollections of Daniel Henry Chamberlain, Once Governor of South Carolina*. Worcester, Mass.: Worcester Antiquity Society, 1908.

"In Memoriam: Reverdy Johnson." In *Proceedings of the Bench and Bar of the Supreme Court of the United States*. Washington, D.C.: Joseph L. Pearson, 1876.

Johnson, Reverdy. *Speeches of Hon. Reverdy Johnson on the Military Reconstruction Bill*. Washington, D.C.: Congressional Globe Office, 1867.

————. "Speech on Grant and the Ku Klux Bill." *Charleston Daily Courier*, 6 November 1871.

Kurland, Philip B., and Gerhard Casper, eds. *Landmark Briefs and Arguments of the Supreme Court of the United States: Constitutional Law*. Arlington, Va.: University Publications of America, 1975.

Lathers, Richard. *South Carolina, Her Wrongs and the Remedy: Remarks of Col. Richard Lathers, Delivered at the Opening of the Taxpayers' Convention in Columbia, S.C., Tuesday, February 17, 1874*. Pamphlet. South Caroliniana Library, University of South Carolina, Columbia, South Carolina.

Leland, John A. *A Voice from South Carolina*. 1879. Reprint, Freeport, N.Y.: Books for Libraries Press, 1971.

Proceedings of the Colored People's Convention of the State of South Carolina. Charleston: South Carolina Leader, 1865.

Shotwell, Randolph Abbott. *The Papers of Randolph Abbott Shotwell.* Edited by J. G. de Roulhac Hamilton. 3 vols. Raleigh: North Carolina Historical Commission, 1936.

"The South Carolina Problem: The Epoch of Transition." *Scribner's Monthly,* June 1874, pp. 129–60.

Stanbery, Henry. "Speech at the Great Democratic Banquet in the City of Washington, 8 January 1868." In *An Appeal to the Senate to Modify Its Policy, and Save from Africanization and Military Despotism the States of the South.* Washington, D.C.: Democratic Executive Committee, 1868.

Statement of Dr. Bratton's Case, Being Explanatory of the Ku-Klux Prosecutions in the Southern States. London, Ontario: Free Press, 1872.

Tillman, Benjamin R. *The Struggles of '76: Address Delivered at the Red Shirt Reunion, Anderson, S.C., August 25th, 1909.* Pamphlet. South Caroliniana Library, University of South Carolina, Columbia, South Carolina.

Secondary Sources

BOOKS

Abbott, Richard H. *The Republican Party and the South, 1855–1877: The First Southern Strategy.* Chapel Hill: University of North Carolina Press, 1986.

Ayers, Edward. *Vengeance and Justice: Crime and Punishment in the Nineteenth Century South.* New York: Oxford University Press, 1984.

Baer, Judith A. *Equality Under the Constitution: Reclaiming the Fourteenth Amendment.* Ithaca, N.Y.: Cornell University Press, 1983.

Baker, Jean H. *The Politics of Continuity: Maryland Politics from 1858 to 1870.* Baltimore: Johns Hopkins University Press, 1973.

Belz, Herman. *Emancipation and Equal Rights: Politics and Constitutionalism in the Civil War Era.* New York: Norton, 1978.

Benedict, Michael Les. *A Compromise of Principle: Congressional Republicans and Reconstruciton, 1863–1869.* New York: Norton, 1974.

Berger, Raoul. *Government by Judiciary: The Transformation of the Fourteenth Amendment.* Cambridge, Mass.: Harvard University Press, 1977.

Blee, Kathleen M. *Women of the Klan: Racism and Gender in the 1920s.* Berkeley: University of California Press, 1991.

Bleser, Carol K. Rothrock. *The Promised Land: The History of the South Carolina Land Commission.* Columbia: University of South Carolina Press, 1969.

Brock, William R. *An American Crisis: Congress and Reconstruction, 1865–1867.* London: Macmillan, 1963.

Brooks, U. R. *South Carolina Bench and Bar*. Columbia, S.C.: State Company, 1908.

Brown, Richard Maxwell. *Strain of Violence: Historical Studies of Violence and Vigilantism*. New York: Oxford University Press, 1975.

Bychowski, Gustov. *Evil in Man: The Anatomy of Hate and Violence*. New York: Grune & Stratton, 1968.

Cash, W. J. *The Mind of the South*. New York: Knopf, 1941.

Channing, Steven A. *Crisis of Fear: Secession in South Carolina*. New York: Simon and Schuster, 1979.

Cooper, William J., Jr. *The Conservative Regime: South Carolina, 1877–1890*. Baltimore: Johns Hopkins University Press, 1968.

Cox, LaWanda, and John H. Cox. *Politics, Principle and Prejudice, 1865–1866*. Glencoe, Ill.: Free Press, 1963.

Cummings, Homer, and Carl McFarland. *Federal Justice: Chapters in the History of Justice and the Federal Executive*. New York: Macmillan, 1937.

Current, Richard N. *Those Terrible Carpetbaggers*. New York: Oxford University Press, 1988.

Curtis, Michael Kent. *No State Shall Abridge: The Fourteenth Amendment and the Bill of Rights*. Durham, N.C.: Duke University Press, 1986.

De Santis, Vincent P. *Republicans Face the Southern Question: The New Departure Years, 1877–1897*. Baltimore: Johns Hopkins Press, 1959.

Dunning, William Archibald. *Essays on the Civil War and Reconstruction and Related Topics*. Columbia, S.C.: State Publishers, 1905.

Fairman, Charles. *Mr. Justice Miller and the Supreme Court, 1862–1890*. Cambridge, Mass.: Harvard University Press, 1939.

———. *Reconstruction and Reunion, 1864–88*. 2 vols. New York: Macmillan, 1987.

Faust, Drew Gilpin. *The Ideology of Slavery: Proslavery Thought in the Antebellum South, 1839–1860*. Baton Rouge: Louisiana State University Press, 1981.

Fitzgerald, Michael W. *The Union League Movement in the Deep South: Politics and Agricultural Change During Reconstruction*. Baton Rouge: Louisiana State University Press, 1989.

Flack, Horace E. *The Adoption of the Fourteenth Amendment*. Baltimore: Johns Hopkins Press, 1908.

Foner, Eric. *Reconstruction: America's Unfinished Revolution, 1863–1877*. New York: Harper & Row, 1988.

Ford, Lacy K. *Origins of Southern Radicalism: The South Carolina Upcountry, 1800–1860*. New York: Oxford University Press, 1988.

Fox-Genovese, Elizabeth. *Within the Plantation Household: Black and White Women in the Old South*. Chapel Hill: University of North Carolina Press, 1988.

Franklin, John Hope. *The Militant South, 1800–1861*. Cambridge, Mass.: Belknap Press of Harvard University Press, 1956.

Friedman, Lawrence J. *The White Savage: Racial Fantasies in the Postbellum South*. Englewood Cliffs, N.J.: Prentice-Hall, 1970.

Friedman, Leon, and Fred L. Israel. *The Justices of the United States Supreme Court, 1789–1969: Their Lives and Major Opinions*. 4 vols. New York: Chelsea House, 1969.

Fry, Gladys-Marie. *Nightriders in Black Folk History*. Knoxville: University of Tennessee Press, 1975.

Genovese, Eugene. *Roll Jordon Roll: The World the Slaves Made*. New York: Random House, 1972.

Gillette, William. *Retreat from Reconstruction, 1869–1879*. Baton Rouge: Louisiana State University Press, 1979.

Goldman, Robert M. *"A Free Ballot and a Fair Count": The Department of Justice and the Enforcement of Voting Rights in the South, 1877–1893*. New York: Garland, 1990.

Graham, Howard J. *Everyman's Constitution: Historical Essays on the Fourteenth Amendment, the Conspiracy Theory, and American Constitutionalism*. Madison, Wisc.: State Historical Society, 1968.

Greenberg, Kenneth S. *Masters and Statesmen: The Political Culture of American Slavery*. Baltimore: Johns Hopkins University Press, 1985.

Griffin, Susan. *Rape: The Power of Consciousness*. San Francisco: Harper & Row, 1979.

Harris, Trudier. *Exorcising Blackness: Historical and Literary Lynching and Burning Rituals*. Bloomington: Indiana University Press, 1984.

Hindus, Michael S. *Prison and Plantation: Crime, Justice, and Authority in Massachusetts and South Carolina*. Chapel Hill: University of North Carolina Press, 1980.

Holt, Thomas. *Black over White: Negro Political Leadership in South Carolina During Reconstruction*. Urbana: University of Illinois Press, 1977.

Hyman, Harold M. *A More Perfect Union: The Impact of the Civil War and Reconstruction on the Constitution*. New York: Knopf, 1973.

Hyman, Harold M., and William M. Wiecek. *Equal Justice Under Law: Constitutional Development, 1835–1875*. New York: Harper Torchbooks, 1982.

Jarrell, Hampton M. *Wade Hampton and the Negro: The Road Not Taken*. Columbia: University of South Carolina Press, 1950.

Jordan, Winthrop D. *White over Black: American Attitudes Toward the Negro, 1550–1812*. Chapel Hill: University of North Carolina Press, 1968.

Kaczorowski, Robert J. *The Politics of Judicial Interpretation: The Federal Courts, the Department of Justice, and Civil Rights, 1866–1876*. New York: Oceana Press, 1985.

Kousser, J. Morgan. *The Shaping of Southern Politics: Suffrage Restriction and the Establishment of the One-Party South, 1880–1910*. New Haven: Yale University Press, 1974.

Lamson, Peggy. *The Glorious Failure: Black Congressman Robert Brown Elliott and the Reconstruction in South Carolina*. New York: Norton, 1973.

Levy, Leonard. *Origins of the Fifth Amendment: The Right Against Self-Incrimination*. New York: Oxford University Press, 1968.

Litwack, Leon F. *Been in the Storm So Long*. New York: Random House Vintage Books, 1980.

Magdol, Edward. *A Right to the Land: Essays on the Freedmen's Community*. Westport, Conn.: Greenwood Press, 1976.

Magrath, C. Peter. *Morrison R. Waite: The Triumph of Character*. New York: Macmillan, 1963.

McFeely, William S. *Grant: A Biography*. New York: Norton, 1981.

McPherson, James M. *The Struggle for Equality: Abolitionists and the Negro in Civil War and Reconstrution*. Princeton: Princeton University Press, 1964.

Miller, Loren. *The Petitioners: The Story of the Supreme Court of the United States and the Negro*. New York: Pantheon Books, 1966.

Nelson, William E. *The Fourteenth Amendment: From Political Principle to Judicial Doctrine*. Cambridge, Mass.: Harvard University Press, 1988.

Nieman, Donald G. *Promises to Keep: African-Americans and the Constitutional Order, 1776 to the Present*. New York: Oxford University Press, 1991.

Perman, Michael. *The Road to Redemption: Southern Politics, 1869–1879*. Chapel Hill: University of North Carolina Press, 1984.

Petty, Julian J. *The Growth and Distribution of Population in South Carolina*. Columbia: State Planning Board, 1943.

Rable, George C. *But There Was No Peace: The Role of Violence in the Politics of Reconstruction*. Athens: University of Georgia Press, 1984.

Randall, James G. *The Civil War and Reconstruction*. Boston: D. C. Heath, 1939.

Randall, James G., and David Donald. *The Civil War and Reconstruction*. 2d ed. Lexington, Mass.: D. C. Heath, 1969.

Reynolds, John S. *Reconstruction in South Carolina*. 1905. Reprint, New York: Negro Universities Press, 1969.

Rhodes, James Ford. *History of the United States, 1850–1909*. 9 vols. New York: Macmillan, 1906.

Roark, James L. *Masters Without Slaves: Southern Planters in the Civil War and Reconstruction*. New York: Norton, 1977.

Rose, Willie Lee. *Rehearsal for Reconstruction: The Port Royal Experiment*. New York: Oxford University Press, 1964.

Simkins, Francis B., and Robert H. Woody. *South Carolina During Reconstruction*. Chapel Hill: University of North Carolina Press, 1932.

Singletary, Otis A. *Negro Militia and Reconstruction*. 1957. Reprint, New York: McGraw-Hill, 1963.

Stampp, Kenneth M. *The Era of Reconstruction, 1865–1877*. New York: Random House, Vintage Books, 1965.

Steiner, Bernard C. *Life of Reverdy Johnson*. 1914. Reprint, New York: Russell & Russell, 1970.

Swinney, Everette. *Suppressing the Ku Klux Klan: The Enforcement of the Reconstruction Amendments*. New York: Garland, 1987.

Taylor, Alrutheus Ambush. *The Negro in South Carolina During the Reconstruction*. New York: AMS, 1971.

ten Broek, Jacobus. *The Antislavery Origins of the Fourteenth Amendment*. Berkeley: University of California Press, 1951.

Thompson, Henry W. *Ousting the Carpetbagger from South Carolina*. Columbia, S.C.: R. L. Bryan, 1926.

Tindall, George Brown. *The Disruption of the Solid South*. New York: Norton, 1972.

———. *South Carolina Negroes, 1877–1900*. Columbia: University of South Carolina Press, 1952.

Trelease, Allen W. *Reconstruction: The Great Experiment*. New York: Harper & Row, 1971.

———. *White Terror: The Ku Klux Klan Conspiracy and Southern Reconstruction*. New York: Harper & Row, 1971.

Williams, Alfred B. *Hampton and His Redshirts: South Carolina's Deliverance in 1876*. Charleston: Walker, Evans & Cogswell, 1935.

Williamson, Joel. *After Slavery: The Negro in South Carolina During Reconstruction, 1861–1877*. Chapel Hill: University of North Carolina Press, 1965.

———. *The Crucible of Race: Black-White Relations in the American South Since Emancipation*. New York: Oxford University Press, 1984.

Wood, Forrest G. *Black Scare: The Racist Response to Emancipation and Reconstruction*. Berkeley: University of California Press, 1970.

Woodward, C. Vann. *Reunion and Reaction: The Compromise of 1877 and the End of Reconstruction*. Boston: Little, Brown, 1951.

Wright, Gavin. *The Political Economy of the Cotton South: Households, Markets, and Wealth in the Nineteenth Century*. New York: Norton, 1978.

Wyatt-Brown, Bertram. *Southern Honor: Ethics and Behavior in the Old South*. New York: Oxford University Press, 1982.

ARTICLES

Avins, Alfred. "The Ku Klux Klan Act of 1871: Some Reflected Light on State Action and the Fourteenth Amendment." *St. Louis University Law Journal* 11 (Spring 1967): 331–83.

Belz, Herman. "The New Orthodoxy in Reconstruction Historiography." *Reviews in American History* 1 (March 1973): 106–13.

Benedict, Michael Les. "Laissez-Faire and Liberty: A Re-evaluation of the Meaning of Laissez-Faire Constitutionalism." *Law and History Review* 3 (1985): 293–331.

————. "Preserving Federalism: Reconstruction and the Waite Court." *Supreme Court Review*. Chicago: University of Chicago Press, 1978.

————. "Preserving the Constitution: The Conservative Basis of Radical Reconstruction." *Journal of American History* 61 (June 1974): 65–90.

————. "The Problem of Constitutionalism and Constitutional Liberty in the Reconstruction South." In *An Uncertain Tradition: Constitutionalism and the History of the South*. Edited by Kermit L. Hall and James W. Ely, Jr. Athens: University of Georgia Press, 1989.

Bickel, Alexander M. "The Original Understanding and the Segregation Decision." *Harvard Law Review* 69 (1955): 1049–86.

Cottrol, Robert J., and Raymond T. Diamond. "The Second Amendment: Toward an Afro-Americanist Reconsideration." *Georgetown Law Journal* 80 (December 1991): 308–61.

Cox, Lawanda. "Reflections on the Limits of the Possible." In Cox, *Lincoln and Black Freedom: A Study in Presidential Leadership*. Urbana: University of Illinois Press, 1985.

Davis, Natalie Z. "The Reasons of Misrule." In *Society and Culture in Early Modern France*. Stanford: Stanford University Press, 1975.

Davis, William Watson. "The Federal Enforcement Acts." In *Studies in Southern History and Politics Inscribed to William Archibald Dunning*. New York: Columbia University Press, 1914.

Diamond, Stanley. "The Rule of Law Versus the Order of Custom." In *The Rule of Law*, edited by Robert Paul Wolff. New York: Simon and Schuster, 1971.

Donald, David H. "A Generation of Defeat." In *From the Old South to the New: Essays on the Transitional South*, edited by Walter J. Fraser, Jr., and Winfred B. Moore, Jr. Westport, Conn.: Greenwood Press, 1981.

Fairman, Charles. "Does the Fourteenth Amendment Incorporate the Bill of Rights? The Original Understanding." *Stanford Law Review* 2 (December 1949): 5–139.

Finkelman, Paul. "Exploring Southern Legal History." *North Carolina Law Review* 64 (1985): 77–116.

Flynn, Charles L., Jr. "The Ancient Pedigree of Violent Repression: Georgia's Klan as a Folk Movement." In *The Southern Enigma: Essays in Race, Class, and Folk Culture*, edited by Walter J. Fraser, Jr., and Winfred B. Moore, Jr. Westport, Conn.: Greenwood Press, 1983.

Ford, Lacy K. "Labor and Ideology in the South Carolina Up-Country: The Transition to Free Labor Agriculture." In *The Southern Enigma: Essays on Race, Class, and Folk Culture*, edited by Walter J. Fraser, Jr., and Winfred B. Moore, Jr. Westport, Conn.: Greenwood Press, 1983.

————. "Rednecks and Merchants: Economic Development and Social Tensions in the South Carolina Upcountry, 1865–1900." *Journal of American History* 71 (September 1984): 294–318.

————. "Yeoman Farmers in the South Carolina Upcountry: Changing Production Patterns in the Late Antebellum Era." *Agricultural History* 60 (Fall 1986): 17–37.

Frank, John P., and Robert J. Munro. "The Original Understanding of 'Equal Protection of the Laws.'" *Columbia Law Review* 50 (February 1950): 131–69.

Franklin, John Hope. "Enforcement of the Civil Rights Act of 1875." *Prologue: Journal of the National Archives* 6 (Winter 1974): 225–35.

Frantz, Laurent B. "Congressional Power to Enforce the Fourteenth Amendment Against Private Acts." *Yale Law Journal* 73 (July 1964): 1353–81.

Fredrickson, George M. "Masters and Mudsills: The Role of Race in the Planter Ideology of South Carolina." *South Atlantic Urban Studies* 2 (1978): 34–49.

Friedman, Leon. "Joseph P. Bradley." In *The Justices of the Supreme Court, 1789–1969: Their Lives and Major Decisions*, 4 vols., edited by Leon Friedman and Fred L. Israel. New York: Chelsea House, 1969.

Fuke, Richard P. "The Freedmen's Bureau and Civil Rights in Maryland." *Journal of Negro History* 37 (July 1952).

————. "Hugh Lennox Bond and Radical Ideology." *Journal of Southern History* 45 (November 1978): 569–86.

Geertz, Clifford. "Local Knowledge: Fact and Law in Comparative Perspective." In *Local Knowledge: Further Essays in Interpretive Anthropology*. New York: Basic Books, 1983.

Gillette, William. "Anatomy of a Failure: Federal Enforcement of the Right to Vote in the Border States During Reconstruction." In *Radicalism, Racism, and Party Realignment: The Border States During Reconstruction*, edited by Richard O. Curry. Baltimore: Johns Hopkins Press, 1969.

Gold, David M. "The Defendant Takes the Stand." In *The Shaping of Nineteenth-Century Law: John Appleton and Responsible Individualism*. New York: Greenwood Press, 1990.

Hackney, Sheldon. "Southern Violence." *American Historical Review* 74 (February 1969): 906–25.

Hall, Jacqueline Dowd. "The Mind That Burns in Each Body: Women, Rape, and Racial Violence." *Southern Exposure* 12 (November 1984): 61–65.

Hall, Kermit L. "The Civil War Era as a Crucible for Nationalizing the Federal Courts." *Prologue: Journal of the National Archives* 7 (Spring 1975).

————. "Political Power and Constitutional Legitimacy: The South Carolina Ku Klux Klan Trials, 1871–1872." *Emory Law Journal* 33 (Fall 1984): 921–51.

Hall, Kermit L., and Lou Falkner Williams. "Constitutional Tradition Amid Social Change: Hugh Lennox Bond and the Ku Klux Klan in South Carolina." *Maryland Historian* 16 (Fall/Winter 1985): 43–58.

Kaczorowski, Robert J. "Revolutionary Constitutionalism in the Era of the Civil War and Reconstruction." *New York University Law Review* 61 (1986): 863–940.

Kelman, Herbert C. "Violence Without Moral Restraint." In *Varieties of Psycho History*, edited by George M. Kren and Leon H. Rapporport. New York: Springer, 1976.

Landon, Fred. "The Kidnapping of Dr. Rufus Bratton." *Journal of Negro History* 10 (July 1925): 330–33.

Litwack, Leon F. "The Ordeal of Black Freedom." In *The Southern Enigma: Essays on Race, Class, and Folk Culture*, edited by Walter J. Fraser, Jr., and Winfred B. Moore, Jr. Westport, Conn.: Greenwood Press, 1983.

Low, W. A. "The Freedmen's Bureau and Civil Rights in Maryland." *Journal of Negro History* 37 (July 1952): 221–47.

McFeely, William S. "Amos T. Ackerman: The Lawyer and Racial Justice." In *Region, Race, and Reconstruction: Essays in Honor of C. Vann Woodward*, edited by J. Morgan Kousser and James M. McPherson. New York: Oxford University Press, 1982.

Morris, Robert C. "Educational Reconstruction." In *The Facts of Reconstruction*, edited by Eric Anderson and Robert W. Moss. Baton Rouge: Louisiana State University Press, 1991.

Olsen, Otto H. "Southern Reconstruction and the Question of Self-Determination." In *A Nation Divided: Problems and Issues of the Civil War and Reconstruction*, edited by George M. Fredrickson. Minneapolis: Burgess, 1975.

Painter, Nell Irvin. "'Social Equality,' Miscegenation, Labor, and Power." In *The Evolution of Southern Culture*, edited by Numan V. Bartley. Athens: University of Georgia Press, 1988.

Perman, Michael. "Counter Reconstruction: The Role of Violence in Southern Redemption." In *The Facts of Reconstruction: Essays in Honor of John Hope Franklin*, edited by Eric Anderson and Alfred A. Moss, Jr. Baton Rouge: Louisiana State University Press, 1991.

Post, Louis F. "A 'Carpetbagger' in South Carolina." *Journal of Negro History* 10 (January 1925): 40–79.

Scott, John Anthony. "Justice Bradley's Evolving Concept of the Fourteenth Amendment from the Slaughterhouse Cases to the Civil Rights Cases." *Rutgers Law Review* 25 (Summer 1971) : 552–69.

Shalhope, Robert E. "The Ideological Origins of the Second Amendment." *Journal of American History* 69 (December 1982): 599–614.

———. "The Right to Keep and Bear Arms: A View from the Past." *Reviews in American History* 13 (September 1985): 347–52.

Shapiro, Herbert. "The Ku Klux Klan During Reconstruction: The South Carolina Episode." *Journal of Negro History* 49 (January 1964): 34–55.

Simkins, Francis B. "The Ku Klux Klan in South Carolina." *Journal of Southern History* 12 (October 1927): 606–47.

———. "New Viewpoints of Southern Reconstruction." *Journal of Southern His-*

tory 5 (February 1939): 49–61.

Smith, Albert C. "Southern Violence Reconsidered: Arson as Protest in Black-Belt Georgia, 1865–1910." *Journal of Southern History* 51 (November 1985): 527–64.

Stagg, J. C. A. "The Problem of Klan Violence: The South Carolina Upcountry, 1868–1871." *Journal of American Studies* 8 (December 1974): 303–20.

Sutch, Richard, and Roger Ransom. "Sharecropping: Market Response or Mechanism of Race Control?" In *What Was Freedom's Price?*, edited by David G. Sansing. Jackson: University Press of Mississippi, 1978.

Swinney, Everette. "Enforcing the Fifteenth Amendment, 1870–1877." *Journal of Southern History* 28 (May 1962): 202–18.

Teiser, Sidney. "Life of George H. Williams: Almost Chief-Justice." *Oregon Historical Quarterly* 47 (December 1946): 417–40.

Thornton, J. Mills, III. "Fiscal Policy and the Failure of Radical Reconstruction in the Lower South." In *Region, Race, and Reconstruction: Essays in Honor of C. Vann Woodward*, edited by J. Morgan Kousser and James M. McPherson. New York: Oxford University Press, 1982.

Williams, Lou Falkner. "The Constitution and the Ku Klux Klan on Trial: Federal Enforcement and Southern Resistance in South Carolina, 1871–1872." *Georgia Journal of Southern Legal History* 2 (Spring–Summer 1993): 41–70.

———. "The South Carolina Ku Klux Klan Trials and Enforcement of Federal Rights, 1871–1872." *Civil War History* 39 (March 1993): 47–66.

Woody, R. H. "The South Carolina Election of 1870." *North Carolina Historical Review* 8 (April 1931): 168–86.

Wyatt-Brown, Bertram. "The Civil Rights Act of 1875." *Western Political Quarterly* 18 (December 1965): 763–75.

Zilversmit, Arthur. "Grant and the Freedmen." In *New Perspectives on Race and Slavery in America: Essays in Honor of Kenneth M. Stampp*, edited by Robert H. Abzug and Stephen E. Maizlish. Lexington: University Press of Kentucky, 1986.

Index

Printed in the United States
22707LVS00005B/1-66

9 780820 326597